Elements of Tragedy in Flavian Epic

Trends in Classics – Supplementary Volumes

Edited by
Franco Montanari and Antonios Rengakos

Volume 103

Elements of Tragedy in Flavian Epic

Edited by
Sophia Papaioannou and Agis Marinis

DE GRUYTER

ISBN 978-3-11-070952-0
e-ISBN (PDF) 978-3-11-070984-1
e-ISBN (EPUB) 978-3-11-070997-1
ISSN 1868-4785

Library of Congress Control Number: 2020946868

Bibliographic information published by the Deutsche Nationalbibliothek
The Deutsche Nationalbibliothek lists this publication in the Deutsche Nationalbibliografie;
detailed bibliographic data are available on the Internet at http://dnb.dnb.de.

© 2021 Walter de Gruyter GmbH, Berlin/Boston
Editorial Office: Alessia Ferreccio and Katerina Zianna
Logo: Christopher Schneider, Laufen
Printing and Binding: LSC Communications, United States

www.degruyter.com

Contents

Acknowledgements

This volume has been a long time in the making, and has benefited from the generous help of a number of people. First and foremost, an immense debt of gratitude is owed to all contributors. We are grateful to them for their insightful readings, their superb cooperation and above all their patience. The frequent exchange of views with them was for the editors a particularly rich and rewarding aspect of the project, while this ongoing discussion shaped the structure of the volume in important ways. We are no less grateful to the two anonymous reviewers for their valuable feedback on the whole volume.

We want to register our gratitude to Carole Newlands, who embraced the project from the outset and offered her expert advice. Her critical reading of the chapters leading to her contribution of the Afterword, which seals the volume, summarizes in a succinct way the innovative character of the volume in hand. Thanks are also due to Annemarie Ambühl and Federica Bessone, for kindly making available their recently published work to us.

From Walter De Gruyter-Trends in Classics Supplementary volumes a number of people deserve our warmest thanks. Antonios Rengakos welcomed our proposal and shepherded it from its early stages. Marco Michele Acquafredda, Anne Hiller and Katerina Zianna followed through meticulously with the production of the book.

A certain level of formatting standardization has been imposed to ensure consistency across the volume, but individual stylistic distinctiveness has been respected.

This book is intended for the specialist scholars of Flavian Epic but also for the graduate students working in the fields of Classics and Literary History. All long quotations of Greek and Latin are accompanied by English translation.

Athens and Patras, August 2020
Sophia Papaioannou
Agis Marinis

https://doi.org/10.1515/9783110709841-203

Sophia Papaioannou and Agis Marinis
Introduction

When Vergil compares, in Book 4 of the *Aeneid* (465–468), the mental upheaval experienced by Dido to the terror felt by Pentheus or Orestes 'on the scene,' he clearly invites us to discern a 'tragic' aspect in his narrative. Yet 'tragic' in what sense? Is the poet intent, for instance, on guiding us to an emotive response akin to that engendered by tragedy? Through this emblematic Vergilian passage the issue of the presence and role of tragedy in epic, namely of the crossing of the two genres, is most forcefully posed. The depiction of Dido in the *Aeneid* effectively highlights the fact that a prime locus of the tragic is the manner in which outstanding characters are portrayed. Such characters may acquire a 'tragic' stature since they arrive at fateful decisions while combining both positive and negative elements in their behaviour. Within this framework, Dido has been regarded as the 'tragic heroine' par excellence of the *Aeneid* — her story having, in fact, prompted a number of scholars to regard her as guilty of *hamartia* ('error') in the Aristotelian sense,[1] namely a moral fault, which may eventually be considered as the cause of her demise.[2]

Hamartia, a key notion in the *Poetics*, is indeed central because it introduces the problem of the tragic agent and his or her intention; it essentially refers to a fault, whereas it may also acquire a moral hue. According to Aristotle, it does not befit tragedy to depict the suffering of someone totally innocent nor of someone who has a distinctly evil purpose. In between we may discern the broader area where, as a rule, tragic heroes act and commit the deeds that form the stuff of tragedy.[3] *Hamartia* is thus related, through either affinity or contradistinction, to the notion of *hubris*, which can be regarded as frequently tainting the tragic protagonists' demeanour. *Hubris* is not, of course, always as clear-cut and accentuated as in the case of Capaneus in Statius' *Thebaid*: a most conspicuous instance of epic character possessing traits evoking the figure of a hubrist, in the manner we are acquainted with in Greek tragedy. In this case, as well, Vergil offers us a 'prototypical' instance — the figure of Mezentius.[4]

---

1 *Poetics* 1453a7–12.
2 See esp. Wlosok 1976; E.L. Harrison 1989. Turnus may also be mentioned here as a further, not totally dissimilar, instance; see Garstang 1950.
3 On *hamartia* see, among a large bibliography, particularly Stinton 1975; Halliwell 1986, 215–226; Witt 2005; Schmitt 2008, 437–476.
4 La Penna 1980.

https://doi.org/10.1515/9783110709841-001

Both *hamartia* and *hubris* effectively lead us towards the key question of characterization. How are 'tragic' persons construed and what is essentially 'tragic' about them?[5] Indeed, the very positing of *hamartia* in a character's demeanour presupposes the existence of a moral dilemma within him or her and, consequently, raises the question of the moral awareness of the human subject. We thus inevitably enter the vexed issue — central to tragedy — of the relation between human autonomy and the impact of supernatural agents: in other words, of the connection between divine and human causality.[6] A related question is that of inherited guilt and its impact on human agents, an issue prominent in Statius' *Thebaid*, as a prime instance.

While *hamartia* refers to the actions of dramatic persons, the tragic plot is primarily characterized by the transformation of their status. A critical factor in realizing this transformation is human ignorance, which is sharply contrasted with divine knowledge. The removal of the veil of ignorance results in *anagnorisis* ('recognition'), which in turn brings about the reversal.[7] Such a momentous change of fortune may indeed be deemed a central tragic motif. It does not occur, however, through an arbitrary stroke of chance, but via the anguished struggle of mortal agents, suffering from and inhabiting their human limitations. The above discussion of *hamartia* and *anagnorisis* inevitably leads us to a further important question. Namely, what place should be awarded to Aristotelian theory within our study of the 'tragic,' as conceived in broadly abstract terms — a question also inevitably emerging with regard to modern theories of the 'tragic.' Indeed, one of the key reasons why the quest for the presence of tragedy in epic is challenging is because we need to contend with the vexed issue of genre, *as well as* its ancient theorization.

Apart from the Aristotelian *Poetics* and the framework it establishes relating to dramatic agents and plot, crucial for the assertion of intergeneric links between tragedy and epic is, of course, the detection of clearly delimited intertextual relations between specific literary works, the evocation of particular scenes or even

---

5 On the influence of Greek tragedy in Vergil, see De Witt 1907; Fenik 1960 [on Euripides in the *Aeneid*]; Maguiness 1963; E.L. Harrison 1972–3; Pavlock 1985; Hardie 1991 and 1997; Weber 2002; Fernandelli 2002–3; Panoussi 2002 and 2009; Galinsky 2003; Polleichtner 2013; Mac Góráin 2013 [on the influence of Euripides' *Bacchae* on, and the presence of Dionysiac element in, the *Aeneid*], and 2018 [on Sophocles' Oedipus in the *Aeneid*]; Kircher 2018 on the 'tragic' element in Homer and Vergil.

6 See esp. Duckworth 1956; Davis 1994.

7 On recognition, see pertinent reflections esp. in Halliwell 1987, 116–119. Also, among numerous studies, Cave 1988 and Sissa 2006.

verbal expressions and tropes from tragedy. Further, more broadly, the conceptualization of the tragic mode involves the detection of distinct narrative patterns and motifs. By this we mean narrative strategies, type-scenes or characters that appear to derive from tragedy.[8] A most typical such pattern, straddling genres, yet unmistakably connected with tragedy, is tragic irony. As further 'tragic motifs,' one may also mention love turned to hate, the idea of the isolation of the hero, or the existence of conflicts of duty.

From a different perspective, the literary articulation of the tragic element is first and foremost realized on stage, and is conveyed through performance. As performance is inherent to civic ideology[9] tragedy becomes a means of expressing political commentary in an impressionable way, and heroic epic, such as Ennius' *Annals* or Vergil's *Aeneid*, a political genre par excellence, becomes an obvious host for inviting at once the articulation and the reinterpretation of 'tragic motifs.' The isolation of the hero and the attendant conflicts of duty are conditioned by different forces in an epic and serve divergent objectives, which nonetheless are inevitably informed by the tragedic precedent.

Of course, we need to take into account that tragedy was amongst the first literary genres to flourish in Rome. Even though its literary lifespan reached an end in the first decades of the first century BCE symbolically with the death of Accius (86 BCE), the last great professional tragedian, the textualization of the dramatic genre that followed and ennobled it as such[10] transformed tragedy into a source for reminiscence and appropriation. Tragedy also became the object of philological study at an early period, while simultaneously reperformance of Republican dramas was being continued as late as the age of Augustus. Characterization, plotlines and plot-twists, themes and motifs, but also textual excerpts verbatim or adapted, and a new overall understanding of how plays were to look and sound, became sources of inspiration in diverse generic contexts[11] and especially in epic (mainly the *Aeneid*). Indeed, epic was subjected to the tragic lens from the

---

8 A valuable overview of the intergeneric influences and interactions between tragedy and Latin epic is now offered by Ambühl 2019, with emphasis on narrative strategies.

9 Roman civic identity is established and affirmed through circles of sacrifices, religious rites, festivals, public speeches, triumphs etc., expressions of public performances that draw inspiration from tragedy, which had established itself as a decidedly political genre by serving and celebrating the civic identity of democratic Athens. On performance as common denominator for Roman tragedy and Roman politics, see Boyle 2006, 3.

10 On the ennoblement of the tragic genre in Late Republican and Augustan Rome, see Beacham 1991, 125–127; Goldberg 1996, 270; Curley 2013, 30–32.

11 On the influence of Republican tragedy on Ovid's elegiac corpus, Filippi 2015; on Republican tragedy and Horace, see Ronconi 1979, 501–524; Aricò 1983, 67–93 and 1998, 73–90.

beginning, since Ennius, the father of Latin epic, was also among the leading representatives of the tragic genre in Rome.[12] Recognizing the tragic element in epic narrative involves the acknowledgement of the active presence of theatricality, which potentially transforms epic action into a spectacle. Ovid's *Metamorphoses* takes this to the extreme,[13] but spectacularity is prominent in all Roman epics and often determines some of the most memorable episodes.

The employment of tragedy, especially in light of Aristotle's theory, as a guide to reader-response in Latin epic has been the subject of increasing critical attention in the past century, since Richard Heinze. For several decades scholarly interest disproportionately focused on the *Aeneid* and critics have suggested manifold ways of responding to the challenge of situating the 'tragic' within the great Roman epic. There is a whole array of issues pertaining to the conceptualization of the tragic and the study of its influence on imperial epic vis-à-vis the earlier epic tradition, and the contributions in the present volume offer new perspectives on precisely this stimulating and multi-faceted issue. The composition of the project at hand is timely, in view of a renewed interest on tragic elements within Roman epic.[14] Taking as a point of departure the valuable scholarship already available on these questions,[15] which nonetheless is limited to small-scale studies, such as articles or chapters in volumes of more overarching orientation, we have produced a volume that is focused exclusively and from a wide range on the presence of tragedy and its association to relevant topics as they are manifested in Flavian epic. The tragic models discussed include principally Classical Greek and Roman Republican tragedy. However, the direct engagement of Flavian epic with Senecan tragedy is also touched upon in several chapters, as a potent intertext, via which older tragic myth and ideology is frequently mediated.

Key themes that are analysed in the eight studies that make up the collection are human and divine causation, the construction of the plot, as well as, more specifically, the tragic motifs of *anagnorisis* and vengeance. The volume equally includes discussions of narrative tropes peculiar to tragedy, the narrative function of tragically coloured narrative units in the progression of the epic story, as well as instances of 'tragic' language and imagery. Finally, individual characters

---

12 On the influence of Republican tragedy on the *Aeneid*, see Stabryla 1970; Wigodsky 1972; Zorzetti 1990, 245–247; Hardie 1997; Scafoglio 2007.
13 Curley 2013
14 See, for instance, the monographs by Panoussi 2009 and Curley 2013, but also studies such as Hulls 2014; Soerink 2014b; Augoustakis 2015.
15 Other publications include Scaffai 1986; Ripoll 1998b; Holford-Strevens 1999; and more recently, Schiesaro 2003; Heslin 2008; Sacerdoti 2008; Buckley 2014; Augoustakis 2015; Marinis 2015; Ambühl 2019.

are examined in specific chapters, focusing on the mode of their transfer from tragedy to epic. The interpretative perspectives and intertextual strategies adopted in each chapter illustrate the many forms of the reception of tragedy in the epic narrative, while the inter-connectedness of the individual contributions enables comparisons between the divergent ways in which tragic motifs are being incorporated into different epic poems.

Antony Augoustakis' study, which opens the volume, introduces a set of important questions on the reception of tragedy in imperial epic. The scant textual evidence from Republican tragedy notwithstanding, it is possible to detect and study the organic presence of the tragic element in the employment of themes and the presentation of mythological heroes in a manner akin to Republican drama. For example, the story of Medus, Medea's and Aegeus' son, who avenges Aeetes by killing the usurper of the throne at Colchis, Perses, Aeetes' brother — a story foretold in a prophecy by Jupiter in *Argonautica* 5 — has a tragic precedent in Pacuvius' *Medus*. Also, Accius' longest fragment from *Medea sive Argonautae* (467–478 Dangel), which describes the arrival of the Argonauts from the perspective of a shepherd as an event of cosmic proportions, is discerned in the subtext of Valerius' depiction of the storm in *Argonautica* 1, which thus focalizes the epic through a tragic vantage point.

Concentrating in the second part of his study on the tragic character of Statius' *Thebaid*, Augoustakis steers away from the obvious Senecan influence and postulates a likely influential contribution of Republican tragedy by identifying a set of fragments from Pacuvius and Accius operable in Statius' subtext. In Pacuvius' *Periboea*, Augoustakis argues, Statius discovers and adapts variants of the myth of the Seven against Thebes, especially involving Tydeus and the murder of Melanippus (fr. 203–230 Schierl). The topic is also treated in Accius' *Melanippus* (532–534 Dangel), with echoes of Tydeus' representation in Statius. More Republican dramas are referenced: for instance, in Accius' *Epigoni,* one finds the continuation of the Statian 'drama' in which Alcmaeon leads the expedition against Thebes; upon returning, he kills his mother Eriphyle (601 Dangel). Further, in Accius' *Alcmeo*, we hear about Amphiaraus' fate, which brings to mind *Thebaid* 8. Also, from *Antigona* (576–578 Dangel) we possess an exchange between Ismene and Antigone (again as in *Thebaid* 8): if it is Ismene speaking, then she comes very close to a Statian character. In light of the above, Republican drama proves an influential filter that enhances the complexity of the tragic element of the *Thebaid.* The issue of tragic influence on epic as regards character drawing, with a focus on Greek tragedy, will be a key concern of Marinis' study of Eteocles and Polynices in the *Thebaid.*

Augoustakis' overarching conclusions are enhanced in the following seven chapters, which look individually at the tragic element in three Flavian epics. **Neil Bernstein**, dealing with Silius' *Punica*, looks at the way distinct and unmistakable tragic motifs inherited from Greek and Roman tragic models are identified and defined accordingly in the context of that epic. The tragic motifs singled out for examination in Silius' text include the articulation of foreknowledge and irony; paternity and its consequences; the figure of the tragic tyrant; and the logic of sacrificial ritual. Particular emphasis is further placed on the sense of narrative inevitability and the ironic mode at work in the *Punica*. A key theme further discussed relates to Silius' incomplete oracles, that are intertextually connected with the multiple visions of the Roman future in Vergil's *Aeneid*. The contrast between Vergilian and Silian prophecy accentuates the sense of Hannibal as tragic figure, while necessitating the sustained reference to Vergil as a filter through which the interaction with tragedy is realized.

Similarly, the amplitude of tyrants in Attic tragedies and their development in Senecan drama against the Neronian historical reality inspired Silius' development of Hannibal's character around the theme of revenge. Revenge for Hannibal is intrinsic to his life, purpose, and identity — it is the, more or less latent, motif behind every decision and accomplishment, and ironically reduces his grand endeavours into expressions of personal struggle without end. A final tragic motif, that of ritual sacrifice, enables Bernstein to allude to the failure of this ritual act in its proper form against the many *piacula* — perverted ritual sacrifices, many of them killings of individuals in the prime of their youth in the *Aeneid*. Silius' Roman leaders, but also Hannibal, who elsewhere is repeatedly portrayed as maddened and revengeful, never perpetrate human sacrifices, a twist that reconditions the tragic character of ritual sacrifice in epic and links it to a new set of epic themes. The motif of ritual sacrifice is also examined in Papaioannou's chapter, with regard to the manner it is articulated in Valerius' epic narrative, encouraging comparative examination of the diverse ways in which Vergil's treatment of ritual sacrifice and its tragic context are received in Flavian epic.

The remaining six chapters explore the presence of the tragic, specifically Greek tragedy, in Valerius Flaccus and Statius respectively. **Robert Cowan** focuses on *anagnorisis*, which is frequently marked in Roman epic as a theme constitutive of 'the tragic,' not merely via intertextual links, but also characteristically through its association with kin-killing and internecine conflict. The various tragic nuances of *anagnorisis* and the role it is called to play in Flavian epic are foregrounded in Cowan's study through the brief examination of a selection of passages from Statius before it focuses on the Cyzicus episode in Valerius' *Argonautica*, a unit that builds on the *anagnorisis* motif in manifold ways. Cowan's analysis is based on the important premise that *anagnorisis* is both a trope for 'recognizing' tragedy and a generic marker by which it can be recognized. Characters and readers undergoing *anagnorisis* are aware of its tragic hue and by extension that of the wider scene in which it is situated. A tension is thus created between the revelation of absolute truth and the destruction of the very basis on which absolute truth can be known, challenging the possibility of extracting a single univocal meaning.

Particularly rewarding for the study of tragic influence in an epic *anagnorisis* are those episodes that involve unwilling kin-killing. For Cowan, these episodes, whose tragedic model is Euripides' *Bacchae*, can be termed 'hypertragic,' because they tend to 'correct' or emphasize the tragic element in a narrative that tends to diverge from it. One such episode is the closing scene of the *Aeneid*, where the recognition of Pallas' baldric acts as a recognition token, changing Aeneas' perception and identification of Turnus from that of a suppliant to be spared to a murderer to be punished. Flavian epic is fond of these perversions of the tragic. Cowan discusses, for instance, the collective augury conducted by Melampus and Amphiaraus in Statius, *Thebaid* 3, which leads the two seers to recognize the arrival of impending disaster instead of the unfolding of an epic vision of manifest destiny as would be expected in epic prophesies.

Following up on Cowan's discussion of inverted tragedy in the *Argonautica*, **Sophia Papaioannou** introduces additional perspectives for the study of the tension between epic and tragedy in the *Argonautica*, as she explores how Vergil's appropriation of influences from tragedy provided a methodological foundation for Valerius. Papaioannou begins by determining the narrative identity of what can be termed 'tragic' units in an epic story. In her definition, tragically coloured epic units operate as elements of "regressive repetition," a term coined by David Quint to capture the function of the tragic element in the *Aeneid*. According to Quint's definition of the tragic, those units develop around events and persons that threaten to impede the linear course of the epic plot. Additionally, the evocation of tragic intertexts, usually well-known and readily detectable, enhances the tragic element within the narrative.

Subsequently, Papaioannou identifies four episodes in the *Argonautica* whose tragic character is conditioned by a combination of tragedic intertextuality and repetition causing delay, and examines the different ways in which they interact with their epic surroundings and the progression (or not) of the leading themes of Valerius' poem. The discussion is divided into two sections, each containing the analysis of two episodes. The first duet includes the suicide of Aeson and Alcimede at the close of *Argonautica* 1 and the Cyzicus episode. Both episodes are underwritten by distinct tragic motifs, respectively suicide and a chain of tragically determined reactions resulting from failed *anagnorisis* (amply discussed in Cowan's chapter immediately preceding) or incomplete knowledge. The tension between epic and tragedy in the *Argonautica* is further observed in two episodes that have been informed by tragic models: the liberation of Hesione by Hercules and Telamon in *Arg.* 2, and the Io story, which is embedded inside Orpheus' song in *Arg.* 4. Both these narratives presuppose at least one Greek tragic model, according to the ancient testimonies, and this tragic influence crucially transforms their epic identity and mission within Valerius' epic.

Valerius' experimentation with tragedy receives one more treatment. Focusing on tragically coloured character-construction, **Gesine Manuwald** deals with the portrayal of Hercules, a less researched character of Valerius' *Argonautica*, and addresses the question of whether the story of Hercules as told in Valerius Flaccus might be read as a 'tragedy' and whether it is possible to trace allusions to particular scenes or motifs from any of these 'Herculean' tragedies. Manuwald splits her argument in two parts: in the first she approaches Hercules' presence in the *Argonautica* as a 'tragic' role that follows a linear course of development, while in the second she considers the similarities possibly shared by certain motifs in Valerius Flaccus' epic with themes and motifs in the long intercultural history of the tragic Hercules.

Manuwald then turns specifically to Valerius' dialogue with the Senecan Hercules, focusing on those details that betray the Roman epic's departure from its primary intertext, Apollonius' *Argonautica*: at these points we may trace the influence of Seneca's tragic treatment of the great hero. For instance, Hercules joins the Argonautic expedition in the Latin epic after having completed his twelve labours, a timeline that puts him in the same position as his counterpart in both of Seneca's *Hercules* plays. Manuwald equally attributes Juno's enhanced role in the Latin *Argonautica* to Seneca's influence and the proximity is clearly illustrated in a discussion of the two monologues concerning Hercules (VF 1.111–119; 3.509–520), as also in the identification of a set of parallel motifs. Manuwald's study of the reception of the Senecan Hercules introduces helpful premises for the epic appropriation of tragedy: Valerius' Hercules is a tragic character but in a different way from the Euripidean or Senecan Hercules. This is illustrated in a variety of episodes, including, for example, the Hesione episode (VF 2.451–578), discussed also by Papaioannou in the previous chapter, where, contrary to the earlier tradition followed by drama, Hercules' erotic feelings for the chained maiden (and all erotic desire for women) are suppressed: a divergence that ingeniously readjusts the tragic lens of the text.

The three last chapters focus on Statius' treatment of tragedy. **Ruth Parkes** seeks in her contribution to delve into the ways in which the presence of the 'tragic' is 'indicated' in Statius' *Thebaid*. Her discussion includes forays into the *Achilleid*, where different generic voices vie for a formative influence on the narrative. A key theme she focuses on is the imagery of the long journey: we may find in epic the 'mapping' of the spatial journey related through the poem onto the textual devolution of narrative, something evident in Books 4 to 7 of the *Thebaid*. Parkes deals further with the problem of disentangling the epic and the tragic. We find a generic crossover both as regards specific human characters, as well as supernatural figures, like the Furies for instance. Besides, tragedy, being naturally connected with staging and spectacle, is able to exploit this fact via metadramatic references; comparable hints can also be found in epic. Another key motif is vengeance, which of course emerges in the *Thebaid* as a key stimulus of action. Again, delay as an obstacle to plot progression is attested in both Seneca and, of course, Statian epic. Parkes focuses on the opening scene of *Thebaid* 8 and the way Dis reacts to Amphiaraus' intrusion into the underworld, by undertaking action that propels the narrative forward. Again here, we may sense allusions not merely to the *Aeneid*, but also to Seneca's *Hercules Furens*. What Parkes underlines is the difficulty of disentangling such a web of intergeneric relationships. This telling case of cross-generic influence is further taken up by Kyle Gervais in the subsequent chapter. In the third section of her contribution Parkes deals with ways in which the tragic is 'marked up' in the text. For instance, Phegeus' cameo appearance as a messenger in *Thebaid* 12 clearly 'flags up' a tragic moment. Parkes rounds off her discussion by pointing out another intergeneric ruse: the assertion by the epic of its identity as a genre, for instance, via specific words or motifs, in order to raise attention to generic intrusion and the concomitant generic derailment.

Kyle Gervais takes up the thread from Ruth Parkes, by pointing out the need to complement the most usual means of comparison between Statius and Seneca, namely one relying on verbal similarities, with a broader examination of theme, structure, and character. Gervais focuses particularly on Book 2 of the *Thebaid*; Laius' apparition to Eteocles in that Book affords a prime instance for a close study of intertextual affinities with Seneca. In Section 2 Gervais engages in a discussion of the intertextual affinities with Seneca's *Oedipus* and *Hercules Furens* present in Book 2. More precisely, *Oedipus* offers a model for Statius' description of the homonymous hero and the Sphinx, whilst *Hercules Furens* contributes to his depiction of the underworld. Gervais proceeds from allusions referring to individual passages to a larger framework of models for heroism in epic. In Section 3 Gervais deals with allusions to Seneca's *Phoenissae* in Book 2 again, where some less conspicuous intertexts (than the well-discussed allusions of Books 7 and 11)

deserve our attention. Gervais focuses particularly on Tydeus' embassy to Eteocles; the Senecan reminiscences help us grasp better specific nuances in Eteocles'
rhetoric concerning the ruler and his relationship to his people, as well as in Tydeus' way of dealing with the Theban king.

In Section 4 Gervais concentrates on Seneca's *Thyestes* and the shared theme
of *odia fraterna*. As he shows, the Senecan influence both complements and complicates an array of epic influences on the *Thebaid*. The comparison with *Thyestes*
ought, however, to include not only details, but also larger elements of narrative
structure. A key difference is that Laius performs his mission willingly, whereas
Seneca's Tantalus hesitates. Among several points raised, it is the assimilation of
Eteocles to both Atreus and Thyestes that effectively builds upon the inescapable
similarities between the Senecan brothers, even as they struggle to differentiate
themselves. Once again, the themes of heroism, power, and madness are problematized with the succour of a complicated web of intertextual relations.

Agis Marinis continues the quest to uncover tragic elements within the *Thebaid* by focusing on the issue of tragic causality. Indeed, we may sense in the
Thebaid the existence of a tragic crux, clearly reminiscent of analogous situations
in Greek tragedy, in which characters stand at the point of convergence of forces
stemming from both their inner 'psychological' constitution and supernatural
factors. This crux is problematized in divergent ways by Aeschylus in *Seven
against Thebes* and Euripides in *Phoenissae*, the two key intertexts. Marinis focuses on the figures of Eteocles and Polynices and the way their motives and im-
pulses to action are depicted, specifically in Books 1 and 11, the first and the last
to see the brothers living and active in the epic.

In Book 1 the narrative is set in motion by Oedipus' imprecation: significantly, both brothers are deemed guilty towards him and both should be susceptible to the influence of Tisiphone, due to their inherited inner tendencies and
their frame of mind. Among other passages, the *aporia* expressed by the narrator
at 1.325–327 is eloquent enough as regards the difficulty of disentangling the real
driving force behind the characters' demeanour. In Book 11, the presence of the
Greek tragic intertext is equally evident throughout the tumultuous narrative
drive towards the final *nefas* of fratricide. As a prime instance, in Aeschylus it is
the chorus of Theban women who try to prevent Eteocles from fighting his
brother, while in the *Thebaid* the Fury fears that *anceps volgus*, the mother, and
Antigone may possibly change the mind of the brothers (11.102–108). We may actually discern here the three facets of the chorus of *Seven*: 'sister,' 'mother,' and
bearer of values pertaining to Thebes as a city-state. Marinis finally aims at a conclusion that seeks to reconcile the potent influence of a supernatural factor with

an intelligibly human substratum on which that influence works: Statius has succeeded in engendering a powerful dialogue on the roots of human behaviour by exploiting the Greek tragic intertext, with all its nuances, and adapting it to his epic mode. The volume concludes with a succinct afterword by **Carole Newlands** who summarizes the important contribution of the volume to the multiperspectivity that underwrites the modern assessment of Flavian Epic.

Antony Augoustakis
Republican Roman Tragedy in Flavian Epic

> Kenntnis der archaischen Litteratur (die klassische der augusteischen Zeit hat nun schon
> ihre Säcularfeier begangen) ist an keinem Punkte nachzuweisen ... In Rom und Italien war
> selbst das Gedächtnis der archaischen Litteratur ausgelöscht ...
>
> (Leo 1912, 27–28)

More than a hundred years ago, Friedrich Leo promoted the thesis that the authors of the Neronian and Flavian periods did not have immediate access to the works of archaic Latin literature but rather had some, incomplete knowledge of the works of Accius, Ennius or Pacuvius and only indirectly through third sources. Seneca, for instance, Leo maintained, returned to the Greek tragedies as his models, not to the plays of the Roman Republican period. Consider Marcus Aper in Tacitus' *Dialogus de oratoribus* who calls for a poetic style that conforms to contemporary standards rather than the rusty and obsolete fashion of the ancient tragedians: *exigitur enim iam ab oratore etiam poeticus decor, non Accii aut Pacuvii veterno inquinatus, sed ex Horatii et Vergilii et Lucani sacrario prolatus* ('for an orator now must use a poetic style that is not defiled by the old fashioned manner of Accius or Pacuvius, but is rather brought forth from the sacred fountains of Horace, Vergil, and Lucan,' Tac. *Dial.* 20).[1] Subsequent scholars have pointed out this gross overgeneralization of this theory of disappearance of the works of the early Roman tragedians from public and private libraries, as one can infer easily from Seneca's reference to the contemporary usage of Republican literature by orators as something 'too recent' for some people: *multi ex alieno saeculo petunt verba, duodecim tabulas loquuntur. Gracchus illis et Crassus et Curio nimis culti et recentes sunt* ('many seek the language of previous centuries, they speak in the style of the Twelve Table. For them Gracchus, Crassus, and Curio are very refined and modern,' *Ep.* 114.13).[2] To be sure, it is a difficult task to identify allusions or verbal echoes of the Republican tragedians in the works of subsequent Latin authors, especially of the imperial age, since the biggest portion of the dramatic corpus of Livius Andronicus, Naevius, Ennius, Accius or Pacuvius is now lost to us. In this chapter, however, I shall try to examine the

---

1 All translations are my own.
2 Jocelyn 1967, 55. Cf. Mart. 11.90.6 on the imitation of the 'old poets.' Jocelyn 1967, 55 n. 2 wonders whether Brittanicus' poem in Tac. *Ann.* 13.16 could have been the canticum from Ennius' *Andromacha* (fr. 27 Jocelyn, fr. 23 Manuwald [*TrRF* v.2]). Persius (1.76–78) alludes to Pacuvius' *Antiopa* and Accius.

https://doi.org/10.1515/9783110709841-002

verbal or lexical points of contact between some of the tragedies of Accius and Pacuvius and the epics of the Flavian period, in particular the mythological poems of Statius (*Thebaid*) and Valerius Flaccus (*Argonautica*). Though such an enterprise is fraught with the particular problem identified above, nevertheless the scant, fragmentary evidence we possess indicates that the Flavian epicists exploited the themes and presentation of mythological heroes from Republican drama.

1 Valerius Flaccus' *Argonautica*

Valerius' Roman *Argonautica* recounts the famous story of Apollonius Rhodius in Latin verse with substantial changes and departures from his Greek and earlier Roman models (most notable Varro of Atax).[3] The poem includes scenes standard in the Argonautic saga, such as Phineus and the Harpies or Jason's labours and subsequent flight of Medea from Colchis but never reaches the conclusion, as it is left unfinished by the Flavian poet.

There is no doubt that the Hellenistic archetype could not have been far enough from Valerius' reach as he composed his version of the centuries-old venture of Jason to retrieve the Golden Fleece from Colchis. There is also little doubt that Valerius combined a myriad of sources in composing his own version of the Argonautic story, from Greek tragedy to Roman epic and Latin epyllion as well as Senecan tragedy. An important aspect, however, followed by Valerius in the footsteps of a long Latin literary tradition, began with Accius: Accius diverges from Apollonius and makes the Argo the first ship to cross the seas. Accius' longest fragment from the *Medea sive Argonautae* (467–478 Dangel) describes the arrival of the Argonauts from the perspective of a shepherd, as Cicero informs us: *atque ille apud Accium pastor, qui navem numquam ante vidisset, ut procul divinum et novum vehiculum Argonautarum e monte conspexit, primo admirans at perterritus hoc modo loquitur* ('and that famous shepherd in Accius, who had never seen a ship before, when from the mountain he looked at the divine and wondrous ship of the Argonauts, he first marveled at it and then spoke thus,' *N.D.* 2.89).[4]

---

3 For a review of the Argonautic myth before Valerius, see Zissos 2008, xvii–xxv, with the Roman Republican tragedians briefly mentioned at xxi–xxii. On Medea in Roman Republican tragedy, see Cowan 2010.

4 Cf. also Prisc. *Inst.* 3.424.15 and Zissos 2008, xxii. On Accius' play, see Arcellaschi 1990, 163–195 and Falcone 2016, 155–195.

In Accius' fragment, possibly from the prologue of the play, the tragedian particularly focuses on the cosmic upset that the arrival of the Argo brings about. This is the moment of Jason's escape with the Argonauts and Medea (*Medea* 467– 478 Dangel):

x – x – x   *tanta moles labitur*
fremibunda ex alto ingenti sonitu et spiritu;
prae se undas volvit, vortices vi suscitat;
ruit prolapsa, pelagus respergit, reflat.
Ita dum interruptum credas nimbum volvier,
dum quod sublime ventis expulsum rapi
saxum aut procellis, vel globosos turbines
existere ictos undis concursantibus;
nisi quas terrestres pontus strages conciet;
aut forte Triton, fuscinae vertens specus
subter radices penitus undante in freto
molem ex profundo saxeam ad caelum eruit.

A great mass glides, roaring with an enormous sound and blast from the deep sea. It makes the waves roll in front of it, it raises whirlpools with its force. It rushes forward and slides, is splashed over the sea, which it also blows back. So you would believe that a dislocated storm cloud was rolling, or that a rock broken off was seized by the winds or the storm up high or that whirlwinds, round as a ball, rose up, struck by the waves, and clashed together. Unless it is that sea that wreaks havoc on land or perhaps Triton, turning a cave upside down with his trident under its roots deep inside the foaming sea, uproots a rocky mass from the deep to the sky.

Accius follows closely Apollonius' fourth book (86–212, 316–319,[5] but also 2.168– 174 and 549–566 on the crossing of the Symplegades) with the departure from Colchis and even the emotive reaction caused by the ship's presence and effect on the deep sea.

While *moles* in the opening line of the passage is used after Accius for the massive structure of the ship, in Vergil and Propertius in particular (*Aen.* 5.118 and 223, 8.693; Prop. 4.6.19),[6] it is nevertheless employed in Valerius to describe the very ship of the Argo as in Accius. At 1.127, Valerius talks about the construction of the ship (VF 1.127–129):

---

5 ἰαμενῇσι δ' ἐν ἄσπετα πώεα λεῖπον / ποιμένες ἄγραυλοι νηῶν φόβῳ, οἷά τε θῆρας / ὀσσόμενοι πόντου μεγακήτεος ἐξανιόντας. / οὐ γάρ πω ἁλίας γε πάρος ποθὶ νῆας ἴδοντο ('In the marshes, rural shepherds left their vast flocks scared by the ships, believing them to be beasts emerging from the monster-harbouring sea'). See Hunter 2015, 126.
6 See *TLL* viii.1341.28–35.

> *constitit ut longo moles non pervia ponto,[7]*
> *puppis et ut tenues subiere latenti acerae*
> *lumina, picturae varios superaddit honores.*

When the bulky structure that was not to be permeated by water, stood ready and when the liquid wax had penetrated the lurking holes of the ship, he (Argus) added the various decorations of painting.

The employment of the noun *moles* can certainly be coincidental and inspired by Vergil or Propertius, where, however, it describes the battle of Actium. But it could well serve as an indication of a window-allusion to Accius through the earlier Augustan poets, especially since it is used by the Republican tragedian to portray the Argo's bulky structure and is then repeated at the end of the fragment again for a rocky mass (*molem... saxeam*).[8]

Most importantly, however, Accius' scene of the Argo's sailing and its cosmic repercussions may have been in Valerius' mind when portraying the storm at sea in *Argonautica* 1 (574–656) after the departure of the Argonauts. In fact, like the *pastor* in Accius, Boreas sees the sailing of the ship from Mt. Pangaeum and reports to Aeolus what he has just witnessed (VF 1.574–577, 598–601):

> *Interea medio saevus permissa profundo*
> *carbasa Pangaea Boreas speculatus ab arce*
> *continuo Aeoliam Tyrrhena quetendit ad antra*
> *concitus ...*
> *'Pangaea quod ab arce nefas', ait, 'Aeole, vidi!*
> *Graia novam ferro molem commenta iuventus*
> *pergit et ingenti gaudens domat aequora velo,*
> *nec mihi libertas imis freta tollere harenis ...'*

Meanwhile, fierce Boreas saw from his citadel on Mt. Pangaeum the sails entrusted to the middle of the sea, immediately he rushed to the land of Aeolus and the Tyrrhenian caves in haste... 'Ah! what monstrous deed, Aeolus, have I seen from the citadel on Mt. Pangaeum! Greek youths have devised a bizarre structure with the axe and now go forward joyfully and try to tame the seas with their huge sails, nor do I have the freedom to stir up the sea from its sandy depths...'

---

7 I follow Ehlers' text and Spaltenstein's (2002, 74) explanation of *puppis* as genitive with *lumina*, not taking *moles* as an apposition as Mozley or Liberman. The noun *moles* is used again at 2.353, when Hypsipyle asks Jason about the provenance of the Haemonian ship.

8 Thomas 1986, 188. Also cf. e.g. Panoussi 2009, 214–215 and n. 60 on Vergil's allusions to Sophocles through Accius or Statius' evocation of Valerius Flaccus and/or Varro of Atax at *Silv.* 2.7.77 (with Newlands 2011, *ad loc.*).

As Andrew Zissos observes, Valerius here "transmutes the scene by providing a divine witness with a stake in what he beholds, whose outrage motivates subsequent narrative developments."[9] Zissos also correctly identifies a nod to Accius in the use of *moles* in 1.599,[10] which Valerius couples with *novam*: the spectacle of launching the Argo stirs a variety of emotions for the beholder; it is new and therefore strange that someone tries to set sail for the first time, which in turn makes Boreas demand retribution for the daring in the form of an epic storm scene to follow, a storm that will have the same cosmic repercussions as the scene does in Accius' description. Boreas' suggestion that he does not have the *libertas* to stir up a storm that would confound the bottom of the sea, the waters, and by extension the winds and land, with the hyperbolic expression *imis freta tollere harenis* points to the middle section of the Accius fragments, in which the sailing of the ship wreaks havoc, with Triton *subter radices penitus... molem ex profundo saxeam ad caelum eruit.*

Valerius of course follows in a long tradition of descriptions of storms in epic and elsewhere, even though in the Argonautic tradition there seems to be no place for such an episode in the versions before the Flavian poet.[11] And yet, Accius' vocabulary offers points of contact, even though again such register belongs to a common heritage regarding the representation of such storms: consider the phrases, for instance, *sublime ventis expulsum rapi, turbines, ictos undis concursantibus.*

Finally, a possible reference to the Accius fragment may be found in *Argonautica* 4, when Valerius describes the cave of the barbarous Amycus (VF 4.177–180):

> *litore in extremo spelunca apparuit ingens,*
> *arboribus super et dorso contecta minanti,*
> *non quae dona deum, non quae trahat aetheris ignem,*
> *infelix domus et sonitu <u>tremebunda</u> profundi.*

> On the tip of the coastal land, a huge cave appeared, covered by the trees above and a cliff hanging over. It was not a cave that received the gifts of the gods or would let in daylight, but it was a terrifying abode, trembling by the sound of the deep.

Valerius adds the details of this grim abode, *infelix domus*, inspired by Cacus' cave in Vergil and Ovid (*Aen.* 8.193–197; *Fast.* 1.555–558), but the last detail of the

---

9 Zissos 2008, 329.

10 Zissos 2008, 337. Cf. Spaltenstein 2002, 236 on *moles* as "suggestif et hyperbolique."

11 Zissos 2008, 328–329 on the inspiration from Vergil, Ovid, Lucan, and the Flavian contemporaries, Statius and Silius Italicus.

sound of the deep which makes the cave *tremebunda* cannot be found elsewhere. As Paul Murgatroyd notes, "the reference will be to the sea pounding the cavern's base and/or side; but the vibration of the rock is extraordinary and unearthly, and adds visual to aural appeal."[12] The reading *tremebunda* is, however, doubtful (found in X and [S], against *remibunda* in L and V), but defended by recent editors, Ehlers and Liberman (who prints *tremibunda*). As Liberman notes, the verb *tremo* is recommended by *Aen.* 9.715: *sonitu Prochyta alta tremit* (also in Luc. 4.766 and Sil. 7.49), but provides a word of caution, since *fremibunda* is found in the Accius fragment, and Heinsius followed this reading to emend the text.[13] In fact, the collocation with *sonitu* could be apt combining the roar with sound, an effective portrayal of the cave and its inhabitant.[14]

Let us now briefly turn to Pacuvius' *Medus*, a play that is the sequel of Euripides' *Medea* and Ennius' *Medea Exul*.[15] The tragedy involves the story of Medus, Medea's and Aegeus' son, who avenges Aeetes by killing the usurper of the throne at Colchis, Perses, Aeetes' brother. Perses is of course a very important person for Valerius Flaccus who recounts the civil war in Colchis in the sixth book of the *Argonautica*, introduced for the first time by Juno who recalls the enmity between the two brothers in 3.492–494: *procerum vi pulsus iniqua / germanique manu (repetis quo crimine) Perses / barbaricas iam movit opes Hyrcanaque signa* ('driven out by the overwhelming force of leading men and the hand of his brother — you remember on account of what charge —, Perses now moves barbarian forces and the Hyrcanian armies [sc. against his brother]').[16] As Maria Falcone observes, the story of Pacuvius' tragedy, a sequel to the Valerian narrative, is foreshadowed in the prophecy by Jupiter in *Argonautica* 5, where the supreme god foretells that there will be a time when Aeetes will be avenged by his Greek grandson (VF 5.685–687):

---

12 Murgatroyd 2009, 111.

13 Liberman 2003, 261–262.

14 It is also important to note with regard to Accius' possible influence on Valerius that in his *Andromeda*, the earlier tragedian recounts the story that becomes famous from Ovid's *Metamorphoses* 4 and 5, one that is long thought to be the model for the Hercules and Hesione episode in Valerius' *Argonautica* 2. Unfortunately, *Io* is too fragmentary to draw any safe conclusions. Naevius' sole *Hesiona* fragment is not included in the 2012 edition of *TrRF* (v.1 ed. Schauer, p. 445), only in earlier editions.

15 See Cowan 2013, 338–340 and n. 86 for further bibliography, as well as the most recent edition and commentary by Schierl 2002, 342–385 (whose numeration I follow) and Falcone 2016, 95–153.

16 See Spaltenstein 2004, 146–147 and Manuwald 2015, 201–202.

Donec Aeeten inopis post longa senectae
exilia, heu magnis quantum licet, impia, fatis,
nata iuvet Graiusque nepos in regna reponat.

until his impious daughter and Greek grandson will help Aeetes, after a long period of exile in his helpless old age (alas, how much powerful fate can do!) and will replace him in his kingdom.[17]

2 Statius' *Thebaid*

Senecan tragedy has long been considered the most definitive tragic predecessor for Statius' account of the story of Eteocles and Polynices, the expedition of the Seven against Thebes, and the eventual fratricide.[18] A look, even a cursory one, at the fragments of Republican tragedy, however, reveals a different picture. For instance, in Pacuvius' *Periboea*, we find references to variants of the myth, which involve especially Tydeus and the murder of his half-brother Melanippus from Oeneus,' his father's, marriage to Periboea (Hyg. *Fab.* 69.1–2), or his cousin Melanippus, son of Agrius, Oeneus' brother (fr. 203–230 Schierl).[19] The scholiast to Statius' poem refers to the pollution on account of Tydeus' murder of a kin at 2.113: *pollutus... sanguine Melanippi fratris sui, quem in venatu incautus occiderat* ('stained by the blood of his brother Melanippus, whom he had killed inadvertently during a hunt').[20] In Statius' account, Melanippus stealthily wounds and kills Tydeus at the finale of *Thebaid* 8.

---

17 Contrast this prophecy to Medea's farewell in 8.14–15 that her father may enjoy peaceful times as king in his old age (*longa placidus... sceptra senecta / tuta*). And cf. fr. 186 Schierl: *cum te expetebant omnes florentissimo / regno, reliqui; nunc desertum ab omnibus / summo periclo sola ut restituam paro* ('when everyone sought you out during the peak of your kingship, I left; now that you are abandoned by everyone I also prepare to restore you at the height of your danger'), where presumably Medea contrasts the "then" and "now" in her father's predicament.

18 For Seneca's influence on Statius, see most recently Bessone 2011 and Augoustakis 2015 for further references. Preliminary thoughts on the Republican tragedians' influence on Statius are offered in Augoustakis 2016a, xxviii, xxxvii.

19 Schierl 2006, 423–467. Pacuvius' fragments leave open the possibility that the tragedy may have involved Tydeus or his son, Diomedes, according to Schierl.

20 Sweeney, the editor of pseudo-Lactantius' scholia, corrects the manuscript reading *Menalippi*. At *Theb.* 1.402–403, the scholiast refers to an alternate tradition of Tydeus killing his mother's brother, Thoas. See Gervais 2017, 105 on Statius' command of the mythographic tradition and the possibility of using different strands thereof at different times.

The topic of Tydeus' *crimen* was also treated in Accius' *Melanippus*, Tydeus' half-brother (523–537 Dangel). It is in Accius' treatment in particular that we find two tantalizing fragments which may be echoed in Statius' scene of Tydeus' cannibalism in *Thebaid* 8:

> hic Melanippum interea traiectus nemorum, in salti faucibus (Accius 532 Dangel)
> constitit cognovit sensit; conlocat sese in locum
> celsum; hinc manibus rapere raudus saxeum grande
> et grave (533–534 Dangel)

> here Melanippus in the passages of the woods, at the entrance of the forest
> He stood, realized, felt. He placed himself in a high place; from there he seized with his hands a huge and heavy lump of rock.

In the first fragment, Accius may be relating the death of Melanippus in the woods, possibly killed by Tydeus.[21] While the subject of the second fragment is unknown (it could be Tydeus himself or Melanippus trying to fight back), I would like to focus on the tricolonic, alliterative asyndeton: *constitit cognovit sensit*. In Statius' *Thebaid*, when the superhuman hero Tydeus is stealthily but fatally wounded by Melanippus who is in the hiding (8.716–750), he demands the head of his attacker and upon looking at it, he commits the atrocity of cannibalism, thus incurring the wrath and disgust of his protectress, Minerva (751–766).[22] In this gruesome moment, Tydeus takes a final look at the dying head of his opponent just before he eats the brains (*Theb.* 8.751–756):

> erigitur Tydeus vultuque occurrit et amens
> laetitiaque iraque, ut singultantia vidit
> ora trucesque oculos seseque agnovit in illo,
> imperat abscisum porgi, laevaque receptum
> spectat atrox hostile caput, gliscitque tepentis
> lumina torva videns et adhuc dubitantia figi.

> Tydeus raises himself and looks at him and, crazed with joy and rage, seeing the gasping face and the fierce eyes and recognizing himself in the other, he orders it to be severed and brought to him. Taking it in his left hand, he glares at the enemy's head with a savage look and swells on seeing the grim eyes of him who is still warm, eyes that are still uncertain to be fixed in death.

---

21 Dangel 1995, 356.
22 Augoustakis 2016a, 344–356.

As I have observed elsewhere, the "description of Tydeus' startling self-realization upon reflection on the mirror-like face of Melanippus is sublime: each word is clearly marked and demarcated between two caesurae, in the second (*trucesque*, iambic), in the third (*oculos*, anapaestic), and in the fourth (*seseque*, spondaic) to accentuate the reflection of Tydeus' face in Melanippus' eyes."[23] The verb *agnovit* is important: this is when Tydeus realizes that he will not survive, he will die like his opponent. The context of the Accian fragment is unknown, and perhaps is a mere coincidence that the verbs of seeing, realizing, feeling are piled up there to capture the many emotions of that moment, but it may not be a coincidence after all if the subject is Tydeus hunting Melanippus down, a situation reversed in Statius but ultimately reproduced in the hero's cannibalism.

Undoubtedly, the Theban cycle provided a plethora of possible tragic topics for the Republican tragedians, especially Accius who seems to be the first to treat the story of the Labdacids on the Roman stage.[24] In Accius' *Epigoni*, one finds the continuation of the story of the Seven in the second attack against Thebes, the sequel to the Statian 'drama' too, with Alcmaeon leading the expedition and upon return, killing his mother Eriphyle (601 Dangel). As Elaine Fantham points out, Amphiaraus is a character of 'tragic grandeur,' and a quick look at the fragments, albeit inconclusive and lacking in many cases, reveals the seer's tragic connections.[25] For instance, Cicero quotes a fragment from an unknown author regarding Amphiaraus' conscious 'sacrifice': *ut in fabulis Amphiaraus sic ego 'prudens et sciens / ad pestem ante oculos positam'* ('as Amphiarus in the tragedies, so I also "in full conscience and knowledge before the danger placed in front of my eyes",' *Fam.* 6.6.6).[26] In Accius' *Alcmeo*, we hear about Amphiaraus' fate, namely his wholesome descent to the Underworld, which becomes the dramatic opening of Statius' *Thebaid* 8:

> *quod di in terram infernam penitus*
> *depressum altis clausere specis* (610–611 Dangel).

> because the gods pushed him down deeply into the earth below and enclosed him in deep caverns.

---

23 Augoustakis 2016a, 347.
24 Dangel 1995, 358 on Accius' *Phoenissae*.
25 Fantham 2006, 147 with an examination of Statius' sources for *Thebaid* 3.
26 Shackleton Bailey 1977, 2.401 suggests Accius' *Eriphyla* or *Epigoni*, but the allusion in Terence (*Eun.* 72) complicates the chronology and possibly points to an earlier tragedy.

Statius emphasizes Amphiaraus' penetration into Hades, a bizarre phenomenon in itself: *penitus* (8.19). At the end of Book 7, Amphiaraus is described as *illum ingens haurit specus et transire parentes / mergit equos* ('a huge cavern swallows him and encloses the horses as they were preparing to cross,' 7.818–819), in the moment when the earth opens up and a cavern engulfs the priest.

Equally important for Statius may have been Accius' *Antigona*, a play that probably combined in *contaminatio* the Sophoclean and Euripidean plays.[27] We have surviving fragments that point to an opening exchange between Ismene and Antigone (576–578 Dangel). The aphorism *iamiam neque di regunt / neque profecto deum supremus rex res curat hominibus* ('and not anymore do the gods or their greatest king care at all about human affairs,' 581–582 Dangel) echoes Sophocles' *Antigone* 922–924, but it is much more forceful and a sentiment that denies the gods any power over world affairs, an outlook fitting in Statius' literary landscape. Finally, the fragment *attat, nisi me fallit in obitu / sonitus* ('Oh! Unless the sound I have just heard deceives me,' 584–585 Dangel) may point to Antigone's burial of Polynices despite Creon's interdiction, as in Statius' *Thebaid* 12, where it is fully developed into a scene.[28]

3 Conclusion

The Republican tragedians displayed a virtuosity in reworking ancient themes and mythological stories and adapting them to fit a Roman perspective and contemporary lifestyles. As Gesine Manuwald points out, for instance, Pacuvius displays a "dexterity in choosing and adapting stories [which] seems to have been complimented by dramaturgical virtuosity... Pacuvius' plays often deal with family relationships, friendship, loyalty and care for each other as well as a well-ordered community life, justice, sensible use of political power and a legitimate 'good' ruler as envisaged goods."[29] Likewise, Accius' "dramas addressed various aspects that could be connected to the social and political struggles in Accius' period. These aspects include the legitimization of power and its potential abuse, elements of a Republican constitution, the role of honour in public life, the conditions of the populace and the relationship between influential individuals as well as between ruler and ruled."[30] Likewise the Flavian epicists adapt Greek

---

27 See Dangel 1995, 362 with further bibliography.
28 See Dangel 1995, 363.
29 Manuwald 2011, 213–214.
30 Manuwald 2011, 223.

myth to answer such concerns in a period where Roman imperial power is consolidated under the Flavians and the distant Republican past more and more seems to be irreversibly lost. Unfortunately, however, the task of identifying the influence of Republican tragedy on the Flavian epicists will remain a speculative enterprise because of our very limited knowledge of the texts.

Neil W. Bernstein

Silius' *Punica* and the Traditions of Greek and Roman Tragedy

Recent studies of Vergil's *Aeneid* and Statius' *Thebaid* have greatly advanced understanding of Roman epic's adaptation of the traditions of Greek and Roman tragedy.[1] Such studies are part of an older and larger tradition of analysis of Roman epic adaptations of Greek poetry, from Homer to Hellenistic epic.[2] Not all Roman epics have received such careful exegesis, however. Through unthinking prejudice, scholars in the nineteenth and twentieth centuries generally dismissed Silius Italicus' *Punica* as unworthy of sustained analysis.[3] Intensive, accurate analysis of the poem only began comparatively recently. Most of the epic's books still lack individual commentaries, and few book-length studies have yet been dedicated to the poem's themes and sources. Study of the multiple genres adapted, emulated, and subsumed by the Flavian poet in his historical epic is accordingly a relatively new project. This chapter is a preliminary discussion of one cross-generic dialogue: it examines how Silius' epic of Roman history adapts some of the familiar motifs of the traditions of Greek and Roman tragedy.

At first glance, the *Punica* appears to engage less directly with tragic influence than the other Flavian mythological epics, Valerius Flaccus' *Argonautica* and Statius' *Thebaid* and *Achilleid*.[4] Valerius and Statius present subjects frequently treated in Greek tragedy: Medea, the Argonauts, and the war at Thebes. Silius' subject is a familiar episode of Roman history. Yet we have little evidence from the few extant fragments of Roman historical drama that would help us see specific adaptation of the *fabulae praetextatae* at work. The gods who typically manipulate the victims of tragedy also play more minor roles in the *Punica* than in the other Flavian epics.[5] Recent studies, however, have emphasized the importance of the poem's

I am grateful to Sophia Papaioannou and Agis Marinis for inviting me to contribute to this volume and for their editorial guidance. Thanks also to Tom Carpenter, Cecilia Criado, Lauren Donovan Ginsberg, Rebecca Futo Kennedy, Leo Landrey, and Rachel Thomas for their many helpful comments and suggestions.

1 For the *Aeneid*, see Panoussi 2009. For the *Thebaid*, see Augoustakis 2014.
2 For Homer, see Knauer 1964. For Hellenistic poetry, see Nelis 2001, Reed 2007.
3 See Dominik 2010 for the history of reception of Silius' *Punica*.
4 See Marks 2010b on Silius' explicit differentiation of his work from those of his contemporaries.
5 See Feeney 1991, 301–312.

https://doi.org/10.1515/9783110709841-003

Hellenistic influences and its characteristically tragic motifs such as feminine lament.[6] As a Neronian courtier whose career included the consulship of 68, Silius may well have known Seneca, the greatest Roman tragedian of the first century.[7] Though Quintilian (*Inst.* 8.3.31) claims to prefer other tragedians, he attests to Seneca's ongoing presence in the Flavian era. It is accordingly not implausible to search the *Punica* for an intertextual dialogue with Greco-Roman tragedy, though the results will not be as striking as those of the mythological epic poems.

The *Punica* is characterized by its abundant use of "window allusion," the poetic technique by which a poem signals both a primary intertext and other secondary intertexts.[8] Though the language of a given passage may adapt the language of a particular Vergilian passage, the narrative context may in fact evoke a different passage of Homer, Ovid, Lucan, or Silius' Flavian contemporaries.[9] Or vice versa: the narrative may reflect a familiar Vergilian story, but do so by employing the language of other Roman epic poets. When Silius reworks the Augustan masters, he rarely does so in a naïve or unreflective mode. Vergil's *Aeneid*, Silius' major intertext, is therefore often the primary filter through which the *Punica* receives all earlier poetry, including tragedy.[10] Many of the motifs discussed in this paper also have counterparts in epic, as Roman epic drew from tragedy from the beginning with Ennius, who worked in both genres.[11]

The present chapter focuses on instances where the *Punica* reworks themes presented in Greco-Roman tragedy. I examine Silius' adaptations of tragic scenes involving foreknowledge and irony (§1); paternity and its consequences (§2); the figure of the tragic tyrant (§3); and the logic of sacrificial ritual (§4). Like Marks' initial accounts of the intertextual engagement of the *Punica* and Lucan's *Bellum Civile*,[12] this is only a preliminary survey of Silius' engagement with the tragic tradition. A more thorough investigation of Silius' verbal adaptation of the Athenian playwrights, Seneca, and the pseudonymous *Octavia* would likely reveal as intense a level of engagement with these scripts as with those of epic and elegy. It must also be remembered that Silius had access to numerous Greek and Roman

---

6 For the poem's Hellenistic influences, see Littlewood 2011. For feminine lament, see Augoustakis 2010, 178–182.

7 For an argument that Silius' aesthetics were formed in the Neronian period, see Wilson 2013.

8 For the concept of window allusion, see Thomas 1999. For examples in the *Punica*, see Ganiban 2010 and Klaassen 2010.

9 For Homer, see Juhnke 1972. For Ovid, see Wilson 2004 and Marks 2020. For Lucan, see Marks 2010a. For Silius' Flavian contemporaries, see Lovatt 2010.

10 See von Albrecht 1964.

11 See Elliott 2008.

12 See Marks 2010a.

tragedies now no longer extant. In particular, these vanished works included the Roman historical dramas that offered an alternative means to historical epic of presenting past events in poetic form.[13]

1 Foreknowledge and irony

Many tragedies operate in the mode of irony. The scripts presuppose that crucial knowledge has been withheld from some of the characters but not others, or from all characters but not the audience. The foreclosure of such knowledge becomes the basis of dramatic tension in scenes such as Tiresias' revelations in Sophocles' *Oedipus Tyrannus* and *Antigone*. The Theban prophet knows who is at fault, but the other principals do not. Thanks to the revelations in the divine prologues of Euripides' *Bacchae*, *Hecuba*, and *Hippolytus*, the audience (but not the other characters) gets to see like Tiresias. They know the motives that drive the remainder of the drama, which the other characters cannot even guess at.[14] The viewer watches the actions of Pentheus, Hecuba, and Hippolytus in the mode of irony. Each of these characters' decisions and statements means something different to them than to a viewer who knows that a god has resolved to destroy them.

Incomplete knowledge drives Silius' epic storytelling as well. The prophecy that opens the *Punica* (1.125–137) emphasizes Hannibal's ignorance of essential details of a future well known to every Roman reader. When Hannibal is but a child (of nine years old, according to the historiographical tradition), his father compels him to swear an oath of eternal hostility against the Romans in the temple of Dido. The incomplete prophecy delivered by Juno's priestess during that ritual dupes the boy with the illusory promise of victory (*Pun.* 1.70–139). The essential detail withheld from the future Carthaginian commander is that the gods will not allow his people to win the second Punic war. All future communication between the Carthaginian commander and the gods simply reinforces this initial error.[15] Mercury guides Hannibal through a deceptive vision to move on from

---

13 See Wiseman 1998. Augoustakis in this volume devotes the second part of his chapter to the likely influence of Republican tragedy on Statius by identifying a set of fragments from Pacuvius (*Periboea*) and Accius (*Melanippus* and *Epigoni*) at work in Statius' subtext.

14 On Tiresias as a "smooth political operator" in Euripides and Sophocles, exploiting hidden knowledge for his own benefit, see Griffith 2009. For the divine prologues of Euripides, see Mastronarde 2010, 153–206.

15 See Vessey 1982, Bernstein 2008, 135–139. Vergil similarly shows Dido deceived by the gods despite her effort to find out their wishes through sacrifice (*Aen.* 4.56–67).

early victory in Spain across the Alps to Italy (*Pun.* 3.163–221). The messenger god lies to Hannibal by promising that he will 'set him victorious before the walls of high Rome' (*Pun.* 3.182 *victorem ante altae statuam te moenia Romae*). The gods will not permit what Mercury promises. After Hannibal's overwhelming victory at Cannae, Jupiter repulses him from attacking Rome with a thunderstorm (*Pun.* 12.605–685). Juno then reveals the gods who are protecting the city to Hannibal, demonstrating to him thereby that it will be impossible for his assault to succeed (*Pun.* 12.701–728). Hannibal himself regrets the limitations of his knowledge as he buries the Roman consul Paulus after Cannae. Even at his greatest moment of victory over the Romans, he remains aware of fortune's mutability: 'Fortune turns our labours yet and compels us to remain ignorant of future events' (*nostros Fortuna labores / versat adhuc casusque iubet nescire futuros*, *Pun.* 10.574–575). Such repeated indications of the limitations imposed by the gods on Hannibal's perspective guide the reader to view him with the sympathy accorded to a tragic victim.

A tragedy such as Aeschylus' *Persians*, based like Silius' *Punica* on an historical narrative of two warring civilizations, offers a comparable case (though evidence of direct influence between the two texts is quite unlikely). Aeschylus similarly shows the enemy commander, son of an earlier commander, deluded by the gods into ambitious conquest and returned to reality by defeat. The parodos of the play introduces a Chorus doubtful whether their monarch Xerxes has triumphed over divine delusion (ἄτη): 'But what mortal man can escape the guileful deception of a god?... For Ruin begins by fawning on a man in a friendly way, and leads him astray into her net, from which it is impossible for a mortal to escape and flee.'[16] Xerxes' mother Atossa receives an omen indicating her son's defeat: a falcon attacks an eagle while she sacrifices at an altar (Aesch. *Pers.* 205–210). The Messenger describes Xerxes as a victim of the gods' jealousy, while the ghost of Darius accuses them both of destroying his son's judgment and assisting in his downfall.[17] To Silius' Roman readers, safely distanced from fear of *Hannibal ad portas*, the Carthaginian's ambition must have seemed equally senseless and doomed.

---

16 Tr. Sommerstein 2008. Aesch. *Pers.* 93–100 (Sommerstein 2008), δολόμητιν δ' ἀπάταν θεοῦ / τίς ἀνὴρ θνατὸς ἀλύξει; / ... φιλόφρων γὰρ <ποτι> σαίνου-/σα τὸ πρῶτον παράγει / βροτὸν εἰς ἄρκυας Ἄτα, / τόθεν οὐκ ἔστιν ὑπὲρ θνα-/τὸν ἀλύξαντα φυγεῖν.
17 Messenger: Aesch. *Pers.* 362, τὸν θεῶν φθόνον. Darius: *Pers.* 725, φεῦ, μέγας τις ἦλθε δαίμων, ὥστε μὴ φρονεῖν καλῶς, *Pers.* 742, ἀλλ', ὅταν σπεύδῃ τις αὐτός, χὠ θεὸς συνάπτεται. See Rosenbloom 2006, 83–103.

The multiple visions of the Roman future in Vergil's *Aeneid* are the primary intertext for many of these prophetic scenes of the *Punica*. The contrast between Vergilian and Silian prophecy accentuates the sense of Hannibal as tragic figure. Vergil's scenes of prophecy include Jupiter's unrolling of fate to an anxious Venus (*Aen.* 1.257–296), Anchises revealing the Roman future to his son (*Aen.* 6.756–792), and the stories of Roman history on the shield of Aeneas (*Aen.* 8.626–731).[18] Vergil's Jupiter conceals some details in his prophecies and appears to be unreasonably optimistic about others.[19] Yet Jupiter does not mislead Venus regarding the crucial details: her son will successfully complete the *translatio imperii* from Troy to Italy, and the Romans will eventually rise to power over their former Greek foes. Venus' revelation to Aeneas of the gods' involvement in the sack of Troy (*Aen.* 2.594–623), the parallel to Juno's revelation to Hannibal of the gods' defense of Rome, removes her son from the role of theomach and saves his life. The gods' contrasting provision of useful information to Hannibal and Aeneas shows that Silius has presented his main character in an ironic mode more characteristic of tragedy. The motif of withheld information is not unique to tragedy and can be easily paralleled in earlier epic. Homer's Hector, for example, famously claims that the gods are fair, despite the abundant evidence of their partiality presented to the audience throughout the *Iliad*.[20] But the particular combination of motifs that shape Silius' presentation of Hannibal — as the enemy commander, son of an earlier successful commander, overly ambitious and deluded into ambition by the gods — point to tragic as well as to epic tradition.

2 Paternity

Heroic paternity is a familiar theme of Roman epic, and Vergil's three generations of Aeneadae are the canonical example.[21] Silius invents an otherwise unattested son for Hannibal so that his commander can also be the middle figure in a three-generation dynasty, inheriting a legacy from his father and expressing his hopes for his son. The *Punica* also enters into dialogue with tragic tradition, however,

---

18 See Hershkowitz 1997.
19 For example, Jupiter neglects to mention the succession crisis involving Aeneas' sons Ascanius and Silvius; Anchises neglects to mention Aeneas' early death in Italy. See O'Hara 1990.
20 Hom. *Il.* 18.309, ξυνὸς Ἐνυάλιος, καί τε κτανέοντα κατέκτα. 'Enyalios is common to all, and he kills the one who would kill.' See Barker 2009, 67–74.
21 See Lee 1982.

in its representation of paternity and its consequences. Fathers can be the destroyers of their families as well as their supporters. At Hera's command, for example, Euripides' Iris summons the personification of madness (Λύσσα) to attack Heracles in his moment of triumph as he returns from the Underworld (Eur. *Her.* 822–874). At Lussa's compulsion, the hero immediately destroys his family in a fit of rage. This type of madness scene proved extremely popular in Roman epic and tragedy. Vergil's Juno summons Allecto to drive Turnus mad (Verg. *Aen.* 7.331–340), Ovid's Tisiphone similarly attacks the family of Athamas (Ov. *Met.* 4.464–511), while Seneca's Fury compels the ghost of Tantalus to pollute his descendants with his ancestral crimes (Sen. *Thy.* 1–121).

In representing the madness of Hannibal, however, Silius remains closer to the tradition represented by Aeschylus' Xerxes in the *Persians*. The Chorus of the *Persians* and other characters make repeated references to Xerxes' delusion, but there is no scene of divine intervention that maddens the monarch. Similarly, there is no scene where a divine actor imparts madness to the Carthaginian commander, as they do in the epics of his contemporaries Valerius Flaccus and Statius. Valerius' Venus drives Medea mad with her kiss (VF *Arg.* 7.251–255), while Statius' Tisiphone implants 'the madness of their house' (*gentilis... furor, Theb.* 1.126) in the feuding brothers Eteocles and Polynices. It is instead a human agent, Hannibal's father Hamilcar, 'skilled at nourishing madness,' who 'sows war with the Romans in the boy's breast' during the ritual in Dido's temple.[22]

Aeschylus' Darius observes that his son Xerxes did not appropriately carry on his legacy of foreign conquest: 'and I invaded many lands with great armies, but I never inflicted on my state such harm as this.'[23] From the perspective of Aeschylus' audience, Darius conveniently overlooks the defeat of his forces at Marathon, but the point he wishes to make to his son remains valid.[24] Just as his father had, Xerxes also failed to conquer the free and unsubdued Athenians. In a similar type-scene, the ghost of Silius' Hamilcar is invited to give his opinion of his son Hannibal's career when Scipio encounters him in the Underworld. This moment falls during Hannibal's period of greatest success, after defeating the Romans at Cannae but before the series of reverses inflicted on him by Marcellus, Nero, and Scipio. Hamilcar accordingly relates his son's victories to his true paternity (*Pun.* 13.744–750):

---

22 Sil. *Pun.* 1.79-80, *sollers nutrire furores / Romanum sevit puerili in pectore bellum.*
23 Tr. Sommerstein 2008. Aesch. *Pers.* 780–781, κἀπεστράτευσα πολλὰ σὺν πολλῷ στρατῷ· / ἀλλ' οὐ κακὸν τοσόνδε προσέβαλον πόλει.
24 See Rosenbloom 2006, 83–103.

> *decimum modo coeperat annum*
> *excessisse puer, nostro cum bella Latinis*
> *concepit iussu, licitum nec fallere divos*
> *iuratos patri. quod si Laurentia vastat*
> *nunc igni regna et Phrygias res vertere temptat,*
> *o pietas, o sancta fides, o vera propago!*
> *Atque utinam amissum reparet decus!*

My boy had hardly passed his tenth year when he conceived war with the Latins at my command. He is forbidden to deceive the gods his father swore by. But if now he is devastating the kingdom of Laurentum with fire and attempting to overturn the Phrygian state — o duty, o holy faith, o my true descendant! And would that he may restore our lost glory! (tr. Duff 1934)

In the manner of Vergil's Anchises, Hamilcar shows only pride in the fact that his son has carried on the family tradition and outdone him at defeating the Romans. Such pride is of course delusive and will be exposed as such a few books later at Zama. Hannibal will indeed prove to be a Xerxes who brings even greater defeat to his people than the humiliation of Carthaginians at the Aegates islands had to his father's generation in the first Punic war. The theme of true paternity (*o vera propago!*), however, provides an additional connection between the *Punica* and the themes of Greek and Roman tragedy.

One piece of crucial information withheld from many characters of Greek tragedy is the details of their true parentage. The negative consequences of such discoveries have functioned as a shorthand for "the tragic" since Aristotle's discussion of the revelation of true parentage in the peripety of Sophocles' *Oedipus Tyrannus* (Aristotle, *Poetics* 11). The action of a tragedy may also furnish characters of proof of true descent from the gods, but rarely with a happy outcome. So, for example, Theseus confirms his true descent from Poseidon when the curse he pronounces on Hippolytus successfully destroys his son. His moment of triumph is shortlived, however, when Artemis reveals that his son was no adulterer but the victim of framing by his wicked stepmother (Eur. *Hipp.* 1282–1341). Seneca's Hercules confirms his true descent from Jupiter by successfully completing the Labours imposed on him by a jealous Juno. Yet soon after, his madness transforms him into his father's Gigantomachic opponent. He threatens to overthrow Jupiter's rule by storming heaven (Sen. *HF* 964–973), which reflects both his maddening by Juno and his hubristic ambition.[25] The revelation of true paternity very rarely has the benign consequences more characteristic of ancient New Comedy or the eighteenth-century English novel of manners. The prime example from

---

25 See Chaudhuri 2014, 116–155.

Greek drama is the tragicomedy *Ion*, where the titular character discovers that his father is the god Apollo.[26]

While Hannibal's paternal legacy leads him to destruction, the revelation of the family romance is benign for the Romans of the *Punica*. During Scipio's journey to the Underworld, his mother Pomponia reveals her son's true descent from Jupiter.[27] This revelation ironizes Hamilcar's claim that his son is his 'true descendant' (*vera propago, Pun.* 13.749). The proud father's statement is factually indisputable, but its consequences point in the opposite direction from Hamilcar's hopes. Hannibal's role as a loser stems in part from being the son of a loser. In the same episode, Scipio learns of his descent from the supreme god Jupiter, and so proceeds to fulfil a destiny of victory rather than repeating his human father's defeat in Spain. The poem's concluding lines relate Scipio's triumph to the truth of his divine descent: 'nor indeed, when it calls to mind your descent from the line of the gods, does Rome lie that you are the descendant of the Tarpeian Thunderer' (*nec vero, cum te memorat de stirpe deorum, / prolem Tarpei mentitur Roma Tonantis, Pun.* 17.653–654). In addition, such an indication of divine parentage does not diminish Scipio's devotion to his presumptive human father, who welcomes his son with joy during the same Underworld visit (*Pun.* 13.650–674) and reappears to guide his attack on Carthago Nova (*Pun.* 15.180–250). Nor does it unsettle the Roman citizens who unite shortly after Scipio's return from the Underworld to propel him to the consulship.[28] Double paternity does not lead to tragic consequences, as it does in the case of Euripides' Theseus and Hercules.

Pomponia's revelation to her son Scipio of her rape by Jupiter also establishes a contrast with the epic's other victims of divine rape. These include Pyrene, who gives birth to a monster after her rape by Hercules (*Pun.* 3.415–441), and Thrasymennus, who cannot prevent Roman defeat by foreign invaders after his rape by the nymph Agylle (*Pun.* 5.1–23).[29] The major contrast evoked by Pomponia's revelation of her rape by Jupiter is with Hannibal's devotion to his human father.[30] Scipio instinctively makes his father his god even before he knows his true parentage when he issues a warning to Roman defectors after the defeat at Cannae: 'I swear by the head of my great-souled father, no less sacred to me than any

---

26 For the play's evocation of autochthonous Athenian origins, see Mueller 2010. For the theme of divine rape in Greek tragedy, see Kearns 2013.

27 See Marks 2005, Augoustakis 2010, 213–222.

28 See Marks 2005 on the omens indicating Scipio's rise.

29 See Augoustakis 2003, Augoustakis 2005.

30 See Bernstein 2008, 135–139.

god.'[31] By contrast, Hannibal's belief that he can achieve success by repeating his father Hamilcar's unsuccessful war with Rome leads only to his country's destruction.

Hannibal's forgiveable ignorance of the gods' plans for him can be contrasted with the willful blindness of the ambitious Roman leaders such as Flaminius and Varro. In their eagerness to win popular favour at Rome, these commanders disregard clear warnings from the gods and choose instead to give battle on unfavourable terms. The results are catastrophic for their followers at Trasimene and Cannae.[32] Their narrative trajectories follow a familiar tragic pattern of hubris punished. Despite his own hubris, Hannibal proves wiser than they: he is capable of listening to some of his advisors, he stands down from his conflict with Jupiter rather than sacrifice himself, and he returns to defend his homeland against Scipio's invasion rather than insisting on giving the battle he wants at all costs. Yet tragedy also colours a different side of the representation of Hannibal: as the terrifying tyrant whose outsized passions propel him to a heinous crime.

The reader's knowledge of Scipio's true descent activated in the Underworld scene is not shared widely, however, with the other characters of the epic. Scipio's subsequent interactions may accordingly be read in the mode of tragic irony — only the tragic consequences redound on those who misperceive Scipio rather than Scipio himself. The Crossroads episode (*Pun.* 15.1–128) and the episodes of diplomacy between Scipio and the African monarchs Syphax and Masinissa (*Pun.* 16.115–274) demonstrate the effect of incorrect assumptions about the Roman commander's identity. The personifications of Virtue and Pleasure visit Scipio shortly before he stands for the consulship, in an episode modelled on Prodicus' famous parable of the Choice of Hercules. Virtus knows that Scipio is descended from divine seed and so destined for greatness, like the series of Jupiter's children to which she compares him (*Pun.* 15.77–83). Voluptas discounts the truth of such descent and its consequences, and thus fails in her attempt to lure Scipio with a life of conventional pleasures (*Pun.* 15.33–67). Her failure to perceive that Scipio is already destined for rewards far greater than those she can promise means that her speech unfolds in the mode of irony for the reader aware of the subsequent course of Roman history.

As Voluptas is only a personification, there are no ill consequences for her except an embarrassing failure to turn Scipio aside from his path of virtue. Nor

---

31 *Pun.* 10.437–438 *perque caput, nullo levius mihi numine, patris / magnanimi iuro.* The revelation of Scipio's true parentage does not come until *Pun.* 13.628–647.

32 See Ariemma 2010 for the association of Varro's contempt for omens with his role as a demagogue.

can her threat to triumph over the Romans in the reader's present day be discounted, however, as it conforms to the view of the moralizing narrator. Her interaction with Scipio emphasizes his difference from the average Roman. But similar ignorance of Scipio's paternity proves fatal to human figures who interact with him. After securing the consulship, Scipio then proceeds to engage in diplomacy with various North African kings in an effort to mobilize opposition to Carthage. Masinissa and Syphax each proceed through political negotiations with Scipio according to their sense of the Roman commander's descent.[33] The pious Masinissa recognizes Scipio's divine descent, hailing him as 'son of the Thunderer' (*nate Tonantis, Pun.* 16.144). He demonstrates his virtue by sticking by his promise to support the Romans against his African neighbours.[34] Syphax misreads Scipio's identity as the son of his human father alone: 'How happily I recall a Scipio's face! Your appearance recalls your father's.'[35] His mistaken sense that he is dealing with a mere human being leads him to treacherously throw his lot in with Hannibal. This serious political miscalculation leads a tragic peripety: the Romans capture him and parade him in triumph (*Pun.* 17.59–145). Like Euripides' Pentheus who thought the Stranger was a mere human being, Syphax's perception of Scipio as the son of a human father proves fatal. As in tragedy, paternity and its perceptions are determinative.

3 The tragic tyrant

The tyrants of Greek tragedy are often violent and implacable. We may think, for example, of Eteocles in Aeschylus' *Seven against Thebes*, Creon in Sophocles' *Antigone* (before the death of Haemon), or Pentheus of Euripides' *Bacchae* (before his "softening" by the vengeful Dionysus). But the raging, sinister, emotionally unstable tyrant is also a signature creation of Roman epic, and one of the significant points of contact between the genres.[36] Senecan tragedy directs action and description to focus on the ethical and physiological consequences of the tyrant's passion. Seneca's Atreus and Lycus stand behind the glowering tyrants of Flavian epic, Valerius' Aeetes, Statius' Eteocles, and Silius' Hannibal. Hannibal's tremendous passions — his *furor* and *ira* — define him, like epic madmen such as Vergil's Turnus and Lucan's Caesar. The affinities between Hannibal and earlier epic

---

33 See Bernstein 2008, 135–139.
34 See Ripoll 2003a.
35 *Pun.* 16.192–193, *quamque ora recordor / laetus Scipiadae! revocat tua forma parentem.*
36 See La Penna 1980.

commanders have been well examined,[37] but there has been little effort heretofore to read Hannibal as a Senecan revenger.

As many studies have shown, Seneca engages with the poetic tradition by granting his revengers awareness of their own identities within that tradition.[38] Atreus, Medea, and others comment metapoetically on the expectations created by their roles. With studied deliberateness, they transform the act of revenge into a spectacle for their victims and for the audience. The characters generate the illusion of voluntary self-creation: their planning and execution of their extraordinary deeds shows their awareness of becoming the figures that the tradition already knows them to be. Medea's self-conscious comments mark the progress of her development into the proverbial murderess: 'Medea abides,' 'I shall become [Medea],' and 'now I am Medea.'[39]

Hannibal's development into the terrifying traditional figure *Hannibal ad portas* is equally self-conscious and revenge-driven. As observed in the preceding section, the *Punica* relates his progress to its dominant theme of paternity and succession. Both Hannibal and his detractors agree on his purpose in life: to exact vengeance on the Romans who defeated his father Hamilcar and to free his people from slavery imposed by the Romans. When Hanno argues against a Carthaginian invasion of Italy, he sneers that Hamilcar's ghost has maddened his son Hannibal: 'his father's shade and furies are driving the young man mad.'[40] Hannibal only confirms such a charge in his apology to his wife Imilce for bringing the war across the Alps (*Pun.* 3.138–146):

> an Romana iuga et famulas Carthaginis arces
> perpetiar? stimulant manes noctisque per umbras
> increpitans genitor, stant arae atque horrida sacra
> ante oculos, brevitasque vetat mutabilis horae
> prolatare diem. sedeamne, ut noverit una
> me tantum Carthago, et, qui sim, nesciat omnis
> gens hominum, letique metu decora alta relinquam?
> quantum etenim distant a morte silentia vitae?
> Nec tamen incautos laudum exhorresce furores...

---

37 See Marks 2010a.

38 The motif pervades the Senecan dramas: see Mader 1997; Schiesaro 1997; Littlewood 2004.

39 *Medea superest* (Sen. *Med.* 166); Nvtrix. *Medea* — Medea. *Fiam* (*Med.* 171); *Medea nunc sum* (910).

40 Sil. *Pun.* 2.296, *exagitant manes iuvenem furiaeque paternae.* Hanno's words echo those of Murrus, one of Hannibal's recently defeated Saguntine opponents: *Pun.* 1.443–444, *quaenam te, Poene, paternae / huc adigunt Furiae?* 'What madness, inherited from your father, brings you hither, man of Carthage?'

Shall I endure the yoke of Rome, and not resent the slavery of Carthage? I am driven on by the spirit of my father that rebukes me in the darkness of night; that altar and that dreadful sacrifice stand clear before my sight; and my brief and changeful span forbids me to defer the date. Am I to sit still, in order that Carthage alone may know my name? And is all the world to be ignorant of my quality? Am I, from fear of death, to abandon the heights of glory? How little does an obscure life differ from death! Yet fear not rashness in my ardour for renown... (tr. Duff 1934)

Hannibal's speech recombines the apology of Vergil's Aeneas to Dido (*Aen.* 4.331–361) for his departure with the tropes of tragic revenge. A life where the world does not know of him is akin to death. Revenge on the Romans for the Carthaginian commander, like revenge on personal enemies for the Senecan characters, accordingly represents life, purpose, and identity. The monumental deeds that he achieves along the way — crossing the Alps in the manner of Hercules, destroying the Roman armies at Cannae, and endeavoring to assault the walls of Rome and being turned away by Jove's thunderbolt like the Giants — are incidental to this larger purpose of taking revenge for his father.

Hannibal's defeat makes most clear the role that revenge has played in his self-creation. His outburst in the sea storm near the conclusion of the *Punica* shows that he remains the implacable, raging opponent of a hostile Jupiter even as he retreats.[41] His crossing of the Alps and repeated efforts to assault Rome in the face of Jupiter's thunderstorm demonstrate his belief that man can transcend nature's boundaries and so need not fear the gods. These predispositions align him more closely with the Senecan revengers than Aeschylus' Xerxes and his Persians. By contrast, the challenge of crossing the frozen river Strymon turns Aeschylus' Persians from contempt for the gods to piety.[42] After the defeat by the Athenians, Darius urges the Chorus to instruct his son Xerxes 'to stop offending the gods with his boastful rashness.'[43]

---

41 *Pun.* 17.225–227, *tunc sat compos, qui non ardentia tela / a Cannis in templa tuli Tarpeia, Iovemque / detraxi solio?* ('Was I in my right mind, when I did not bring burning missiles straight from Cannae against the Tarpeian temple and drag Jupiter from his throne?'). See also 17.606–609, *caelum licet omne soluta / in caput hoc compage ruat terraeque dehiscant, / non ullo Cannas abolebis, Iuppiter, aevo, / decedesque prius regnis, quam nomina gentes / aut facta Hannibalis sileant.* ('Though the earth yawn asunder, though all the framework of heaven break up and fall upon my head, never shalt thou, Jupiter, wipe out the memory of Cannae, but thou shalt step down from thy throne ere the world forgets the name or achievements of Hannibal.') For Hannibal as a theomach, see Chaudhuri 2014, 231–255.

42 Aesch. *Pers.* 497–499, θεοὺς δέ τις / τὸ πρὶν νομίζων οὐδαμοῦ τότ' ηὔχετο / λιταῖσι, γαῖαν οὐρανόν τε προσκυνῶν, 'those who had never before paid any regard to the gods now addressed them with prayers, making obeisance to earth and heaven' (tr. Sommerstein 2008).

43 Aesch. *Pers.* 831, λῆξαι θεοβλαβοῦνθ' ὑπερκόμπῳ θράσει; tr. Sommerstein 2008.

In Senecan tragedy, a blocking figure often attempts to restrain the would-be revenger from carrying out his or her vengeance. Seneca's Medea outmaneuvers a series of such characters through dissimulation, while Atreus disposes of the reasonable arguments voiced by the Satelles in the "passion-restraint" scene of Act Two of the *Thyestes*. Wise counselors similarly attempt to restrain Oedipus from his fateful pursuit of Laius' killer in the Greek and Latin *Oedipus* plays. In the two Carthaginian senate debates of the *Punica*, Hanno plays the role of the wise counselor who tries to restrain the tyrant and guide him toward a moderate path. He argues that madman Hannibal will eagerly drag his city to destruction in pursuit of revenge. In the first debate, Silius assigns the role of rebutting Hanno's argument to Gestar, a figure invented to voice the majority position of the Carthaginian senate (Sil. *Pun.* 2.270–390 ~ Livy 21.11.1). In the second debate, Hannibal's brother Mago reports the overwhelming victory at Cannae to the Carthaginian Senate, and no Carthaginian senators care at that point to listen to Hanno's counsels of defeat (Sil. *Pun.* 11.483–611 ~ Livy 23.11–13). As an ironic rebuttal to Seneca's *Thyestes*, Silius' Hannibal does not even need to answer his moderate critics directly: his minions do instead. Hannibal the revenger carries the day, the moderate voice raised against revenge is silenced, and the result is devastation for both Hannibal and Carthage.

4 The logic of sacrifice

Vergil's *Aeneid* makes the perversion of ritual sacrifice one of its major tragic themes. As Panoussi's recent study of Vergil authoritatively demonstrates, the murders of Laocoon, Priam, Turnus, and others disfigure conventional Greco-Roman notions of appropriate communication with the gods through sacrifice.[44] Subsequent epics extend and develop this motif into greater horror: familiar scenes include the murder of Pelias in Ovid, Erictho's necromancy in Lucan, Medea's magic in Valerius Flaccus, and the *devotio* of Menoeceus and the ban on burial in Statius' *Thebaid*.[45] The *Punica* shows a generally more positive view of ritual. In ostentatious contrast to the Creon of Sophocles' *Antigone* or Statius' *Thebaid*, Hannibal buries the Roman consul Paulus with full honours at Cannae (*Pun.* 10.513–577). He is further forced to stand down from his Gigantomachic attempt to storm the Capitol, and learns from taking a blow from Jupiter's thunderbolt on

---

44 See Panoussi 2009.
45 On the perversion of ritual in Statius' *Thebaid*, see Bernstein 2013a and Dee 2013.

his shield not to follow in the fatal path of Statius' Capaneus (*Pun.* 12.622–626). There are none of the necromancies, murders at altars, ritualized suicides, or prohibitions of burial that characterize the transformation of religious action into horror in the other epics. Such activities are usually associated with peoples besides the Romans, such as the Carthaginians who sacrifice their children at the tophet of Carthage, or the Spanish brothers who fight to the death and then burn on a divided pyre like the feuding brothers of the Theban tragedies.[46]

Yet sacrifice still plays a determinative role in the *Punica*. The narrative logic of the sacrificial act still evokes the traditions of Greek and Roman tragedy — only in reverse. Vergil's stories of sacrifice focus on the ritualized murder of individuals; Silius' *Punica* presents a contrasting narrative of sacrifice averted. Fabius rescues Minucius and his men and becomes like a second father to them, rather than (as his son suggests) delight in seeing them die in order to exact revenge for his loss of dictatorial authority (*Pun.* 7.536–750). Varro escapes from Cannae in shame (*Pun.* 10.605–614) rather than accept the self-sacrificing death of his consular colleague Paulus. Hanno demands the literal sacrifice of Hannibal's son at the tophet in conformity with both Carthaginian religious tradition and epic tradition, but Hannibal forbids it.[47] On the psychological level, such concern for his family humanizes a commander portrayed throughout the epic as maddened and violent. The Carthaginian appears more "Roman" in his aversion to human sacrifice than his countrymen, and the father appears more sympathetic than exemplary Roman figures such as Brutus or Manlius Torquatus who condemn their own sons to death.[48] Hannibal the politician, meanwhile, recognizes the demand for his son's death as yet another example of Hanno's endless scheming against him and his clan.[49] Yet on the mythological level, it is likely a poor choice for Hannibal to deny the sacrifice, which might well have been necessary, if not sufficient, for the Carthaginians to win the war.

In one episode, however, Silius presents human self-sacrifice, and on a grander scale than the individual death. The city of Saguntum, the first battlefield of the second Punic war, becomes the sacrificial substitute for Rome. Though the

---

46 *Pun.* 16.533–548. See Ariemma 2008 and Lovatt 2010.

47 Pun. 4.763–829; see Enn. *Ann.* 214, *Poeni soliti suos sacrificare puellos* with Skutsch's note.

48 The Romans did, however, engage in human sacrifice at various crisis points: see Várhelyi 2007.

49 For Hanno's hostility, see *Pun.* 2.276–277, *olim / ductorem infestans odiis gentilibus Hannon.* ('Hanno, long hostile to the leader because of familiar hatred'). For a tragic parallel, see Tiresias' demand for Menoeceus' death at Eur. *Phoen.* 834–976, with Griffith 2009. Tiresias' condemnation of Menoeceus is an assault by one branch of Cadmus' descendants against another.

Spanish city is hundreds of miles distant from Rome, on the other side of the Pyrenees and Alps, the *Punica* repeatedly frames Hannibal's capture of the city as the first step to the assault on Rome.[50] The besieged Saguntines, meanwhile, choose to sacrifice themselves *en masse* rather than surrender themselves to the Carthaginians (Sil. *Pun.* 2.592–707). They burn their arms, their household gods, and then their bodies on a communal pyre, thereby obliterating their identity and their ties with the Romans.[51] In a variation on the tragic motif that the gods departed in advance from captured Troy (e.g., Eur. *Tro.* 15–27), the Saguntines believe that the ghosts of their ancestors leave their tombs in advance of the city's fall (Sil. *Pun.* 2.592–594). The Carthaginians capture a city that has been emptied of its people and its wealth. Silius exaggerates the historiographical accounts of the Saguntine siege, which tell a more plausible if still frightening story of leading citizens destroying themselves and their goods on a communal pyre, but leaving captives and goods for their victors.[52]

The women of Saguntum furnish the episode with a tragic chorus and tragic ironies. As Hannibal's approach strikes terror into the Saguntine champion Murrus, 'both sides cry out, as if all Saguntum were flashing with flame.'[53] The women watch from the walls as Theron, the next and last Saguntine champion, stands briefly against Hannibal and then runs: 'the matrons call out, and a call mixed with lamentation resounds from the high summit of the wall.'[54] A scene involving the Saguntine matrons offers a sophisticated reworking of the speeches of Andromache in Euripides' *Trojan Women* and Vergil's *Aeneid*. In a speech modelled on Eur. *Tro.* 641–683, Vergil's Andromache tells Aeneas that Polyxena was lucky to die at Troy and so avoid the fate of enslavement that she herself suffered (Verg. *Aen.* 3.321–329). Silius assigns a similar speech to the Fury in disguise as Tiburna, the widow of the Saguntine champion Murrus. She tells the Saguntine women to kill themselves in order to avoid enslavement by the Carthaginians, and for the young men to pursue virtue by assisting their elders to death (*Pun.* 2.555–579). Speaker and context provide this scene with multiple layers of irony. It is a basic Stoic argument that suicide is preferable to loss of liberty. Yet the argument

---

50 See *Pun.* 1.270, *Hannibal extremis pulsat Capitolia terris* ('Hannibal striking at the Capitol from the edge of the world'); 3.564, *casus metuit iam Roma Sagunti* ('Rome already fears the fall of Saguntum'); and discussion at Dominik 2003, 474–480.
51 See Augoustakis 2010, 113–136.
52 See Livy 21.6–21, Polyb. 3.17–33, Diod. Sic. 25.15–16, App. *Hisp.* 7–13.
53 Sil. *Pun.* 1.502–503, *conclamant utrimque acies, ceu tota Saguntos / igne micet.* See Bernstein 2017, *ad loc.*
54 See Bernstein 2017, *ad loc. Pun.* 2.251–252, *conclamant matres, celsoque e culmine muri / lamentis vox mixta sonat.*

comes from the mouth of a disguised Fury who intends only to send her victims to a maddened death, and so has no philosophical force.[55] In the end, it matters little what the Saguntines hear. Like Euripides' Pentheus or Hippolytus, their death is inevitable. Juno has resolved to kill them, and all that remains to be seen is the manner in which she will achieve it.

5 Conclusion: The logic of inevitability

The sense of narrative inevitability characterizes folk understandings of the "tragic." The drama's outcome is typically made apparent to the viewer early on in many Greek and Roman tragedies. It is immanent in the tragedian's selection of a particular episode of myth, the opening words of the god or the human re-venger may threaten it, or the chorus's forebodings may announce it. Whatever their intentions may have been before the action begins, the tragic victims must fall. Aeschylus' Agamemnon enters the palace to be murdered by Clytemnestra, Euripides' Phaedra yields to her passion and destroys herself and Hippolytus, and Seneca's Hercules yields to madness in his moment of triumph and kills his family. The choruses' expressions of desire for a narrative alternative provide a preliminary model for the audience's reaction.

The tragic motifs of Silius' *Punica* discussed in the preceding sections simi-larly follow the logic of inevitability. The epic establishes from its opening scene that its major character's progress occurs in the mode of irony. The fact of his birth dooms Hannibal to repeat his father's failed invasion of Rome, with graver consequences for his country than in his father's generation. Restraining charac-ters such as Hanno perceive the inevitable outcome but cannot dissuade Hanni-bal. On the Roman side, the preliminary episodes before the battle of Cannae point most clearly to the motif of tragic inevitability (*Pun.* 8.617–9.180). The con-sul Varro reacts with contempt to the ghastly omens that unmistakably signal the terrible defeat to follow. He similarly derides as mere cowardice his consular col-league Paulus' recommendations to give battle at a more favourable time and place than Cannae. Fabius, Paulus, and the narrator play the role of the chorus who attempt to restrain the protagonist from dragging himself and others to their doom.

---

55 The scene is modelled on the speech of Vergil's Iris, disguised as the Trojan woman Beroe, which deceives the Trojan women and leads them to burn the ships (Verg. *Aen.* 5.604–640). For the connections between her speech and Hecuba in Euripides' *Trojan Women*, see Smith 2011, 123.

Yet the seventeen-book *Punica* is far more capacious than any tragedy, and so its narrative trajectory does not conclude with defeat at Cannae. The battle instead represents the nadir of Roman fortunes, and the epic's subsequent books represent the return to the zenith of Scipio's triumph. The defeat can even be described as a *felix culpa*. Defeat at Cannae establishes a standard for virtue from which Silius' contemporaries have declined, as the famous lines that conclude the Cannae episode suggest (*Pun.* 10.656–657): 'This was Rome then: if it stood fixed in Fate that its morals would change after you [fell], Carthage, would that you still remained!'[56] As Jupiter confirms in his prophecy to Venus encapsulating Roman history (*Pun.* 3.570–629), there is nothing here that is without god.

---

56 *Haec tum Roma fuit: post te cui vertere mores / si stabat fatis, potius, Carthago, maneres*, Sil. *Pun.* 10.657–658. For discussion, see Littlewood's note, Fowler 2000, 115–137, and Tipping 2007.

Robert Cowan
Knowing Me, Knowing You: Epic *Anagnorisis* and the Recognition of Tragedy

1 Recognizing tragedy

Anagnorisis was born in epic and later led a happy second life in comedy, but had its true home in tragedy.[1] The successive recognitions of Odysseus by the members of his household, from Argus to Penelope, and especially that by his nurse Euryclea using the physical token of his scar, were seminal examples of the motif with immense influence on its development in Greek, Roman and later Western and World literature.[2] Equally influential has been New Comedy's appropriation of the late Euripidean use of *anagnorisis* to reunite separated families and lovers, and restore kidnapped children to their rightful status.[3] Yet, as Hunter notes, comic *anagnorisis* remained a 'motif which comic poets clearly regarded as a borrowing from the tragic repertoire ... it seems that this link between tragedy and the recognition was never lost.'[4] For it is indeed with tragedy that *anagnorisis* became and remained inextricably connected.[5] It was not only the happy, if problematic, reunions of all three Electras with their Orestes, the catastrophic self-recognition of Sophocles' Oedipus, and the narrow avoidance of catastrophe when Iphigenia recognizes Orestes and Creusa Ion that forged this connection. At least as important was Aristotle's theorizing of *anagnorisis*, in the *Poetics*, as not only a distinctive formal feature of tragedy but fundamentally bound up with its essence. While we should by no means underestimate the significance of the numerous actual *anagnoriseis* in numerous actual tragedies, it is arguably the *idea* of *anagnorisis* and its intimate relationship with the *idea* of tragedy that is of primary importance for this chapter. As with Hinds' notion of 'essential epic,' an

---

1 The ancient novel is the other genre closely associated with *anagnorisis*, on which see Robiano 2008, Montiglio 2012. Yet even here the motif is marked as generically tragic or comic, sometimes even dramatizing the tension between the two dramatic modes, on which see Montiglio 2012, 148–152, 227–230.
2 On *anagnorisis* in the *Odyssey*, see esp. Ar. *Po.* 1459b, Richardson 1983, Murnaghan 1987, Goldhill 1991, 1–24, Gainsford 2003. On the topos in literature more broadly, see esp. Cave 1988, Mleynek 1999, Adams 2000, Kennedy and Lawrence 2008, Russo 2013, Kennedy 2016.
3 On *anagnorisis* in comedy: Hunter 1985, 130–136, Anderson 2002, Munteanu 2002.
4 Hunter 1985, 130.
5 On *anagnorisis* in Attic tragedy, see esp. Segal 1999–2000, Sissa 2006, Torrance 2011, Zeitlin 2012, McClure 2015, Wohl 2015, 63–88; in Seneca: Cordes 2009, Bexley 2016.

https://doi.org/10.1515/9783110709841-004

idea of 'essential tragedy' need not correspond to every, or even any, actual play.[6] For I wish to explore the ways in which *anagnorisis* served as a formal generic marker for tragedy, or at least the idea of tragedy, in the alien genre of Roman epic. The strong claim would be that *anagnorisis* was, at least by the first centuries BCE and CE, considered sufficiently 'tragic' to serve as a generic marker for tragedy on its own, but the majority of the instances I shall discuss do not require this. The weak claim is that *anagnorisis* can act in this way when supported by one or more other generic markers of tragedy, be they intertextual (such as allusion to actual tragedies), contextual (theatrical imagery of acting or viewing), or thematic (killing of φίλοι, perversion of norms, divine persecution, madness).

Although the passage is extremely familiar, it is important for the purposes of this argument to revisit Aristotle's famous definition of *anagnorisis* (Arist. *Po.* 1452a29–37):

> ἀναγνώρισις δέ, ὥσπερ καὶ τοὔνομα σημαίνει, ἐξ ἀγνοίας εἰς γνῶσιν μεταβολή, ἢ εἰς φιλίαν ἢ εἰς ἔχθραν, τῶν πρὸς εὐτυχίαν ἢ δυστυχίαν ὡρισμένων· καλλίστη δὲ ἀναγνώρισις, ὅταν ἅμα περιπετείᾳ γένηται, οἷον ἔχει ἡ ἐν τῷ Οἰδίποδι. εἰσὶν μὲν οὖν καὶ ἄλλαι ἀναγνωρίσεις· καὶ γὰρ πρὸς ἄψυχα καὶ τὰ τυχόντα ἐστὶν ὡς ὅπερ εἴρηται συμβαίνει, καὶ εἰ πέπραγέ τις ἢ μὴ πέπραγεν ἔστιν ἀναγνωρίσαι.

> Recognition, as the very name indicates, is a change from ignorance to knowledge, leading to friendship or to enmity, and involving matters which bear on prosperity or adversity. The finest recognition is that which occurs simultaneously with reversal, as with the one in the *Oedipus*. There are, of course, other kinds of recognition too, since what has been stated occurs, after a fashion, in relation to inanimate and even chance things, and it is also possible to recognise that someone has or has not committed a deed.[7]

Anagnorisis is a complex notion, encompassing recognition of far more than personal identity. The change from ignorance to knowledge can include persons, objects, events, actions and agencies, but though Aristotle taxonomizes these into separate categories, literally 'other recognitions' (ἄλλαι ἀναγνωρίσεις), each set apart by a coordinating but differentiating καί, in practice they tend to be interrelated. On a relatively simple level, the recognition of inanimate objects (ἄψυχα) which thus become functionally recognition tokens is a common mechanism for the recognition of persons. The relationship of the *anagnoriseis* of persons and actions is more complex. To follow Aristotle's practice of using Sophocles' *OT* as an example, Oedipus' triple recognition of personal identities (his own, Jocasta's and Laius') entails a recognition of both the nature and the

---

6 Hinds 2000. For 'essential tragedy' in Seneca: Cowan 2017.
7 Translations of the *Poetics* are those of Halliwell 1995.

agent of two acts (murder as parricide, marriage as incest, Oedipus the perpetrator of both) and beyond that a less tangible recognition of the nature of the universe (harsh and cruel, but inscrutably ordered by divine will). *Anagnorisis* scenes foreground not only the nature and identity of the persons, acts and objects recognized, but the very cognitive act of perception, interpretation, and comprehension which constitute recognition.

This foregrounding of the process of recognition inevitably enlists the reader or audience in the same process, sometimes focalizing through characters undergoing their own *anagnorisis*, sometimes enjoying the ironic distance afforded by superior knowledge. Thus, *anagnorisis* can serve as a trope for the audience's or reader's act of recognition. Goldhill has drawn attention to the double sense of the verb ἀναγιγνώσκειν as 'to recognize' and 'to read,' and hence the participation of the reader in the process of recognition.[8] This participation can easily be extended from the parallel recognition by characters and reader of identities and situations within the world inside the text, to a metatextual recognition — primarily by the reader, but troped by the characters — of features of the text itself.[9] Indeed, recognition, without its tragic connotations of *anagnorisis*, has been identified as an important intertextual trope, symbolizing the reader's identification of a feature of the target text which she has 'seen before' in the source text. The classic instance of this is the moment towards the end of Book one of Lucan's *Bellum Civile* when the possessed *matrona* 'recognizes' in her prophetic vision of the decapitated Pompey (*BC* 1.685–686):

> *hunc ego, fluminea deformis truncus harena*
> *qui iacet, agnosco.*

> This man, who, misshapen, headless, in the river sand
> lies, I recognize.

The *matrona*'s recognition of the corpse's identity, despite the distortion of its characteristic form and absence of its distinguishing head, tropes the reader's recognition of the allusion to Vergil's description of Priam's corpse, which itself

---

8 Goldhill 1991, 1–24, esp. 5: "There is... to be recognized in the first words of the *Odyssey* the (self-)involvement of the reader or audience in comprehending the narrative of recognition."
9 "As a stock feature of tragic poetry, the recognition scene is... an obvious mechanism through which to invite audience recognition of metapoetic suggestions and narrative." Torrance 2011, 199.

alluded to the historical Pompey's death, perhaps as described in Pollio's history.[10]

In this chapter, I suggest that recognition scenes were sometimes deployed in Flavian (and earlier) epic in a way which combined their generic association with tragedy and their status as tropes for metatextual interpretation. *Anagnorisis* is both a trope for 'recognizing' tragedy and a generic marker — almost a recognition token — by which it can be recognized. Characters and readers undergoing *anagnorisis* recognize the tragic nature of that *anagnorisis* and by extension that of the wider scene, and perhaps even of the entire epic, in which it is situated. Yet the relationship between the two levels of recognition — by character and reader — is not purely one of trope or metaphor. Rather there is an interrelation between the recognitions of one's own and/or another's identity, of the implications which that identity has for one's actions, and for a wider *Weltanschauung*. The tragic associations of *anagnorisis* mean that it can act both as a formal marker of generic affiliation — an episode is marked as 'tragic' because it contains an *anagnorisis* — and as a trope for 'recognizing' the 'tragic' (in the wider sense of the worldview associated with the genre) quality of an episode, the wider epic and even the universe.

This notion of 'recognizing' the nature of the universe carries with it certain dangers. Inherent in recognition is the idea of absolute truth, truth which is of course obscured and concealed, but which is ultimately susceptible of discovery and of unchallengeable authority once it is discovered. Oedipus' true identity as the son of Laius and Iocasta was obscured by a chain of circumstances and, perhaps, a series of failures to draw the obvious conclusion, but, once recognized by himself and others, its status as truth is unassailable. Likewise, the recognition of his personal identity entails recognition of his acts of homicide and marriage as parricide and incest.[11] Translated onto the metatextual, generic plane, this could result in an absolute, positivist view of what texts 'really' mean, closing down the dialogue of genres and the negotiability of interpretation. Yet, as Cave notes near the start of his influential study of recognition, "*anagnorisis* conjoins the recovery of knowledge with a disquieting sense... that the commonly accepted co-ordinates of knowledge have gone awry."[12] By the very act of revealing that the 'truth' is very different from what concealment, disguise, misperception, and misunderstanding had led characters and readers to believe it was, recognition

---

10 Verg. *Aen.* 2.557–558; on the *matrona*: Narducci 1973, Hinds 1998, 8–10; on Priam as Pompey: Serv. *ad loc.*, Bowie 1990; on Pollio: Moles 1982–3, Morgan 2000.

11 Ahl 1991 does argue for Oedipus' innocence, but his arguments have convinced few.

12 Cave 1988, 2.

cannot but throw into question the extent to which one can be confident that the newly-revealed facts are any more absolutely true and any less likely to be lies or misapprehensions. Once epistemological instability has been released from the box, it cannot easily be put back in. Recognition thus produces a tension, even a paradox, between the revelation of absolute truth and the destruction of the very basis on which absolute truth can be known. So far from producing a univocal meaning for the texts in which it occurs, *anagnorisis* challenges the very possibility of such a meaning.

2 Recognizing kin-killing

Kin-killing, and the murder of other *philoi*, is a central feature of tragedy both in practice and in Aristotelian theory.[13] Instances abound in both extant and lost tragedies. Yet perhaps more important for the purposes of discussing elements which are marked as 'tragic' in other genres is the fact that scenes of kin-killing are often selected as emblematic of the genre.[14] It is striking that, both in actual tragedies and in evocations of 'essential tragedy,' kin-killing is closely connected with *anagnorisis*. In his discussion of the best kinds of tragic plot, Aristotle singles out those which combine recognition with kin-killing or its narrow avoidance (Arist. *Po.* 1453b29–36, 1454a2–7):

> ἔστιν δὲ πρᾶξαι μέν, ἀγνοοῦντας δὲ πρᾶξαι τὸ δεινόν, εἶθ' ὕστερον ἀναγνωρίσαι τὴν φιλίαν,
> ὥσπερ ὁ Σοφοκλέους Οἰδίπους· τοῦτο μὲν οὖν ἔξω τοῦ δράματος, ἐν δ' αὐτῇ τῇ τραγῳδίᾳ
> οἷον ὁ Ἀλκμέων ὁ Ἀστυδάμαντος ἢ ὁ Τηλέγονος ὁ ἐν τῷ τραυματίᾳ Ὀδυσσεῖ. ἔτι δὲ τρίτον
> παρὰ ταῦτα τὸ μέλλοντα ποιεῖν τι τῶν ἀνηκέστων δι' ἄγνοιαν ἀναγνωρίσαι πρὶν ποιῆσαι. ...
> τὸ δὲ πρᾶξαι δεύτερον. βέλτιον δὲ τὸ ἀγνοοῦντα μὲν πρᾶξαι, πράξαντα δὲ ἀναγνωρίσαι...
> κράτιστον δὲ [5] τὸ τελευταῖον, λέγω δὲ οἷον ἐν τῷ Κρεσφόντῃ ἢ Μερόπη μέλλει τὸν υἱὸν
> ἀποκτείνειν, ἀποκτείνει δὲ οὔ, ἀλλ' ἀνεγνώρισε, καὶ ἐν τῇ Ἰφιγενείᾳ ἡ ἀδελφὴ τὸν
> ἀδελφόν...

> Alternatively, the agents can commit the terrible deed, but do so in ignorance, then subsequently recognise the relationship, as with Sophocles' Oedipus: here, of course, the deed is

---

13 The most comprehensive study is Belfiore 2005, but see also Seaford 1994, esp. 338–367, McHardy 2005. For the purposes of brevity and elegance, I shall often use the term kin-killing as shorthand for the killing of φίλοι outside the family such as friends and allies, since my attempted coinage philoktony lacks euphony and recognizability.
14 Oedipus, Atreus, Procne, Medea, and Orestes are particularly often used in this paradigmatic way, particularly in satire and epigram, as at Pers. 5.7–9, Mart. 4.49 and Juv. 6.634–644, 8.215–221.

outside the play, but cases within the tragedy are, for instance, Alcmaeon in Astydamas, or Telegonus in *Odysseus Wounded*. This leaves a third possibility, when the person is on the point of unwittingly committing something irremediable, but recognises it before doing so. ... Next worst is execution of the deed. Better is the act done in ignorance, and followed by recognition: there is nothing repugnant here, and the recognition is thrilling. But best is the last option: I mean, for example, in *Cresphontes* Merope is about to kill her son, but recognises him in time; likewise with sister and brother in *Iphigeneia* [*among the Taurians*]...

Although Aristotle does not include it in his taxonomy of *anagnoriseis*, the scenario where belated recognition follows the crime implicitly entails another recognition scene, a failed one where recognition before the crime does not occur. This, of course, is also the non-enactment of the other scenario, where recognition occurs in time to prevent the crime. In some cases, such as Oedipus' killing of Laius as recounted by both Sophocles and Seneca, the possibility that son might have recognized father (or vice versa) but failed to do so is not even raised and hence there is no developed sense that belated recognition is the sequel to failed recognition.[15] In contrast — and in an example which is particularly relevant to this discussion — Agave's belated recognition in Euripides' *Bacchae* that the head she is holding belongs, not to a lion, but to her son Pentheus, is preceded by a marked instance of failed recognition. The messenger describes Pentheus' desperate attempts to make his Maenadic mother recognize him and thus initiate the type of *anagnorisis*-scene which averts kin-killing (Eur. *Ba.* 1115–1121):

> ὃ δὲ μίτραν κόμης ἄπο
> ἔρριψεν, ὥς νιν γνωρίσασα μὴ κτάνοι
> τλήμων Ἀγαύη, καὶ λέγει, παρηίδος
> ψαύων· Ἐγώ τοι, μῆτερ, εἰμί, παῖς σέθεν
> Πενθεύς, ὃν ἔτεκες ἐν δόμοις Ἐχίονος·
> οἴκτιρε δ' ὦ μῆτέρ με, μηδὲ ταῖς ἐμαῖς
> ἁμαρτίαισι παῖδα σὸν κατακτάνῃς.

> But he cast the head-dress
> from his hair, so that recognizing him she might not kill him

---

15 Soph. *OT* 800–813, Sen. *Oed.* 768–772. Jocasta's version at Eur. *Phoen.* 30–45 gestures towards the irony of the failed recognition as both father and son are, with "deliberate... parallelism" (Mastronarde 1994, 154) heading to Delphi 'wanting to find out' (ἐκμαθεῖν θέλων, 34 ~ μαστεύων μάθειν, 36) about each other's identity. This contrasts with Sophocles' version where Oedipus has already been to Delphi and leaves Corinth now believing that Polybus and Merope are indeed his parents and hence in danger (787–799). The only detail there about Laius' journey is Creon's that he was θεωρός (114), probably a consulter of the oracle, but maybe simply a pilgrim to a festival, and in any case the reason for consulting the oracle would be more naturally be taken as being the Sphinx than unprovoked speculation about his long-since exposed son.

wretched Agave, and he said, touching
her cheek, 'Look, mother, it is I, your son
Pentheus, whom you bore in the house of Echion:
pity me, my mother, and do not because of my
errors kill your son.'

Pentheus removes the disguise which might prove a hindrance to recognition and appeals to three of Agave's senses, sight, touch, and hearing, then emphasizes their bonds of kinship and finally entreats her explicitly not to commit filicide. Agave's failed *anagnorisis* is further combined with Pentheus' belated recognition of his own transgression, anticipating his mother's.[16] A similar moment in the messenger speech of the *Heracles* has the eponymous hero's second son tell his crazed father that he is his son, not Eurystheus', and beg him not to kill him.[17] In Seneca's version of the killings, staged rather than narrated, his wife explicitly calls on Hercules to 'recognize Megara' (*agnosce Megaram*, Sen. *HF* 1016), but he fails to do so, convinced that he is holding his stepmother Juno (*teneo novercam*, 1018). Such failed recognitions are almost more tragic than tragedy, indicating the counterfactual scenario which could lead to a happy ending — and indeed does so in tragedies such as *IT* and *Ion* — only to intensify the horror of the unwitting kin-killing which actually ensues. As such, they almost serve to 'correct' tendencies to diverge from an essentialized idea of tragedy and are thus particularly suited to constructions of the tragic, or perhaps the hypertragic, in other genres like epic.

A related but distinct example of such hypertragic recognition in Roman epic may be found in what is perhaps that genre's most famous and certainly its most controversial scene. Among the many ways in which the final scene of the *Aeneid* can be read is as a perverted recognition scene. Aeneas has been affected by Turnus' words of submission and is increasingly tending towards clemency until he fatally notices Pallas' sword-belt (Verg. *Aen.* 12.940–946):

et iam iamque magis cunctantem flectere sermo
coeperat, infelix umero cum apparuit alto
balteus et notis fulserunt cingula bullis

---

16 "...Pentheus' equally ineffectual *anagnorisis* in *Bacchae*. There the king finally acknowledges his past errors (1120–1), and realizes that his end is close (1113), but to no avail: the divine force of Dionysus should have been recognized and obeyed earlier... Agave's recognition of her own deeds, too, is tragically belated": thus Schiesaro 2003, 135, comparing the failure of Seneca's *Thyestes* to recognize Atreus' true nature.

17 ὦ φίλτατ', αὐδᾷ, μή μ' ἀποκτείνῃς, πάτερ: / σός εἰμι· σὸν παῖδ, οὐ τὸν Εὐρυσθέως ὀλεῖς. Eur. *Her.* 988–989, accepting Elmsley's conjecture for the MS reading σὸς παῖς.

> *Pallantis pueri, victum quem vulnere Turnus*
> *straverat atque umeris inimicum insigne gerebat.*
> *ille, oculis postquam saevi monimenta doloris*
> *exuviasque hausit*

> Slowly but surely, the words take effect. He's begun hesitating,
> But when a harness catches his gaze, high on Turnus's shoulder,
> Gleaming with amulet studs, those pleas have no chance of fulfilment:
> Pallas's oh so familiar belt, which Turnus had shouldered
> After defeating and killing the boy. It's the mark of a hated
> Personal foe. As his eyes drink in these mementoes of savage
> Pain, these so bitter spoils...

Of course, Aeneas already knows who Turnus is and that he has killed Pallas, so that there is no literal *anagnorisis* of identity or agency here, no change from *agnoia* to *gnosis*.[18] As Tarrant puts it, "it is tempting to see A[eneas] as having his own moment of recognition... but the emphasis here seems to be on recollection."[19] Yet perhaps it would be better to say that it is not recognition as it is commonly conceived, since the third of Aristotle's five types is in fact that 'by means of memory... when one's awareness is roused by seeing something' (διὰ μνήμης, τῷ αἰσθέσθαι τι ἰδόντα, *Po.* 1455a1). Certainly, the sword-belt stirs a painful memory in Aeneas and rouses his awareness when he sees it. In relation to the more common notion of *anagnorisis*, it acts as a recognition token, changing Aeneas' perception and identification of Turnus from that of a suppliant to be spared to a murderer to be punished. The usual function of such tokens in recognition scenes is, as we have seen, to avert at the last moment inadvertent kin-killing. Here it produces the precisely the opposite effect. *Anagnorisis* does not avert killing but rather causes it when it was on the point of being averted, effectively averting the aversion. La Penna has attractively suggested that there may be an allusion here to a scene in Accius' *Eriphyla*, where Alcmaeon's resolution to kill his eponymous mother and avenge his father Amphiaraus may have been triggered by the sight of Harmonia's necklace, the bribe which induced Eriphyle to betray her husband.[20] If so, then Vergil is exploiting an actual tragic subcate-

---

18 It could of course also be objected that Turnus is hardly Aeneas' φίλος, but the status of the Trojan-Latin conflict as a proto-Roman civil war renders its final confrontation sufficiently internecine.

19 Tarrant 2012, 335 *ad* Verg. *Aen.* 12.942. He makes a strong case elsewhere for Turnus' "recognition scene" at 12.614–696 as giving him a "claim... to tragic status" (*ibid.* 11) using the word "in a strict generic (i.e. Sophoclean) sense." (*ibid.* 11 n. 40).

20 La Penna 2002.

gory of *anagnorisis*, albeit one which in itself could be conceived of as a perversion of the Aristotelian type which forestalls kin-killing. If not, then it stands as an instance of hypertragedy within epic, perverting a potentially positive tragic type-scene into a negative and hence more essentially 'tragic' one.

Several scenes in Flavian epic exploit the tragic potentialities of *anagnorisis* and, before focusing in detail on the motif in Valerius Flaccus' Cyzicus episode, I shall briefly glance at two examples from Statius' *Thebaid* and Silius' *Punica*.[21] As might be expected from an epic which so pervasively and self-consciously acknowledges its generic pull towards tragedy, the *Thebaid* has numerous moments of tragic *anagnorisis*.[22] In the collaborative augury conducted by Amphiaraus and Melampus in Book 3, instead of unfolding an epic vision of manifest destiny like the grand prophecies of the *Aeneid*, the two seers recognize a disastrous future which combines the anti-epic nihilism of Lucan with the out-of-joint universe of tragedy, parallel antitheses to the glorious teleological epic of the winners.[23] Stover has demonstrated how the paired seers appear to be about to imitate the contrasting generic world-views of Valerius' tragically pessimistic Mopsus and epically optimistic Idmon, but in fact reinforce Statius' grim outlook by both predicting disaster.[24] As Walter puts it, "in the formation of the birds in the sky, Amphiaraus recognizes an image of future events at Thebes — and thus also of the *Thebaid* itself."[25] As a surrogate reader-interpreter of the poem, Amphiaraus recognizes in the allegory of the birds not only individuals and events, but the nature — and especially the generic nature — of the *Thebaid* itself. This act of readerly recognition climaxes in an exquisitely complex moment as he recognizes himself as one doomed to die: *quid furtim in lacrimas? illum, venerande Melampu, / qui cadit, agnosco.* ('Why do you hide your tears? That man, venerable Melampus, who falls, I recognize.' 3.546–547). The clear allusion to Lucan's *matrona* and her vision of Pompey's headless corpse, quoted above, continues the chain of intertextual tropes linking Amphiaraus to Pompey to Priam full-circle to Pompey, but it also constitutes a recognition that the *Thebaid* belongs in a tradition including the internecine *Bellum Civile* and the tragic *Aeneid* 2. Yet the

---

21 The various recognitions in Statius' *Achilleid* more subtly balance the tragic, comic, and epic associations of *anagnorisis*, and, though it would be illuminating to examine them through the lens of the current argument, such an analysis would be beyond the scope of this chapter.
22 Among the extensive studies of tragedy and the *Thebaid*, representative are Ripoll 1998b; Heslin 2008; Soerink 2014b; Augoustakis 2015; Marinis 2015.
23 On this scene, see esp. Fantham 2006, 149–158, Stover 2009.
24 Stover 2009, 450–453.
25 "In der Formation der Vögel am Himmel erkennt Amphiaraus ein Abbild der künftigen Ereignisse um Theben — und damit auch der *Thebais* selbst," Walter 2014, 169.

further twist in Amphiaraus' recognition is that it is a *self*-recognition.[26] The seer recognizes himself, an archetypal tragic figure, killed in a fratricidal war through the treachery of his wife. *Anagnorisis* of person, event and text converge as Amphiaraus recognizes himself, his death, and the epic *Thebaid* as quintessentially tragic.[27]

One of the most remarkable episodes in Silius' *Punica* takes place on the eve of the battle of Cannae and combines the motifs of *anagnorisis* and kin-killing, as a Roman soldier, Solimus, unwittingly kills his father, Satricus, a POW from the First Punic War employed by the Carthaginians as an interpreter.[28] The complexity of this episode is considerable, combining allusions to Ovid, Lucan, and even a recent incident in the civil wars of 69 CE.[29] However, here I wish briefly to focus on its exploitation of *anagnorisis* and in particular the latter's implications for issues of identity and kin-killing. Satricus sneaks out of the Carthaginian camp to try to return home but, fearing to proceed unarmed, takes a shield from the corpse of a soldier, unaware that it is that of his elder son, Mancinus (9.83–89). Here we have the first failed *anagnorisis*, leading to Satricus' *de facto* desecration of his son's corpse. The second failed *anagnorisis* occurs when the younger son, Solimus, exploiting his guard-duty to try to bury his brother's corpse, throws a spear at his unrecognized father, who in a further twist assumes that the weapon was thrown by the Carthaginians from who he is escaping: both Romans misrecognize the spear-cast as being made by and at a Carthaginian. Solimus now successfully recognizes the token of Mancinus' shield (*notis... armis*, 9.107) but misinterprets its significance, taking it not as an accidental sign of kinship (his father carrying his brother's shield), but rather as a successor to Pallas' sword-belt, a negative *anagnorisma* leading towards enmity rather than friendship (9.111–118). However, the further act of parricide (even though Satricus' first wound does eventually prove to be mortal) is averted by the father's timely recognition of his sons' names (9.121) and his explicit determination that Solimus not be guilty of kin-killing (9.125–126). There is a further recognition topos when Satricus removes

---

26 Limitations of space prevent my discussing here the dying Tydeus' even more complex self-recognition when looking at the dead Melanippus' (not yet severed) head (*sese agnovit in illo*, 'he recognized himself in him,' 8.753), but I hope to do so elsewhere.

27 Cf. Lovatt 2013a, 137: "he is graphically erased from the epic narrative by the resurgence of his traditional tragic fate."

28 Sil. 9.66–178. On the episode, see esp. Hardie 1993a, 67–69, and the items in the next footnote.

29 Ovid: Bruère 1959, 229–232, Wilson 2004, 228–229; Lucan: Fucecchi 1999, 315–322, 332–336, Marks 2010a, 137–138.

his helmet, and then the despairing Solimus foregrounds the horror of his belated *anagnorisis* (9.159–162):

> *felix o terque quaterque*
> *frater, cui fatis genitorem agnoscere ademptum.*
> *ast ego, Sidoniis imperditus, ecce, parentem*
> *vulnere cognosco.*

O brother, thrice and four times happy, from whom the recognition of our father was taken by death. But I, not killed by the Carthaginians, see, I recognize my father with a wound.

There is an almost Lucanian sense of 'ignorance is bliss' here, where the knowledge (or recognition) of a crime or suffering is actually worse than the crime itself.[30] And indeed recognition is very much to the fore. It is recognition itself (*agnoscere*, 9.160), rather than brother or life, of which Mancinus is deprived. The belatedness and futility of Solimus' *anagnorisis* is wittily — and hypertragically — expressed by replacing the recognition token that prevents kin-killing with the wound that is its enactment: it is only by the parricidal wound that Solimus recognizes his father.

Yet Satricus has already tried to absolve Solimus from kin-killing on the grounds that 'when you hotly hurled the spear at me, I was a Carthaginian' (*iaceres in me cum fervidus hastam | Poenus eram*, 9.129–130). This could be taken simply as a reassuring point about intention: Solimus did not intend to kill his father, or any fellow-Roman, because his perception was that Satricus was a Carthaginian. However, the bold existential statement *Poenus eram* offers an equally bold reinterpretation of the whole episode: Solimus defended his familial and national honour by killing someone who *was* a Carthaginian, in keeping with the epic narrative of Roman victory over Carthage. Yet the *anagnorisis* insists on recognizing a different narrative and generic pattern: one of kin-killing and civil war. The man Solimus killed, as he himself recognizes, was not a Carthaginian but his father. This is the interpretation which Solimus accepts and which drives him to suicide. This is the interpretation with which the narrator has framed the episode, declaring that a 'wicked mistake polluted the night' (*noctem sceleratus polluit error*, 9.66): the almost paradoxical collocation of crime and mistake (ἁμαρτία) conflates two key aspects of tragedy. Throughout the *Punica* there is tension between the (essential) epic narrative of glorious *bellum externum* and the tragic-Lucanian narrative of civil war, kin-killing, and decline. The competing interpretations of Satricus' death by Satricus himself and his son Solimus stand as a *mise-en-abîme* for these competing interpretations of the poem as a whole. Moreover,

---

30 Esp. *BC* 2.1–15.

they centre on moments of *anagnorisis*, recognizing a father or an enemy, a parricide or an act of war, a tragedy or an epic. These parallel acts of *anagnorisis* by characters and readers are played out more extensively in the Cyzicus episode of Valerius Flaccus' *Argonautica* 3, to which the rest of this chapter will be devoted.

3 Recognizing tragedy in Valerius' Cyzicus episode

In Book 3 of the *Argonautica*, the Argonauts leave the land of Cyzicus after a pleasant stay with their friendly hosts but, as part of Cybele's vengeance against King Cyzicus for killing her sacred lion, they drift back into port, where mutual lack of recognition leads to a battle and the death of many Cyzicans, including the king. The tragic quality of the episode, in the fullest generic sense of the word, has been widely acknowledged by scholars, and most fully elaborated by Garson, who carefully categorizes a number of key elements including *hubris, peripeteia,* and irony, but not *anagnorisis*.[31] Yet *anagnorisis* is a pervasive motif throughout the episode and is fundamental to the generic and ideological tension between epic and tragedy, heroic Gigantomachy and tragic civil war, crudely speaking, optimism and pessimism, which is particularly prominent here, but is also of central importance to the interpretation of the poem as a whole.

Already at the start of the episode proper, when Tiphys falls asleep and the Argo drifts unwittingly back into the port of Cyzicus, there is an ironic hint of failed recognition. (VF 3.43–45):

> *ut notis adlapsa vadis, dant aethere longo*
> *signa tubae vox et mediis emissa tenebris:*
> *'hostis habet portus, soliti rediere Pelasgi!'*

> As it rode into the shallows it had known, trumpets sounded alarm far through the air, and a voice cried in the midst of the darkness: 'The enemy have seized the harbour, our customary foes the Pelasgians have returned!'[32]

---

31 Garson 1964, 267–270. Buckley (2013) looks at *anagnorisis* in the Lemnian and Colchian episodes, but focuses on the recognition of the divine, specifically Venus. Antoniadis (2017, 645–650) explores elegiac elements in the episode, esp. Clite's lament. Blum 2019, 77–81 on how "the Cyzicus episode diverts the Argonauts' quest for epic glory into tragedy and civil war" (77) appeared too late to be taken full account of but is complementary to the present discussion.
32 Translations from Valerius are based on Mozley 1934, but often considerably altered to remove archaisms and to bring out key verbal motifs.

The inadvertently internecine nature of the imminent conflict has already been flagged by the narrator's reference in the previous line to the 'friendly port' (*portu amico*, 3.42), but the reference to 'familiar shallows' increases the irony. On a surface reading, *notus* is colourless, almost a cliché, like the 'familiar' sands of Sicily toward which Aeneas' fleet turns, the 'familiar' ridges which Actaeon fills with mournful complaints, or in the *Argonautica* itself, the 'familiar' woods in which Diana meets Apollo while he is Admetus' herdsman, among many other examples.[33] At best it could serve as an Alexandrian footnote or an intertextual trope, signalling the familiarity of the episode in Apollonius, Varro Atacinus, and other pre-Valerian texts.[34] Yet its very conventionality intensifies the jarring effect of its defamiliarizing incongruity in the present context. For the most important issue in the whole narrative is that, though the port *should be* familiar to the Argonauts — both in the purely cognitive sense that the Argo has so recently left it, and with the regular additional emotional colour that it is the home of their close friends — it fatally is not. The port does not appear familiar (*notus*) to them and it is clear that they do not recognize (*noscere*) it.[35] This failed *anagnorisis* is brutally underlined by juxtaposing the 'familiar port' with the almost disembodied voice issuing through the mimetically befuddling shadows, misrecognizing the Argonauts as Pelasgians, misconstruing the situation as 'the enemy has the port' (*hostis habet portus*, 3.45), a pointed inversion of what the narrator has just told us is the true state of affairs, that this is a port friendly to the Minyae (*portu... amico*, 3.42). Soon afterwards, it is made explicit that the Argonauts do not recognize the city of Cyzicus any more than its citizens recognize them, as they do not perceive what territory they are in or what dangers they face (*nec quae regio aut discrimina cernunt*, 3.75). All of this could have been presented as merely a misrecognition or a neutral non-recognition, but the seemingly banal reference to *nota vada* subtly signals that both port and Minyae should have been recognized, so that this is a failed recognition.

During the battle itself, two episodes of failed recognition and the attendant failure to avert the killing of a friend are tellingly juxtaposed. In the first, Hercules

---

33 *et tandem laeti notae advertuntur harenae*, Verg. *Aen.* 5.34; *maestisque repleta iuga nota querellis*, Ov. *Met.* 3.239, where the context is also one of failed *anagnorisis*, though the ridges are tangential to the hounds' inability to recognize the metamorphosed Actaeon; *famulo notis soror obvia silvis*, VF 1.447.

34 On such tropes, see esp. Barchiesi 1995; Hinds 1998, 1–16.

35 As often, Spaltenstein (2004, 18) notes the oddity, which other commentators miss, but not its full implications: "*Notis* est illogique puisqu'ils ne s'en avisent pas, mais cette épithète doit rappeler l'élément central de cette péripétie, qui est le paradoxe."

kills a Cyzican whose name is lost through textual corruption and who recognizes the identity of his killer too late (3.167–172):

> *levis ante pedes subsederat †Hidmont.*
> *occupat os barbamque viri clavamque superne*
> *intonat 'occumbes' et 'nunc' ait 'Herculis armis,*
> *donum ingens semperque tuis mirabile fatum.'*
> *horruit ille cadens nomenque agnovit amicum*
> *primus et ignaris dirum scelus attulit umbris.*

> The nimble †Hidmon† had sunk at his feet; Hercules seized his chin and beard and brought down his club's thunder-stroke upon him from above, and 'Now will you fall,' he cries, 'by Hercules' own weapon — no slight gift and a fate ever to be wondered at by your kin.' The other shuddered as he fell, for he straightway recognized his friend's name; and he bore the horrid deed down to the unwitting shades.

Dinter, in his discussion of epigrammatic motifs in the *Argonautica*, identifies Hercules' flyting as "an 'anti-epitaph,' which excludes the name of the dead man but preserves the memory of the killer."[36] There is already, therefore, a perversion of an epic convention, "that the slain bestows fame on the slayer."[37] Yet it is not mere literalism to point out that Hercules does not use his victim's name because he does not know it, or rather does not know that he knows it — and it is a strangely appropriate accident of transmission that modern readers do not know his name either.[38] The inversion of the epic convention corresponds to an inversion of the tragic *anagnorisis*.[39] Slayer is named rather than slain, which means that the recognition token of the name is passed in the wrong direction, failing to enable Hercules identify his victim and thus avert the killing, causing the victim alone, belatedly and futilely, to recognize his killer and hence the full horror of the act.[40] *Nomenque agnovit amicum.* He recognizes a friend's name, but also that

---

36 Dinter 2009, 542.

37 Dinter 2009, 541, citing Hom. *Il.* 7.89–91.

38 It seems likely that *Hidmon* derives from a scribe's eye slipping to *Idmon* in the same *sedes* at 3.175, in which case it may offer no palaeographic assistance in determining the lost name, but it is tempting to see a further confusion of categories by having a similarly-named Argonautic killer and Cyzican victim in quick succession.

39 It should be acknowledged that the use of the imminent victim's name as a recognition token averting kin-killing does not occur in extant Attic or Roman tragedy, though it is clearly analogous to other, visual tokens. If Hyg. *Fab.* 100 can be used to reconstruct Sophocles' *Mysians*, then Auge's call to her rapist Hercules leading to her son Telephus' recognition of her and hence preventing his killing her (100.4) would be a close parallel.

40 The victim's recognition of a name has greater effect when Orestes hears Iphigenia's name, setting in motion the chain of *anagnoriseis* which averts her sacrifice of him: ΙΦ: Ἦ 'ν Αὐλίδι

the name is that of a friend, and hence that it is a friend who is killing a friend in tragic internecine slaughter.[41]

Immediately following this comes Idmon's killing of his particular guest-friend among the Cyzicans, Ornytus, who is pathetically apostrophized (3.173–177):

> nec tibi Thessalicos tunc profuit, Ornyte, reges
> hospitiis aut mente moras fovisse benigna
> et dapibus sacrasse diem, procul advenit Idmon
> oblatumque ferit, galeam cristasque rubentes
> (heu tua dona) gerens.

Nothing availed it in that hour, Ornytus, that you had cherished the Thessalian princes in friendliness, or with kind intent had sought to delay them and had kept the day holy to your household gods; Idmon draws hither from close by and strikes you in the encounter, wearing the helmet with its scarlet plume, that was, alas! your gift.

Idmon, the seer, the one who knows (ἴδμων), does not recognize his host and benefactor.[42] Manuwald is of course quite right to detect here an instance of the topos whereby a warrior's admirable behaviour was of no benefit in preventing his death.[43] Yet here once more, Valerius takes the established convention and gives it a twist suited to the context of tragic confusion and failed recognition. The *quid profuit?* topos, as Nisbet and Hubbard term it, tends to have a primarily moral implication, lamenting that a premature death was the only reward for a virtuous life, with the attendant implication about the injustice of the universe or the indifference of the gods.[44] These implications are present here too, of course.

σφαγεῖσ' ἐπιστέλλει τάδε / ζῶσ' Ἰφιγένεια, τοῖς ἐκεῖ δ' οὐ ζῶσ' ἔτι —/ OP: ποῦ δ' ἔστ' ἐκείνη; κατ-θανοῦσ' ἥκει πάλιν; / ΙΦ: ἥδ' ἣν ὁρᾷς σύ: ('IPH: She who was killed in Aulis, Iphigenia, alive, send this — OR: Where is she? Has she who died come back again? IPH: This is she whom you see.' Eur. *IT* 770–773). On *anagnorisis* and (averted) kin-killing in *IT*, see Belfiore 2000, 29–34. The motif also appears a little later in Silius' Satricus episode, discussed above.

41 "narrative elements typical of internal, not external conflicts... Friend kills friend." Davis 2015, 166, on this episode.

42 On the etymological connotations of Idmon's name, see Zissos 2008, 198 *ad* 1.228 and esp. Wijsman 1996, 15 *ad* 5.2–3, including the calque *non inscius*.

43 Manuwald 2015, 111 *ad* 3.173–174, citing Verg. *Aen.* 11.843–844 and Hor. *Carm.* 1.28.4–6.

44 In different contexts, of course, it can serve as a more morally neutral reflection on the universality of death (sometimes even as a form of *consolatio*), since wealth, power, and other worldly goods profit their bearers nothing. E.g. *quid genus aut virtus aut optima profuit illi | mater, et amplexum Caesaris esse focos?* Prop. 3.18.11–12 (on Marcellus), 4.11.11–12 (on Cornelia).

Ornytus is praised for his practice of the virtue of hospitality, a virtue which profited him nothing on two levels, since the gods did not reward his moral excellence and the Argonauts — treated almost as gods themselves (*dapibus sacrasse diem*)—reciprocated his *xenia* with death. Yet, while divine justice, both Cybele's excessive vengeance and Jupiter's permissiveness, is a pervasive theme of the Cyzicus episode, the Argonauts themselves are not deliberately and wickedly repaying hospitality with murder. In this perverted context, the almost bathetic implication of the *quid profuit?* topos is that Ornytus' hospitality was profitless, not because his virtue was unrewarded, but because the close acquaintance which he established with the Argonauts was not sufficient for Idmon to recognize and hence refrain from killing him. Valerius retains the cosmic pessimism of the *quid profuit?* topos, but ironically combines it with a witty twist on failed *anagnorisis*.

The connection with (failed) *anagnorisis* is further strengthened by the presence of (failed) recognition tokens. Idmon is wearing the armour which Ornytus had given to him as a guest-gift (*heu tua dona*, 3.177). Valerius could easily have had the Argonaut ironically kill his host with the Cyzican's own sword or spear, introducing the motif of the deadly gift comparable to, yet distinct from, the role Hector's sword plays in the suicide of Sophocles' Ajax.[45] Such a move would also have meshed with the episode's imagery of internecine conflict, as Ornytus would become the victim not only of his guest but of his own weapon. But Valerius chooses not to do this. Instead it is a helmet with red crest (*galeam cristasque rubentes*, 3.176) which Ornytus gave and which Idmon wears.[46] The emphatically distinctive and conspicuous item of clothing ought to be the perfect recognition token, producing *anagnorisis* and averting xenocide.[47] However, the failure of *anagnorisis* here is even more complete than with the belated

---

45 Esp. Soph. *Aj.* 815–818.

46 There is also an intriguing, if elusive, web of intertextual engagements with the Nisus and Euryalus episode in *Aeneid* 9. The phrase *cristasque rubentes* occurs only here and in the description of the spoils which Ascanius offers to Nisus before the night expedition: *ipsum illum, clipeum cristasque rubentis | excipiam sorti, iam nunc tua praemia, Nise* ('That [sc. Turnus'] horse and shield and ruddy crest I will except from the lot; even now they are your rewards, Nisus,' Verg. *Aen.* 9.270–271). This itself picks up the Vergilian narrator's description of Turnus exhorting the Latins earlier in the book (*maculis quem Thracius albis | portat equus cristaque tegit galea aurea rubra*, 'a Thracian horse with white spots carries him; a golden helmet with a ruddy crest covers his head,' 9.49–50).

47 The detail that the *anagnorismata* were a gift might even evoke the motif of the parent giving trinkets to the exposed, abandoned or otherwise surrendered child, which later trigger recognition.

recognition of Hercules, as Ornytus does not recognize his guest-friend by means of his tokens and thus misses even the chance of averting xenocide.

Among all these failed recognitions, throwing them into sharp relief, is one successful *anagnorisis* which prevents kin-killing (VF 3.186–189):

> accessere (nefas) tenebris fallacibus acti
> Tyndaridae in sese. Castor prius ibat in ictus
> nescius, ast illos nova lux subitusque diremit
> frontis apex.

> There meet (unspeakable!) the sons of Tyndareus, embroiled by the treacherous darkness:
> Castor was the first about to strike unknowing, when a strange light and a sudden radiance
> on their brows separated them.

The internecine nature of the conflict is here massively intensified. Instead of hosts fighting guests, friends killing friends, we have two members of the same side turning on each other, and worse than that, brothers, fratricide being one of the most potent metaphors of civil war.[48] Nor are these dysfunctional twins like Eteocles and Polynices, or Romulus and Remus. The Dioscuri are paradigms of fraternal concord and devotion.[49] It is even tempting to see in the bold use of *in sese* for *inter se* a hint that, in attacking his twin, each is actually attacking himself. This is *nefas* indeed. Of course, as with all the killings in Cyzicus, the attack is the result, not of wickedness, but of non-recognition. This element is particularly explicit here, as the brothers are 'driven by the deceptive shadows' (*tenebris fallacibus acti*, 3.186) and Castor is about to strike the first blow 'unknowing' (*nescius*, 188).

However, fratricide is averted, as in the best Aristotelian plot, by *anagnorisis*, produced by a combination of recognition tokens and an implicit divine intervention. The light with which Jupiter had distinguished his sons back at the Argo's launch (1.568–573) is doubly transformed here. The elaborate conflation of ideas, combining features of hendiadys and *schema Horatianum*, makes the 'new light' into a sort of helmet, 'the sudden peak of their forehead,' precisely the token which has just failed to produce recognition between Idmon and Ornytus. While *nova* might be stretched to refer to Jupiter's comparatively recent bestowing of the light, *subitus* cannot, and there is hence the subtle implication that Jupiter is only now intervening to prevent fratricide, conforming to the pattern of divine

---

48 Bernstein 2008, 215 n. 74, Davis 2015, 166. Cf. Stocks 2018 on fratricide and civil war in Silius.
49 E.g. V. Max. 5.5.3.

intervention to forestall kin-killing.[50] In extant tragedy, such intervention is not combined with *anagnorisis*. Theoclymenus in Euripides' *Helen* about to kill his sister Theonoe and the eponymous hero of the *Orestes* his cousin (and future wife) Hermione are in full knowledge of their identities when, respectively, the Dioscuri and Apollo appear *ex machina* to forbid them.[51] Euripides' Heracles, in his madness, does not recognize his father Amphitryon, but Athena prevents the parricide not by producing *anagnorisis*, but by knocking him out with a rock.[52] One might also think of Ovid's two very tragic depictions of the moment when Arcas almost kills his mother Callisto, not recognizing her metamorphosed bear-form[53] In the *Metamorphoses* version, she 'resembled one who recognized' (*cognoscenti similis fuit*, Ov. *Met.* 2.501), before Jupiter 'prevented' him (*arcuit*, 505) and 'removed the unspeakable crime' (*nefasque sustulit*, 505–506) by katasterizing them both. Failed recognition does not prevent kin-killing, so divine intervention is required.[54] With the Dioscuri in Cyzicus we have another instance of tragic epic's being more tragic than tragedy, combining two common, but generally separate, tragic ways of not killing a kinsman, *anagnorisis*, and divine intervention.

The successful *anagnorisis* of Castor and Pollux successfully averts fratricide. In part, this throws into relief all the surrounding failed *anagnoriseis*, highlighting the alternative path which the plot does not take for Ornytus and the other Cyzicans. However, as with all 'pessimistic' readings, we must beware of adopting too monolithically gloomy an approach and of forcing even positive elements into a uniformly negative pattern. Certainly, the averting of the fratricide does set

---

50 *Pace* Manuwald 2015, 115: "The light is 'new' because Jupiter had only given it to Castor and Pollux at the start of the voyage." Spaltenstein 2004, 64 comes closer: "[elle] brille subitement à ce moment pour les séparer: si elle brillait sans cesse, ils se seraient reconnus aussitôt... leur père intervient miraculeusement."

51 Eur. *Hel.* 1642–1657, esp. 1656: ἀλλ' ἴσχε μὲν σῆς συγγόνου μέλαν ξίφος; *Or.* 1627–1628, though the emphasis is less on their existing blood-kinship (through all four parents) than on their predestined marriage: ἐφ' ἧς δ' ἔχεις, Ὀρέστα, φάσγανον δέρῃ, / γῆμαι πέπρωταί σ' Ἑρμιόνην (1654–1655).

52 Eur. *Her.* 1001–1009. Seneca's Amphitryon despairingly invites parricide, but it is prevented by a more naturalistic loss of consciousness (*HF* 1039–1059). Since Juno's prologue reveals that the apparently naturalistic onset of the madness is in fact the work of the Furies, this ending could more implicitly be all that mortal spectators (on stage and off) can see of a similar divine intervention.

53 Ov. *Met.* 2.496–507 and *Fast.* 2.183–188.

54 Robinson 2010, 176 *ad* Ov. *Fast.* 2.183-188 on "the focus on Callisto and Arcas and this tragic moment of failed recognition." Cf. Trinacty (2017, 176–179) on the allusion at Sen. *Oed.* 1051 (*siste, ne in matrem incidas*) to Arcas' chancing across Callisto (*incidit in matrem*, Ov. *Met.* 2.500).

a limit on the internecine conflict, and indeed confines this ultimate transgression of bonds to those between Argonauts and Cyzicans, not those between members of the same side. However, the moment of relief is brief and in the *Todeskette* of Cyzican victims whom the Dioscuri immediately proceed to slaughter, Valerius deftly includes an Itys (3.189), namesake of the tragic victim of Procne's filicide, and a Thapsus (3.191), eponym of an emblematic civil war battle. The tragic and Lucanian quality of the episode is emphatically reasserted.

Before turning to the most significant *anagnorisis* in the Cyzicus episode, it is worth briefly glancing at two moments of recognition which follow the slaughter. The women of Cyzicus search the battlefield for the bodies of their menfolk (VF 3.274–276):

> *tum super exsangues confertae caedis acervos*
> *praecipiti plangore ruunt, agnoscit in alta*
> *strage virum sua texta parens, sua munera coniunx.*

> Then the mourners rush wildly upon the dense heaps of bloodless slain; among the high-piled corpses of the heroes a mother recognises her woven work, a wife her gift.

This is a conventional type-scene in both epic and historiography, as Pagán has skilfully shown, and it regularly includes "verbs of discovery or visual perception."[55] Yet the recognition is usually of the corpses themselves.[56] Valerius even leads the reader to think that it is 'a man' or 'a husband' who is recognized, as the ambiguous form *virum* appears accusative singular before the actual object, *sua texta*, leads to its recognition as genitive plural. The Cyzican mothers and wives recognize (*agnoscit*), not the bodies themselves but their own woven garments, their own gifts, recognition tokens which fail to avert the death of kin, not because they are unsuccessful in producing *anagnorisis*, but because they do so too late and in the wrong people. The final failed *anagnorisis* offers a further, painfully ironic variation on the motif. It comes at the funeral as Jason looks at the corpse of Cyzicus and finds it unrecognizable (VF 3.286–289):

> *ille ubi concretos pingui iam sanguine crines*
> *pallentesque genas infractaque pectore caro*

---

55 Pagán 2000, esp. 432–433 for the "eight common elements," quoting from 432. The Cyzicus scene is not part of the representative sample she draws from Sallust, Livy, Tacitus, Lucan, Statius, and Silius.

56 Again, Spaltenstein 2004, 90 picks up the oddity but not its implications: "Val. substitue ingénieusement la reconnaiscance des cadeaux à celle des morts."

tela neque hesternos agnovit in hospite vultus,
ingemit atque artus fatur complexus amicos:

He, when he saw the locks now matted with rich blood and the pallid cheeks and the darts shattered on the breast he loved, nor recognised in his host the face known but yesterday, groaned, and clasping his friend's limbs cried...

The irony of course is that Jason, who fatally failed to recognize Cyzicus when he was about to kill him, does actually do so here.[57] So *neque... agnovit* must convey a notion closer to Aeneas' *quantum mutatus ab illo / Hectore* (Verg. *Aen.* 2.274–275). Yet Valerius' decision to phrase the idea that Cyzicus is 'unrecognizable' in terms of failed *anagnorisis* inevitably and agonizingly foregrounds the role which recognition and its failure have played in the episode.

However, the most important in the chain of *anagnoriseis* comes a little earlier, at the moment when the Argonauts for the first time belatedly recognize their victims and what they have done to them (VF 3.262–266):

illi autem neque adhuc gemitus neque conscia facti
ora levant, tenet exsangues rigor horridus artus
ceu pavet ad crines et tristia Pentheos ora
Thyias, ubi impulsae iam se deus agmine matris
abstulit et caesi vanescunt cornua tauri.

But they can neither utter a groan nor lift their guilty eyes; freezing horror binds their strengthless limbs; even as the Bacchant pales at the sight of the hair and sad face of Pentheus, when the god has withdrawn from the frenzy-driven mother's troop, and the horns of the slain bull fade away.

The Argonauts' gradual, horrified recognition of the Cyzicans and hence of the internecine nature of the slaughter is compared in a simile to Agave's recognition of Pentheus' head and hence the fact of her filicide.[58] The parallels with the exodos of Euripides' *Bacchae* are striking. They extend even to the roles of Cyzicus and Pentheus as — albeit to vastly different degrees — theomachs, punished by Cybele and Dionysus respectively through their *philoi*, though Agave is another object as well as the instrument of the latter's vengeance, where the Minyae are

---

57 "*Neque agnovit vultus* surenchérit avec un paradoxe: Jason a reconnu Cyzicus, mais ne le retrouve pas tel qu'il était." Spaltenstein 2004, 93–94.
58 On this simile, see Fitch 1976, 117; Hershkowitz 1998a, 39–41; Manuwald 1999, 82, and 2015, 134–135; Spaltenstein 2004, 88–89. Gärtner (1994) disappointingly only includes it in her catalogues of similes.

innocent tools. However, the most striking thing about this passage is the multiple ways in which it exploits the tragic motif of *anagnorisis*. The generic intrusion of tragedy into epic is marked, as with the earlier failed recognitions, by the distinctively tragic formal motif of *anagnorisis*, in this case the belated recognition which reveals rather than averting kin-killing. Yet, unlike the other instances in the Cyzicus episode, where the allusion was purely formal, here the generic link is reinforced by intertextuality with a specific tragic text. The fact that the intertextual link occurs within a simile further intensifies the effect, as it does with the simile comparing Dido's dream to the explicitly tragic Pentheus and Orestes.[59] Similes are privileged textual sites where the reader is encouraged to consider a full range of points of comparison. Not only is Jason like Agave and the Cyzican battle like a filicide, but the *Argonautica* is like the *Bacchae*, an epic like a tragedy. The comparative function of the simile acts in parallel with the recognitive function of *anagnorisis*, as readers and characters compare the situation to tragedy and recognize it as a tragedy. The implications are further enriched by intertextuality with Lucan's simile at 7.777–780 when the haunted Caesarean troops after Pharsalus are compared to the tragic kin-killers Orestes and Agave. Valerius not only triangulates the intertextuality, linking to Euripidean tragedy and Lucanian civil war, but also produces a window allusion, alluding to Lucan's own allusion to Euripides and asserting that civil war is itself tragic.

Just as the generic affiliation with tragedy operates on multiple levels, so does the function of the *anagnorisis*. The parallelism between recognition of person and of deed — I recognize my *philos* and therefore I recognize that my act of killing them was internecine — is an integral part of the pattern of failed and belated *anagnorisis*. Here, however, the greater, almost explicit attention which Valerius draws to the generic dimension encourages the reader to reflect more on her own *anagnorisis*, her recognition of what kind of narrative this is. Stover has made a strong case, as part of his interpretation of the *Argonautica* as a strongly pro-Vespasianic poem, for the Cyzicus episode as a gigantomachy, a war with internecine elements reflecting the Flavian war against the Vitellians, but one where there is nevertheless a clear distinction between heroes and villains: "what [Valerius] delivers is a most un-Lucanian civil war. The winning side unambiguously possesses a moral superiority over the defeated. The episode is indeed tragic, but it is not a senseless tragedy."[60] Though Stover accommodates a sort of

---

59 Verg. *Aen.* 4.469–473.

60 Stover 2012, 113–150, quoting from 125. On Gigantomachy in Flavian propaganda, see also Rebeggiani 2018, 132, 143–146, 246–247, 253–254. For a different view on heroes and villains in

tragedy into his reading, it could be argued that it corresponds more closely to (at least an essentialized notion of) epic. Gigantomachy is, of course, the archetypal subject-matter of epic narrative, but more significantly epic is the genre of the victors on their teleological path to glory.[61] Certainly there are many elements in the Cyzicus episode which encourage such a reading, but this moment of *anagnorisis* challenges them. The reader is invited to focalize through the Argonauts as both she and they, with Stover, interpret their victory as an epic gigantomachy, only for the tragic *anagnorisis* to force both her and them to recognize that this is in fact a tragedy of civil war.

4 Coda

Even this short chapter has shown how diverse are the ways in which the tragic motif of *anagnorisis* can be and is exploited by epic poets, and I hope that it has also demonstrated the potential for further work in this area. It would be reductive to offer too constrictive a definition of the role of tragic *anagnorisis* in Roman epic. However, there are three key points that are worth restating. Epic tends to treat *anagnorisis* as distinctively tragic and a generic marker of tragic *contaminatio* within its own generic code. It is debatable whether the association is strong enough for *anagnorisis* to evoke tragedy entirely on its own, but in most cases epic poets combine it with other clear generic markers acting in tandem. Epic tends to make *anagnorisis* 'hypertragic,' more tragic than its occurrences in many actual tragedies and corresponding more closely to a notion of 'essential tragedy,' especially in its exclusion or perversion of recognitions which lead to happy outcomes. Finally, *anagnorisis* invites the reader to enact her own recognition, not only of the characters and events of the text, but of its generic nature, so that *anagnorisis* serves as both a trope for and the token of the recognition of tragedy.[62]

---

the *Argonautica*, see Cowan 2014. A representative example of a pessimistic reading of the *Argonautica* is Davis 2010.

61 "The combination of gods and battle makes the Gigantomachy the grandest theme of martial epic." Innes 1979, 166. See also Ov. *Am.* 2.1.11–16 with McKeown 1998, 10–11 *ad loc.* for further references. Epic and victory: Quint 1993, 19–96; the title of Stover's monograph is of course itself an allusion to Quint's.

62 Versions of this paper were delivered to Homer Seminar IX at the Australian National University, ASCS 39 at the University of Queensland, and the University of Sydney Classics and Ancient History research seminar. I am grateful to all three audiences for helpful questions and comments.

Sophia Papaioannou

Apollonius' 'Further Voices': Cameo Appearances of Greek Tragedy in Valerius Flaccus' *Argonautica*

1 Introduction

Greek drama sits firmly at the foundation of the Roman epic plot and determines its character as early as Ennius, the *pater* of Roman poetry, who wrote the quintessential epic of Republican Rome but began and ended his literary career as a composer of *tragoediae*.[1] In the *Aeneid*, Attic tragedy, in terms of emotional effect and formal structure — distinct techniques of tragic drama as specified in Aristotle's *Poetics* —, has, since Heinze, been recognized as an organic part of the epic text, aiding Vergil to accomplish his ultimate poetic goal, which was "to arouse a sense of the sublime in his audience" (383). The accommodation of Greek tragedy inside Vergil's epic text is directed by an ongoing antagonism of variant 'further voices' (Panoussi, Putnam, Lyne),[2] which alternatively has been defined more abstractly as "dualism" (Hardie 1993a).[3]

In a way, Valerius' dynamic engagement with the *Aeneid* was unavoidable. The *Aeneid* very shortly after Vergil's death had assumed the status of a classic, to which any epic poem written thereafter would be compared. Given the fundamental role of Greek tragedy in determining the character of Vergil's epic voice, it must be assumed that for every epic successor of Vergil, starting with Ovid,

---

1 His last tragedy, *Thyestes*, premiered in 169 BCE; cf. Conte 1994, 76. Ennius, *Thyestes* 1.295–312 Klotz (1953).

2 The quotation reproduces, of course, the title of Lyne's *Further Voices in Vergil's Aeneid* (1987), that first pointed at the systematically distracting and persistent, though discrete, influence of other poetic genres, most prominently tragedy, on the formation of Vergil's epic voice. The works of Putnam (1995) and Panoussi (2009) build on Lyne, as they focus on identifying the antagonistic generic trends (exclusively tragedy in the case of Panoussi) at the interface of Vergil's epic narrative. According to Panoussi, the employment of tragedy offered Vergil the literary means to express his skepticism about Augustus' new regime in Rome (1–7). Other leading modern studies on the influence of Greek tragedy on Vergil include Hardie 1997 and Conte 2007.

3 A trend which Hardie believes to have originated already in Ennius (Hardie 1997, 323).

https://doi.org/10.1515/9783110709841-005

Greek tragedy was read, more or less consciously, through the lens of the *Aeneid*.[4] Vergil's reception of tragedy in the *Aeneid* is the rule that dictates the shaping of Valerius' tragic appropriation politics, even on those occasions when Valerius' epic narrative is in direct and explicit dialogue with some Greek tragedy, as, most conspicuously, in the *Hypsipyle* episode.[5] The visible, even though often uncomfortable, coexistence of epic and tragedy in the *Aeneid*[6] sets a paradigm for the reception of the Greek tragic voice in the *Argonautica*, the first Roman mythological epic in the traditional mould after the *Aeneid*, and becomes the leading premise of my study, for Vergil's *Aeneid*, more than any other product of the epic tradition, has influenced Valerius' own view of Greek tragedy. The latter, in his effort to legitimize himself as the successor of Vergil, revisits and refines the tension between epic and tragedy. Recent readings on the reception of Greek tragedy in Ovid through the prism of Vergil will offer crucial instruction to my examination,[7] even though Ovid's reception politics of the Vergilian epic (and traditional epic more broadly) was markedly different from Valerius' own.

I have chosen to study the tension between epic and tragedy in the *Argonautica*, in four different episodes that may be defined as tragic either because their literary sources include some surviving Greek tragic model, or because they exhibit distinct tragic themes and modalities.[8] In the former category belongs, most conspicuously, the Lemnian episode and Jason's brief love affair with Queen Hypsipyle, which draws, among others, on Euripides' *Hypsipyle*. This episode has attracted considerable attention by Valerian scholars, not least because of its distinct tragic subtext, and as such is excluded from my study, which focuses on a set of other narrative units, shorter and less explicit in the way they

---

4 Critics agree that Roman tragedy claims an equally important contribution to the development of Vergil's tragic voice, but the absence of extant Latin plays as a rule does not allow the extraction of firm conclusions to that extent. On Roman tragedy in Vergil see Wigodsky 1972, esp. 80–97; Zorzetti 1990; Hardie 1997, 323–325; Galinsky 2003, 290–293; Scafoglio 2007, 781–787.

5 For a list of Athenian plays that deal with the Argonautic cycle, see Vian 1974, xxxvi–vii.

6 Cf. Conte 2007, 161: "for Virgil... destabilizing the meaning of his text by fuelling it with internal contradictions is a genuine strategy of composition, a strategy by which the 'ambiguous' manner of Greek tragedy infects the language of epic."

7 A topic that has not yet received systematic and exclusive study; some discussion of this important issue of generic reception in the Latin epic tradition is recorded recently in Curley 2013, esp. 50–58 and 221–230; and *passim* in all five chapters of Paschalis 2015.

8 Obviously one should acknowledge that many Greek tragedies had inspired the composition of Latin tragedies under the same title and of similar plot, and also the fact that these *tragoediae* are now lost; thus one may only hypothesize of their influence on the epics of Vergil and his successors; the interaction between the surviving fragments of *tragoediae* and the epics of Valerius and Statius is studied in Augoustakis' chapter in the present volume.

use their tragic background as backdrop for the interpretation of their epic function: these include the liberation of Hesione by Hercules and Telamon in *Arg.* 2,
and the Io story, which is embedded inside Orpheus' song in *Arg.* 4. Both these
episodes presuppose at least one Greek tragic model, according to the ancient
testimonies, and their tragic backdrop will be explored in the second half of my
paper. In the first half of my discussion I shall turn to a couple of tragically coloured units with no traceable tragedy as literary source. One such unit is the Cyzicus episode, which was written under the influence of Vergilian episodes of
tragic character. Before turning to Cyzicus, I shall discuss the death by suicide of
Jason's parents at the close of Book 1. This episode is hardly expected to feature
in an epic narrative — suicides take place primarily in tragedies. The only epic
victim of a suicide, Ajax, is driven to this act by the consequences of his actions
under the possession of madness — itself a state that distinguishes characters of
tragedy, associated as it is with ecstasis which is a state of (subconscious and
involuntary) acting. My analysis of the Aeson episode will serve a programmatic
function in my study, because it will map out Valerius' thoughtful employment
of Greek tragedy both in episodes that are explicitly relying on dramatic models
and in those that are less obviously inclusive of tragic elements. Further, it will
discuss the predilection for specific tragic subtexts that have previously been
used to infuse with tragic elements key Vergilian characters and episodes, and
will illustrate the interpretative impact of this generic intersection in the Vergilian epic context upon Valerius' appropriation of the tragic Vergil.

Before we analyse the Greek tragic subtext behind each of the four narratives
under study, it might be useful to identify also their special and distinct *narrative
identity* as tragic narratives, which is reflected in their function in the narrative
trajectory. For this identification, too, I shall turn to the *Aeneid* and the appropriation of tragedy therein. Tragically coloured epic narratives do not conform to the
"epic code"[9] but rather operate as elements of "regressive repetition," according
to Quint's definition of the tragic. For Quint, tragedy in the *Aeneid* is to be found
in all those episodes developing around events and persons that threaten to impede the linear course of the epic plot, Aeneas' predestined mission, which is the
foundation of a new city at Latium. Dido's unit, for example, qualifies as a tragic
one, not only because the performance of Dido is constructed against that of a
series of well-known heroines from Greek (and Roman) tragedy, but also because

---

9 A term coined by Conte in order to describe the generic characteristics of an epic poet, "the
objective narrative structure, conventions, expectations defined by epic as a literary genre, for
example heroic combat, divine interventions, extended similes, and so forth"; see Segal's fore-
word in his translation of Conte 1986.

her erotic passion for Aeneas threatens to impede the hero from realizing the foundation of the Roman nation. And Aeneas is a tragic hero, at least in the books of the Carthaginian unit, because, in his eagerness to put an end to his *labores*, he repeatedly misreads the signs, which results in abortive efforts to found Rome, or he readily forgets his mission and needs to be reminded thereof by divine intervention — in Quint's understanding, Aeneas risks terminating the linear trajectory of the epic plot before completion. Quint, further, notes that the tragic element in the books of the Carthaginian unit, especially in *Aeneid 3*, is enhanced by the numerous evocations of tragic intertexts, including Euripides' portrayals of Hecuba and Andromache, and of course, of Medea and Phaedra.[10]

The leading external agent/cause of "regressive repetition" in the *Aeneid* throughout the poem is the irate Juno, directly (when she stirs up the storm in Book 1 or invites Allecto in Book 7) or indirectly (when she allies with Venus to cause Dido fall in love with Aeneas). Juno operates metapoetically as an antagonist to Vergil and tries to advance her own version of Aeneas' post-Iliadic destiny, which is fluid and open to revisions but excludes settlement at the predestined site of Latium. The intervening Juno in Valerius is mindful of that role of her Vergilian counterpart, and in the *Argonautica* operates under the exact opposite motives: she wishes for Jason's epic mission to continue, therefore at the opening of Book 2 she prevents the news of Aeson's and Alcimede's suicide from reaching the hero, lest this will cause him to terminate his expedition and turn back to avenge his parents.[11]

One additional detail: Panoussi's study of the *Aeneid*, her political interpretation of the phenomenon (the 'tragic,' anti-Augustan voice) aside, has crucially stressed the significance of ritual and its proper appreciation in the context of an epic narrative. Ritual is a traditional ceremony that observes a set protocol. It is a performance that adheres to a prescribed order, and as a performative act it is tightly connected with theatrical action and Greek tragedy more explicitly. The performative dimension of ritual is a sound reason that explains the considerable presence of ritual activities in Greek drama,[12] and favourite such rituals include the sacrifice and the funeral. *Agamemnon, Trachiniae, Heracles, Orestes* or *Iphigeneia at Aulis* are tragedies that develop around, and obtain meaning on the basis of, the rite of sacrifice. *Seven against Thebes, Antigone,* and *Ajax* develop around death and funeral. Sacrifices and funerals are two ritual ceremonies with

---

10 See the full argument in Quint 1993.
11 See the comments on Juno's role, in Bernstein 2008, 49.
12 On the entwinement of ritual action and theatrical action see Sourvinou-Inwood 2005, 7–24; ead. 1994, 269–290; and Easterling 1988, 87–109 (with earlier bibliography in nn. 2–7).

recurrent presence not only in the *Argonautica* but in epic narratives in general, and as such they furnish an obvious point of intersection between epic and tragedy. Finally, before I embark on my examination of the function of ritual in the tragic subtext of the four Valerian episodes noted above, I should note that ritual in epic is often perverted (or interrupted), and that this ritual failure communicates the tension between the forming new epic text and its various distinct tragic influences from Greek drama.

2 Tragic Models

2.1 Aeson and Alcimede

As noted earlier, the suicide of Aeson and Alcimede at the end of Book 1 (*Arg.* 1.730–850) will presently furnish my starting point.[13] This episode, which has no precedent in Apollonius but is one of Valerius' innovative additions to the Argonautic legend, is the first major tragic narrative in the epic, and plotwise it is the tragic culmination of Pelias' uncontrolled reaction to the news that his youngest son Acastus has joined Jason's crew, a decision of which the king of Iolkos was unaware (*Arg.* 1.700–729). Pelias also ignores that Acastus joined the expedition on his own free will, eager to acquire *kleos*. Convinced that the expedition is a death mission, he is certain that his son is doomed and mourns him. The combination of a cruel royal father (Pelias is one of the four rulers in the *Argonautica* whom Valerius calls 'tyrants') and an adolescent idealistic son who pines for glory, calls to mind the Vergilian pair of Mezentius and Lausus.[14] The tension between epic and tragedy is expressed in at least three different ways, as tragic intertextuality, narrative regression, and ritual are all visibly influential and interlocked.

Firstly, the obvious association with contemporary politics aside,[15] the episode that records the enforced death of Aeson and his wife and the murder of

---

13 On the episode in general see Vessey 1973, 245–248; Adamietz 1976, 26–29; Perutelli 1982; Franchet d'Espèrey 1988, 193–197; Hershkowitz, 1998b, 128–136; Ripoll 1998b, 204–205, 376–382, 393–394; Manuwald 2000; Spaltenstein 2002, 274–305; Kleywegt 2005, 425–492; Zissos 2008, 379–420.
14 Scaffai 1986, 257; Bernstein 2008, 37–38 and Zissos 2008, 374 *ad* 709–711 and 712–724.
15 Aeson's suicide has repeatedly been seen to allude to a series of political deaths by enforced suicide executed at the orders of Domitian; cf. e.g. McGuire 1997, 24–28, has read Aeson's suicide in light of the suicide of Thrasea Paetus in Tac. *Ann.* 16.33.5; Hershkowitz 1998b, 246, argues that

their young son at the end of *Arg.* 1 comprises a miniature tragedy also because it has no impact on the course of the epic plot, even though it could potentially impede the linear trajectory of the *Argonautica* had Jason heard of it, and prove disruptive to the epic code. According to Panoussi, the performance of ritual is a typical closural theme in epic and tragedy, yet in the *Aeneid* a series of inter-rupted or perverted rituals underscore the failure to reach closure.[16] The same lack of catharsis underscores the end of *Arg.* 1, as the incomplete sacrifice and the multiple ritual perversions (the employment of witchcraft; suicide) anticipate and prohibit, yet eventually replace, perverted (human) sacrifice.

Secondly and most prominently, the tragic element in the narrative, via the manifestations of tragic themes and the simultaneous evocation of well-known intertexts, underwrites the conduct of all characters involved. Pelias is experienc-ing a loss that generates feelings of grave emotional suffering. As he watches the departing Argo from the towers, the enraged king evokes two famous deserted Roman heroines of acknowledged tragic background, the helpless Ariadne of Ca-tullus 64 watching Theseus' ship moving out of her sight and, by association, the furious Dido[17] sensing that the Trojans are preparing to sail away:

> *Saevit atrox Pelias inimicaque vertice ab alto*
> *vela videt nec qua se ardens effundere possit.*
> *nil animi, nil regna iuvant; fremit obice ponti*
> *clausa cohors telisque salum facibusque coruscat.* (*Arg.* 1.700–703)

Savage Pelias rages as from a high peak he beholds the sails of his enemy, and knows not how his anger can find vent. Nor courage, nor empire avail; hemmed in by the barrier of the sea his soldiers chafe, and the brine sparkles with their weapons and torches.[18]

> *Nam fluenti sono prospectans litore Diae,*
> *Thesea cedentem celeri cum classe tuetur*
> *indomitos in corde gerens Ariadna furores,*
> *nec dum etiam sese quae visit visere credit* (Cat. 64.53–55)

---

the depiction of deception and tyrannical conduct in the *Argonautica* is meant to evoke Tacitus' depiction of Domitian in the *Histories* and Tiberius in the *Annals*.

16 Panoussi 2009; on ritual perversion specifically associated with altar violation as core theme that runs through the *Aeneid*, see also Gladhill 2009.

17 On the broad similarities of the curse of Valerius' Pelias to Dido's curse at *Aen.* 4.590–627, see Eigler 1988, *ad loc.* 27–28. Adamietz 1976, 28 n.65; Kleywegt 2005, 408 observe structural resemblances between the Aeson episode and the end of *Aeneid* 4 ("place of departure, last scene of the book, curses, suicide"); see also Spaltenstein 2002, 273–274.

18 All translations of the *Argonautica* are from Mozley 1934.

Looking out from the wave-sounding shore of Diae, Ariadne bearing unconquerable anger in her heart, as she watches Theseus' swift fleet receding in the distance, and she does not yet believe that she has seen what she has seen.

At regina dolos ...
praesensit, motusque excepit prima futuros
omnia tuta timens. Eadem impia Fama furenti
detulit armari classem cursumque parari.
saevit inops animi totamque incensa per urbem
bacchatur, qualis commotis excita sacris
Thyias, ubi audito stimulant trieterica Baccho
orgia nocturnusque vocat clamore Cithaeron. (*Aen.* 4.296–303)

But the queen sensed his tricks ...
and was first to anticipate future events, fearful even of safety.
That same impious Rumour brought her madness:
they are fitting out the fleet, and planning a journey.
Her mind weakened, she raves, and, on fire, runs wild
through the city: like a Maenad, thrilled by the shaken emblems
of the god, when the biennial festival rouses her, and, hearing the Bacchic cry, Mount Cithaeron summons her by night with its noise.[19]

The double subtext casts Pelias in a sympathetic light: the aching and deserted father briefly replaces the cruel and deceitful king. And his decision to murder Aeson and Alcimede is described as motivated by irrational, bacchic-like fury for revenge. The semiotics evoke Euripides' *Bacchae*,[20] only in reverse. The king in the story, Pelias, and his army perform the part of the frenzied Bacchants, while their victims are the helpless family of Jason (the mutilation theme is stressed in the employment of the verb *diripio*, 'tear apart,' to describe the treatment of the bodies of Jason's parents (*diripiat laceretque*, 'he tears apart and cuts into pieces,' 1.813) as well as the murder of Jason's young brother, Promachus, *Arg.* 1.824–825).[21] The reversal in the roles, in this respect, is paired with a reversal in the movement of the agents: the victims are residents of the countryside while the king, who marches against them from the city, is a bacchant in rage.

The bacchic element not only determines the king's action, but in a way transforms Pelias' identity. Once the king's lament for the departure of his son is

---

19 The translations of the *Aeneid* passages follow Kline 2002.
20 Mac Góráin 2009 recently has shown how the plot of Euripides' *Bacchae* may be taken as a key to a reading of the plot of the *Aeneid* as a whole, thus suggesting the presence of play in the subtexts of Vergil's epic successors.
21 The same verb, *diripio*, describes the attack of the Bacchae on Orpheus in Ovid, *Met.* 11.20 ff. (*direptos*, 11.29), which brings about the death and mutilation of the bard.

completed, Pelias is furious and eager for revenge, so much so that the intensity of these emotions transform his appearance and his conduct: he becomes a deranged bacchant in the possession of Dionysus (*Arg.* 1.726–730):

> *Bistonas ad meritos cum cornua saeva Thyoneus*
> *torsit et infelix iam mille furoribus Haemus,*
> *iam Rhodopes nemora alta gemunt, talem incita longis*
> *porticibus coniunxque fugit natique Lycurgum.*

Even such, when Thyoneus has turned his savage horns against the guilty Thracians, and now the mountains of unhappy Haemus filled with madness a thousandfold, now the tall forests of Rhodope groan — such was Lucyrgus before whom wife and sons in flight speed down the long colonnades.

From a complementary perspective, Valerius' description of the mourning father Pelias reminds of the mourning Aeson and Alcimede, and suggestively points to the strong intertextual influence of the Vergilian Evander and his relationship to his young son Pallas. The Evander model has already been employed in *Arg.* 1, to describe the farewell scene between Jason and his parents (1.184–349). The farewell speech, divided between Alcimede and Aeson, seemingly follows the Apollonian bipartition but actually is modelled on Evander's farewell speech to Pallas (*Aen.* 8.560–583). Alcimede speaking first (1.320–334) recalls the second half of Evander's speech; Aeson next (1.336–347) engages with the same points as in Evander's opening part.[22] The Evander model is connected to Pelias as well, and this connection is two-directional. One of the models behind Vergil's Evander sacrifice to Hercules at *Aen.* 8.102–103 is Pelias' sacrifice to his father Poseidon, set as the introductory scene to the narrative of Apollonius' *Argonautica* (1.13–14). Aware of this association in Vergil, the Vergilian Valerius reverses the order and portrays his Pelias with Vergil's Evander in mind: Pelias' mourning for Acastus' departure suggestively recalls Evander's mourning the death of Pallas, especially in light of the proximity of Acastus to Pallas, as the former's first meeting with Jason in *Arg.* 1.162–163 is similar with that of Pallas and Aeneas in *Aen.* 8.124.[23] The association of both elderly and rival brothers to Evander originates in

---

22 The models of Valerius' farewell speech, Apollonius and Vergil's Evander at *Aen.* 8.558–584, and also other less prominent, are listed in Dräger 1995, 486. On the bipartition of Evander's farewell speech between Aeson and Alcimede, see Dräger 1995, 476–478, citing also Mehmel 1934, 62; and Fuà 1986, 271. Finkmann 2014, 76 n. 16 adds that "the same pairing and order of speeches (Alcimede: 1.763–766; Aeson: 1.788–822) occurs before their suicide and the end of Book 1."

23 Hershkowitz 1998b, 113 n. 38.

tragedy — Roman tragedy this time. Accius' *Atreus*, a play popular in the tragic theatre at least as late as the Late Republic, and the leading model for Seneca's dramas on the Atrides saga, introduces a genealogy that connects Evander, an important culture hero of proto-Rome as early Fabius Pictor and Cato Maior,[24] to the tyrant Atreus, thus inscribing the saga of Atreus in Rome's past.[25]

The scholarly recollection of Atreus encourages deeper research into the tradition of the Pelias-Aeson relationship. The tense relationship between Aeson and Pelias is recorded in the Greek tradition as early as Pindar's fourth Pythian Ode (ll. 106–115).[26] According to Pindar, Aeson was originally the king of Iolkos but Pelias usurped the throne and imprisoned Aeson.[27] Fraternal strife is at the core of several Greek tragedies, usually culminating in fratricide. Valerius innovates on Aeson's death (in no other version prior to Valerius does Aeson commit suicide in order not to become a murder victim at the hand of his brother),[28] an innovation that brings to the fore the theme of fratricide in the story of Pelias and Aeson,[29] and evokes the feud between Atreus and Thyestes, which had received numerous tragic treatments, Greek and Roman alike. Notably, Valerius never mentions the fraternal feud over the throne; instead, he states very soon after the beginning of the poem that Pelias held the rule of Iolkos 'from his earliest years' (*primis... ab annis*, *Arg.* 1.22).

Thirdly and finally, the staging of the double suicide by the altar projects the self-immolation against an actual ritual sacrifice. The tragic element is further stressed by the prophetic utterance of Cretheus' ghost (*Arg.* 1.741–751).

> 'mitte metus, volat ille mari, quantumque propinquat
> iam magis atque magis variis stupet Aea deorum
> prodigiis quatiuntque truces oracula Colchos.
> heu quibus ingreditur fatis, qui gentibus horror
> pergit! mox Scythiae spoliis nuribusque superbus   745
> adveniet — cuperem ipse graves tum rumpere terras —,

---

24 Cf. Bispham et al. 2013, 667.

25 Boyle 2006, 178–179.

26 In Valerius Flaccus this tension is only implicit.

27 Aeson in Valerius Flaccus is a marginal figure but is not imprisoned. He is briefly mentioned early at 1.72–73 as a figure to be pitied — judged so by Jason himself — but his stance in the closing episode, and his overall conduct that is portrayed in distinct epic tones, are "setting [him] as an exemplum of traditional epic heroism" (Heshkowitz 1998b, 130). In Apollonius, Aeson is a frail and bedridden old man, and receives only a cursory mention in 1.263–264.

28 Perutelli 1982, 137–138.

29 As Stover (2006, 126 n. 219) notes at *Arg.* 1.747 Cretheus describes the civil strife between Aeson and Pelias as a *triste nefas*, a phrase that is immediately glossed as *fraterna arma*.

sed tibi triste nefas fraternaque turbidus arma
rex parat et saevas irarum concipit ignes.
Quin rapis hinc animam et famulos citus effugis artus?
i, meus es, iam te in lucos pia turba silentum   750
secretisque ciet volitans pater Aeolus arvis.'

"Banish all fear! He is flying over the ocean, and as he draws ever nearer more and more does Aea marvel at the manifold miracles of heaven, and fierce Colchis is shaken by the prophecies. Alas! To what destinies does he move forward! His coming is the terror of nations! A little while and he shall return glorying in the spoils and the brides of Scythia; then would I, even I, long to burst the weight of earth. But against you the violent king prepares a deadly crime and arms, brother against brother, and is nursing the fierce fires of his passion. Why do you not snatch away your life, and quickly escape from these trembling limbs? Come then, you are my son, already the silent throng of the sanctified call you to their glades, and Aeolus the father who flits in the sequestered fields."

The portrayal of prophecy in Flavian epic is distinguished, according to Lovatt, by "a self-conscious theatricality, in which staging and performance come to the fore."[30] Cretheus encourages Aeson to *perform* his death; to commit suicide by perverted sacrifice in order to prevent fratricide. Not least, the enforced death of Aeson by the poisoned blood of a sacrificial victim evokes the multiple expressions of ritual pollution that surrounds the death of Priam in *Aeneid* 2, who was murdered beside altars by the son of Achilles, in a way that resembles a perverted sacrifice, amidst the blood of his slain son Polites, and before the eyes of his wife and daughters-in-law who at the same time clutch the altars: *vidi ipse furentem /* *caede Neoptolemum... , / vidi Hecubam centumque nurus Priamumque per aras /* *sanguine foedantem quos ipse sacraverat ignis* ('I saw Neoptolemus myself, on the threshold, mad with slaughter...: I saw Hecuba, her hundred women, and Priam at the altars, polluting with blood the flames that he himself had sanctified,' 2.499–502).[31]

2.2 The Cyzicus episode

In a recent monograph, Christoph Sauer has argued that Valerius' narrative is deeply informed by Aristotle's theory of dramatic plot as developed in the *Poetics*. The core of Sauer's study, the parts of Valerius' epic most conspicuous for their dramatic character, is Book 1 in its entirety (built on the concept of fame — for

---

30 Lovatt 2013b, 55.
31 On the resemblance between Aeson and Priam of *Aeneid* 2 but in reverse, "in a comparison that is definitely to Aeson's advantage," see Hershkowitz 1998b, 128–129.

Sauer Book 1 is a tragedy developing around the fatal consequences of the quest for glory/*fama*) along with the Cyzicus episode that spreads over the last thirty-something lines of Book 2 (627–664) and a little over the first half of Book 3 (1–461). Sauer successfully identifies in the episode all the components of Aristotelian tragedy, especially *peripeteia* and *anagnorisis*,[32] delivered in the context of a civil war of prolonged fight and an involuntary quasi-fratricide due to mistaken identity soon to come to the fore.[33] Briefly, the episode at the land of King Cyzicus is the first martial engagement of the Argonauts — and a perverted one at that. At the end of *Argonautica* 2, the Argonauts arrive at Cyzicus' kingdom. The king welcomes them and offers hospitality. The Argonauts depart from Cyzicus at the opening of Book 3 (3.1–14), but divine intervention causes a storm that drives the Argonauts back to the land of their former hosts (15–42). Since they arrive during the night they do not realize where they are: the people of Cyzicus, who mistake them for invaders, attack them, and a battle ensues during which Jason kills King Cyzicus (43–248). When Jupiter ends the fighting and the horrified Argonauts realize what they have done, they bury Cyzicus and the other dead with honours, while Jason assumes the role of Cyzicus' substitute son and delivers a funeral speech (249–361). Subsequently the seer Mopsus officiates at a purification and atonement ritual and thereafter the Argonauts depart for Colchis (362–461).

According to all evidence the Cyzicus story was added to the Argonautic legend by Apollonius but Valerius has expanded the story (in the Latin *Argonautica* it is more than twice as long) and has emphasized different themes.[34] The structure of the episode repeatedly has been compared to a tragedy, as it features distinct Aristotelian elements, namely a 'prologue,' an exposition of the situation, an *anagnorisis, peripeteia*, and resolution.[35] Further, Vergil's influence on the transformation of the model is both visible and catalytic, and duly acknowledged by Gesine Manuwald.[36] More important for the present argument is the realization

---

32 Sauer 2011, 68 f. and *passim*. On the Cyzicus episode see foremost Manuwald 1999. On Valerius' interaction with tragedy via his employment of *anagnorisis* especially as this is manifested in the Cyzicus episode see Cowan (in the present volume).

33 Garson (1964, 267–270, esp. 269) is the first detailed study which defines the Cyzicus episode as a tragic narrative featuring a dramatic plot and the elements of *hubris, peripeteia*, irony, quasi-choric interludes, and speeches (Garson omits *anagnorisis*).

34 Garson 1964, 267–268 illustrates the differences in a comparative table; see also Sauer 2011, 151–157; Manuwald 2015, 61–63.

35 Garson 1964, 168–169; Sauer 2011, 183; Manuwald 2015, 61.

36 Nicely summarized in 2015, 61: "While Apollonius Rhodius has provided the outline for Valerius Flaccus' version, Virgil's *Aeneid* has inspired its tone and motifs: the sequence of a friendly welcome for a band of sailors by the ruler of a foreign kingdom, including a banquet and an

that the Vergilian subtexts transport into Valerius' text their own complex engagement with Greek tragedy, as I am concerned with the tension produced when Greek tragedy filtered through Vergil affects Valerius' direct engagement with the text of the *Argonautica*. In the Cyzicus episode Valerius discusses from his own epic perspective two central themes of Greek tragedy, ignorance and guilt.[37] The two protagonists of the episode, Jason and Cyzicus, have committed crimes unintentionally and unbeknown to them. While hunting at Mount Didymus Cyzicus killed one of Cybele's lions (*Arg.* 3.20–31). The slight to her honour led Cybele to plan vengeance against the king. Cyzicus is unaware of having killed one of Cybele's lions, and this lack of knowledge protects him from feelings of guilt or shame. His sacrilege matters only as an explanation for his tragic accidental death, a *tisis* for a *hubris* he never knew he had committed, at the hands of Jason, who only a few hours earlier was his *xenos*. Excessive guilt, on the other hand, takes hold of Jason when he realizes that during the nocturnal battle he has killed Cyzicus, a dear friend and, as shown during the funeral, a substitute father figure.

Both Cyzicus' ignorance of his doomed death and Jason's ignorance of his murder evoke the fate of Oedipus,[38] the leading example of tragic ignorance leading to murder (of his father) and eventually to utter destruction. The echoing of Oedipus is likely deliberate[39] in order to underscore the tragedic nucleus of the Cyzicus drama: according to Aristotle, Oedipus was the gold standard of tragedy: in the *Poetics*, Aristotle refers to the *Oedipus Tyrannus* ten times (cf. Halliwell 1987, 42–45): most notably, twice in connection with Thyestes, in chapter 13, as possessing the best sort of subject matter for tragedy (1453a11, 20); twice in chapter 11, as an example of *peripeteia* (reversal of the action) and an *anagnorisis*

---

exchange of gifts, followed by the death of the host, caused by the leader of the guests, recalls the encounter between Aeneas and Dido (Virg. *Aen.* 1.4), and the meeting of Aeneas and Evander with the subsequent death of Pallas (Virg. *Aen.* 8, 10, 11). The night-time battle evokes the nocturnal fighting in Troy narrated in *Aeneid* 2 (with Priam's death at the end), and there are allusions to the battles in Italy in the *Aeneid*'s second half. Clite's grief at the death of her husband is similar to that of Euryalus' mother in *Aeneid* 9 (9.473–502)"; see also the remarks on Valerius' Vergilian intertextuality in Garson 1964, 270–271.

37 On Jason's and Cyzicus' guilt, see recently Manuwald 2015, 62.

38 The tragedy of Oedipus is in the subtext of another important episode in Valerius Flaccus, the Phineus episode, which in turn had its own long history on the Greek tragic stage; see Lovatt 2015, 415; and Gantz 1993, 349–356 for the surviving evidence of Greek tragedies about Phineus (at least three, one by Aeschylus and two by Sophocles).

39 The fates of Cyzicus and Sophocles' Oedipus have been viewed as parallel already in Levin 1971, 96, studying the version of the story in Apollonius, Valerius' model, who invented the Cyzicus episode. Despite the several obvious differences from the model, Valerius builds on the same narrative core.

(recognition of persons) coincident with the *peripeteia* (1452a24–33); and again in chapter 14, as a tragedy containing an *anagnorisis* of *philia* (kinship: 1453b31). Chapter 13 in the *Poetics* is particularly important because it numbers *hamartia* (a great error) among the main elements of a good tragic plot.

> "A well-formed plot will be simple rather than (as some people say) double, and it must involve a change [*metaballein*] not *to* good fortune *from* bad fortune [*eis eutukhian ek dustu-khias*], but, reversely, *from* good fortune *to* bad fortune [*ex eutukhias eis dustukhian*]. And this must be due not to depravity [*dia mokhtherian*], but to a serious error [*di' hamartian megalen*], on the part of someone of the kind specified, or better than that, rather than worse [*beltionos mallon e kheironos*]." (*Poetics* 1453a26–27).[40]

Further, both Jason and Oedipus suffer from guilt for the crimes they committed. Judged on the basis of objective criteria, the two heroes are not guilty because those crimes (murder of father/father-like figure[41]) were not intentional. It is the effect of these involuntary actions that triggers their guilt, which is caused by emotions — the personal experiencing of these actions.[42] Guilt takes over Oedipus who punishes himself with blindness; the particular punishment is laden with irony, as the leading motif of the tragedy is the binary knowledge/ignorance often described as blindness of the mind, and Oedipus, who brags about his mental faculties, the brightness of his mind, ultimately realizes that he has been mentally blind. He condemns himself to eternal darkness because he refuses to 'see' mentally his involuntary error, or rather to accept that he can be so prone to error as to commit such a damning *hamartia* (great error). The theme of blindness is no less prominent in Jason's accidental killing of Cyzicus, for the tragedy took place during the night, when the warriors were visually impaired. The darkness/light dichotomy is a motif in Valerius Flaccus throughout,[43] and a theme at the foundation of Jason's tragedy, as it transforms the maiden battle of the Argonauts into a civil war.[44]

---

40 Tr. Heath 1996.

41 On Cyzicus as a father-figure for Jason who acts in place of the king's son, lifting the dead body onto his pyre (*Arg.* 3.338–339), see recently Bernstein 2008, 52–53.

42 Noted already in Adam Smith, *The Theory of Moral Sentiments*, London: A Millar 1790 (publ. first date 1759), 156, on the distinction between subjective and objective guilt, with Oedipus as his case study. For Smith, the feelings of subjective guilt, or rather, to have incorrectly assumed a guilt that is not rightly his, is at the core of Oedipus' real tragedy. Valerius Flaccus' emphasis on Jason's excessive lamentation underscores the same *hamartia* of assigning unjustified guilt to himself.

43 Manuwald 2015, 140, 142 and elsewhere.

44 Several critics have noticed Valerius' presenting the fight between the Argonauts and the people of Cyzicus in terms of a civil war; see for example Hull 1979, 406; Burck 1981, 456; Hardie

The conclusion of the Cyzicus episode with the two laments, by Jason and the king's widow Clite, brings to the fore the interpretative prominence of the tragedic subtext and at the same time ascertains the filtering of Greek tragedy through Vergil's *Aeneid*, for the mourning over the funeral pyre of Cyzicus is modelled on the mourning of Aeneas over the dead body of Pallas.[45] The intertextuality between the two passages has been amply discussed, as well as the association of Cyzicus with Pallas more broadly,[46] but what has not received due attention is the bridging function of the intertextual dialogue between Valerius' Jason and the protagonists of Vergil's Pallanteum with another point of departure, the farewell encounter between Jason and his parents in *Argonautica* 1.320–334. The latter presupposes knowledge of Evander's speech to Pallas on his departure in *Aeneid* 8.569–583.[47] The establishment of this cross-textual relationship through the employment of the same intertext effectively signals the closure of the Cyzicus episode as a new beginning for the Argonauts — the real beginning of their epic *labor*, in a way.

Even so, Jason's persistent feelings of guilt get the better of him, so much so that he forgets how the epic hero should behave: *ipse etiam Aesonides, quamquam tristissima rerum / castiganda duci vultuque premenda sereno, / dulcibus indulget lacrimis aperitque dolorem* ('Aesonides himself, though as chief he must repress the extremity of sorrow and hide it beneath a tranquil countenance, indulges the sweetness of lament and lays bare his grief,' *Arg.* 3.369–371). The negative phrasing describing Jason's conduct means to point out tongue-in-

---

1993a, 87; McGuire 1997, 108–113; Manuwald 1999, 159, and the detailed analysis in Stover 2012, chapter 5 ('Gigantomachy and Civil war in Cyzicus'); also Manuwald 2015, 62, and (from a metaliterary perspective, extending the civil war theme onto the level of agonistic epic poetics) Heerink 2016, 511–525. The civil war theme is at the core of the sequel to the Oedipus story in the Theban legend, the conflict between Oedipus' sons; as a matter of fact, the treatment of the fraternal conflict in Statius' *Thebaid* has been convincingly proven to have been inspired by the attack of the Argonauts on the Doliones as recorded in Valerius; see Parkes 2014, 332.

45 Garson 1964, 270–271 proves that the Cyzicus narrative integrates several *loci Vergiliani* also from the 'tragedic' Aeneas-Dido unit.

46 Stover 2006, 123, has keenly noted that Cyzicus welcomes Jason and the Argonauts with a gesture copied from Evander's Pallas as he welcomes Aeneas to Pallanteum: *Arg.* 2.638, [Cyzicus] *miraturque viros dextramque amplexus et haerens / incipit*, 'and gazed [Cyzicus] in wonder at the heroes, and as he clasped and clung to their right hand he thus began' ~ *Aen.* 8.124, *excepitque manu dextramque amplexus inhaesit*; and that the first departure of Jason early in Book 3 is described in light of the farewell scene between Evander and Aeneas in Vergil's epic (Stover 2006, 123–124).

47 See the analysis of the intertextual interaction in Hershkowitz 1998b, 131–132, and my discussion of the Aeson/Alcimede episode above.

cheek what Jason is not — the protagonist of an epic. His behaviour is the exact opposite of the model epic leader Aeneas, who in *Aen.* 1.208–209, *curis... ingentibus aeger / spem vultu simulat, premit altum corde dolorem* ('sick with heavy cares, he feigns hope in his face; his pain is held within, hidden'). And the incessant mental anguish of the Argonauts (*aegro adsidue mens carpitur aestu*, their invalid minds are consumed by unceasing turmoil,'*Arg.* 3.365) which causes them to lose any desire for deeds, echoes the mental suffering of the love-afflicted, tragic Dido (*regina gravi... saucia cura, vulnus alit venis, et caeco carpitur igni*, *Aen.* 4.1–2), and her fall into inertia and neglect for her political responsibilities (*non coeptae adsurgunt turres...*, *Aen.* 4.86).

To recover their epic *amor laborum*[48] and hence to exit the tragedic frame of conduct the Argonauts will turn to ritual and the intervention of the *vates* Mopsus.[49] Interestingly, Mopsus is a Valerian addition to the Argonautic myth, he makes his appearance early in Book 1 and immediately prior to Idmon, the 'traditional,' Apollonian seer of the legend. Like his colleague, he enters the epic narrative with a prophecy (*Arg.* 1.211–226) which, however, talks of toil, hardships and sacrifices, and as such is ridden by pessimism, in stark contrast in style and content from the one delivered by Idmon immediately afterwards (*Arg.* 1.227–239), which is considered optimistic and traditionally epic in character. The juxtaposition of the two prophecies is aligned with the structural dichotomy of Valerius' *Argonautica*, which among the various binaries includes the interaction and interchange between the epic and the tragic elements.[50] The tragedic essence of Mopsus' introduction in the epic is underlined by the fact that the diction of his introductory prophetic speech draws on the phraseology and pessimistic spirit of the so-called Argonautic Odes in Seneca's *Medea* (*Med.* 306–379, 579–

---

48 *Arg.* 3.367–368, *patria ex oculis acerque laborum / pulsus amor segnique iuvat frigescere luctu* ('lost to view is the homeland, forgotten the keen love of enterprise, and their joy is to grow cold in the languor of distress').

49 The unanticipated intervention of Mopsus has been pointedly compared to that of a tragic *deus ex machina* in Garson 1964, 270.

50 See Zissos 2004. According to this study, by placing the two prophets side by side, "Valerius ingeniously exploits the vatic 'surplus' offered by the literary tradition in order to give expression to the duality inherent in the received *Argonautica* myth" (Zissos 2004, 320). This duality is particularly prominent in the generic fluidity of the epic. For Krasne 2011, who develops further the dualism theme in the *Argonautica*, the inclusion of Mopsus' prophecy next to Idmon's own underscores the incongruence resulting from the pairing of pessimism and optimism, as "Mopsus' and Idmon's pair of prophecies, conflicting and even competing in their generic sensibilities and overtones, provides an early and striking locus of doubling in Valerius's epic" (p. 127).

669).[51] Yet, at the end of the Cyzicus episode, when the Argonauts are in deep depression and have given up on their epic mission, it is Mopsus and his purification rituals (3.377–458) that will effectively heal the guilt and suffering of internecine war tormenting Jason and his men, and lead them out of their unepic passivity and readjust the generic focus of their mission.[52]

3 Tragic influences

3.1 Hesione

In the rescue of Hesione by Hercules (*Arg.* 2.451–578),[53] Valerius introduces from an epic standpoint[54] a narrative that had inspired both tragedies and comedies in the Greek tradition, producing intertexts suitable for generic experimentation. The Hesione episode is not part of Apollonius' epic.[55] The only other extant source prior to Valerius that makes the rescue of Hesione a stop on the Argo's itinerary is Diodorus Siculus 4.32, 42, which nonetheless records a very different version, so much so that direct dialogue with Valerius should be excluded.[56] Still, these two divergent accounts share an important detail: in both the plight of Hesione is distinctly described along the lines of Aristotle's tragic definition for the reversal of fortune, *peripeteia*. Dionysius uses the very term at Diodorus 4.42.5, while Valerius' Hesione describes the tragic reversal in her fortune in a paraphrasis of *peripeteia*: *nos Ili felix quondam genus, invida donec / Laomedontos*

---

51 On the Valerian Mopsus' prophetic speech echoing Seneca's tragic language and pessimistic interpretation of the Argonautic myth, see Boyle 1997, 126–127; Buckley 2014, 311–313; also Biondi 1984; Zissos 1997.

52 See Stover 2012, 172–178, discussing how Mopsus' purification rituals contribute to the renewal of Jason's epic mission, and at the metaliterary level to the renewal of the epic genre as poetry of hope, in the wake of Lucan's pessimistic *Bellum Civile*.

53 Detailed account of the myth in *RE* 8.1: 1240–1242; *LIMC* s.v. Hesione.

54 On making the death of a beautiful maiden the catalyst of heroic action in Roman epic, see Keith 2000, 128–129.

55 Recent thorough discussion of the myth, its prehistory and the function in Valerius Flaccus is Manuwald 2004, 145–163.

56 Harper Smith 1987, 194–195; *contra* Poortvliet 1991, 240; recently Galli 2014, 148–151 suggested that Valerius draws on Diodorus' primary source, Dionysius Scytobrachion, because Dionysius, unlike Diodorus, includes in his Argonautic account both the Lemnos episode and the Hesione story; Galli offers a detailed exposition of the differences between the two narratives; on Dionysius as Diodorus' source on Hesione, see also Harper Smith 1987, 195–196.

fugeret Fortuna penates, 'our family sprang from Ilus, a happy family until envi-
ous Fortuna fled the household gods of Laomedon,' *Arg.* 2.473–474).[57] The happy
ending of the story (eventually Hesione is rescued) is combined with an emphasis
on the reversal of fortune and the impending destruction of Ilium at a later time,
as a result of Laomedon's refusal to abide by his promise to Hercules. Also, the
prominence of the visual element in Valerius' narrative throughout explains why
this myth has exercised such a strong attraction over the dramatists, leading to
the production of both tragic and comic treatments of the story.

The myth of Hesione, in addition to its firm place in the epic tradition as part
of the Trojan legend,[58] had inspired possibly at least one tragedy, by a certain
5th c. tragedian Melanthius.[59] Grammarians, further, have recorded evidence of a
4th c. comedy with the title *Hesione* by Alexis,[60] while the tragedian Demetrius
wrote a satyr play entitled *Hesione*.[61] At the same time, the story of Hesione ex-
hibits many parallels to the story of Andromeda which was even more popular
with the ancient dramatists;[62] the tragedic reproduction of Andromeda in Euripides inspired among others the version recorded in Ovid, *Metamorphoses* 4.668
ff.,[63] which in all evidence is the leading intertext behind Valerius Flaccus; the

---

57 Galli 2014, 150, on the proximity.

58 *Iliad* 20.145–148; also Hellanicus *FGH* 4 fr. 26b, and in the Hellenistic times Lycophron, *Al-
exandra* 31–36.

59 Referred to as a glutton, according to Athenaeus, by several of his contemporary comic poets,
including Eupolis, Leucon, Pherecrates, and Archippus (Athen. 8.343c, with Leucon F 3 K.-A.;
Ar. *Peace* 803–811; Pherecrates F 148 K.-A.; Archippus F 28 K.-A.); the fragments are recorded in
Farmer 2016, 38 with n. 79. Further, in the Archippus fragment described by Athenaeus, Archippus in his comedy *Ichthyes* ('Fish') depicted Melanthius being devoured by fish, and Eu-
stathius (in *Il.* p. 1201.3) elaborating on the same scene compares Melanthius' depiction to that
of Hesione being sacrificed to a sea monster, making clear that in Archippus' comedy
Melanthius' death *à la* Hesione was enacted paratragically; see Farmer 2016, 39, citing Miles
2009, 103–104.

60 *Hesione* fr. 85–86 Kock; see Arnott (1996, 232), also arguing that there is evidence suggesting
that a tragic play with the same title did exist; cf. Farmer 2016, 39 n. 82.

61 Snell 1971.

62 Of the several Greek plays produced under the title *Andromeda*, the best known are Euripides' version, which Aristophanes parodies in the *Thesmophoriazousae* 1001–1135, and Sophocles' own. Notably, popular in Roman times was a Roman version by Accius, from which a little
over 20 lines have survived, while Ennius, too, had composed an *Andromeda*; cf. Falcetto 1998,
55–71; Collard and Cropp 2008; on Euripides' *Andromeda* (and the other two — surviving — escape-tragedies, *Helen* and *Iphigeneia at Tauris*, see now Wright 2005).

63 Most recently Marshall 2014, 169–179; also Anderson [1997, 484, generally noting that
"Ovid's genial, humanized account probably goes back to Euripides' romantic tragedy of 412,

two myths inform each other already in Classical Greek iconography.[64] It is my contention that the tension between tragic and epic that determines the structure and interpretation of the story of Perseus and Andromeda in Ovid follows after Vergil's revisiting the norms of the epic genre by folding Greek tragedic material into a Roman epic context. Valerius' experimentation with generic tension in the Hesione narrative, in short, reaches back to Vergil through Ovid.

Ovid's Andromeda episode is part of the 'Perseid,' a longer unit devoted to Perseus' heroic decapitation of Medusa. As a matter of fact, Perseus' encounter with Andromeda happens by accident. The hero had accomplished his heroic deed and was on his way home, when Andromeda's cries made him change his course. This sidetracking leads Perseus into sequential deeds (the killing of the *cetos*; the petrification of Phineus and his people) that mock traditional epic, and especially the *Aeneid*, the primary model behind Ovid's Perseus and Andromeda story,[65] at its most heroic — the prolonged, gruesome conflict on the battlefield between rival suitors for the hand of a beautiful princess in marriage. Ovid's employment of Greek tragedy as building block for the construction of his mock-'Perseid' establishes generic dissonance, and this determines the mock-epic tone of the Ovidian narrative.

At the core of the generic tension and intertextual complexity in Ovid's Andromeda narrative stands the element of visuality. In light of the emphasis on the spectacular, culminating on the comparison of both Ovid's and Valerius' chained maidens to a statue (*Met.* 4.673–675; *Arg.* 2.465–467),[66] recent critics consider Euripides' tragedy as the very model of the depiction of the chained maiden in distress on the rock, since, in addition to the spectacular aspect of a dramatic performance, Euripides' text also features a comparison of the chained Andromeda

---

which Aristophanes also comically exploited in *Thesmophoriazusae* of 411"], and more specifically, Klimek-Winter 1993, 11.

64 On Ovid's treatment of Andromeda as the model behind Valerius' account of Hesione see in detail Burck 1976, 221–238; also Harper Smith 1987, 196; and Spaltenstein 2002, 438–439. Ogden 2008, 93–99 offers detailed comparative study of the two tales, and records a series of vases that depict the mutual exchange of plot elements between the two stories.

65 The 'Perseid' has been read as a reworking of the *Aeneid* already in Otis 1970, 159–165; and more recently, Keith 2002, esp. 241–245, who further discusses the engagement of the 'Perseid' with the Homeric epics, especially *Odyssey* 22.

66 Decisive evidence for proving Valerius' reliance on the generic tension conspicuously advertised in Ovid's 'Perseid,' is the detail that the sacrifice of a maiden to the *cetos* in both the Andromeda and the Hesione story is directed by the oracle of Ammon, the Egyptian counterpart of Zeus (*Met.* 4.671; also 5.17 ~ *Arg.* 2.482); the Aethiopian location of Andromeda's adventure may justify the replacement of Zeus, but the reference in Valerius is out of place — it operates clearly as an Alexandrian footnote to the Ovidian model; cf. Harper Smith 1987, 208 *ad* 482.

to a statue (Eur. *Andr.* fr. 125 Kannicht, παρθένου τ᾽ εἰκώ τινα ἐξ αὐτομόρφων λα-ΐνων τυκισμάτων, σοφῆς ἄγαλμα χειρός; 'And what image of a maiden from the natural rock, a stone-chiselled statue crafted by a skilled hand?').[67] Philip Hardie, no less, suggests that we appreciate Ovid's statuesque Andromeda by looking back to Vergil, and specifically the scene in *Aeneid* 1 inside the temple of Juno when Aeneas' "stupefied gaze turns suddenly from an artistic representation of the Amazon queen Penthesilea to the flesh-and-blood Dido (*Aen.* 1.490–7)."[68] For Hardie, Perseus' stupor (*Met.* 4.673; 676–677, *vidit... et stupet et visae correptus imagine formae / paene suas quatere est oblitus in aëre pennas*, '[when Perseus] saw... dumbly amazed and entranced by the beautiful vision before him, he almost omitted to move his wings and he hovered in the air,' tr. Raeburn 2004) is inscribed in the amazement of Aeneas expressed in marked similarity (*Aen.* 1.494–495, *Haec dum Dardanio Aeneae miranda videntur, / dum stupet, obtutuque haeret defixus in uno*, 'while these wonderful sights are viewed by Trojan Aeneas, while amazed he hangs there, rapt, with fixed gaze ...'). The reaction of Valerius' Hercules (*Arg.* 2.462, *constitit... visuque enisus*, '[Hercules] halted, and straining his gaze upwards...') similarly discloses wonder, and emphasizes the intensity of the heroic viewer's gaze.[69] This interfusion of tragic (Euripidean) and epic (Vergilian) intertexts behind the depiction and performance of Ovid's Andromeda conditions the portrayal of Valerius' Hesione. The Vergilian element is more clearly stressed in the simile that likens the lamenting maiden to a bellowing bull (*Arg.* 2.458–461). The employment of the bull (usually as victim of lions) in similes is very common in Homeric epic,[70] but Valerius presently, when he compares Hesione to a bull and describes her cries with the term '*gemitu*' (*Arg.* 3.458–459 *qualiter, implevit gemitu cum taurus acerbo / avia...*, 'even as when a bull fills the wild places with his harsh bellowing...'), has in mind specific Vergilian passages, *G.* 3.223, and especially *Aen.* 12.722 where '*gemitu*' is used to describe the bellowing of a bull in the famous last simile of Vergil's epic, which compares Turnus (shortly before he dies at the hand of Aeneas) to an exiled bull coming back to

---

67 Harper Smith 1987, 201 *ad* 465–467, where additional scholarship is noted.
68 Hardie 2004, §20.
69 Harper Smith 1987, 200–201 *ad loc.*
70 *Il.* 5.161–164, 16.487–491, 17.542; also *Il.* 12.293, where Sarpedon advances against the Greeks like a lion against oxen, and *Il.* 18.579–583, where an attack of lions against bulls is not a simile, but is depicted on Achilles' shield. Identified and discussed in detail in Scott 2009, *passim*, with table 2 (pp. 194–197).

attack his rival and avenge the loss of his love.[71] The intertext from *Aeneid* 12, in turn, is tied to another important passage from the same epic, for the simile likening Turnus to a charging bull is modelled on Hercules' attack on Cacus as described in *Aeneid* 8[72] — an episode that is suggestively in the subtext of the fight between Hercules and the *cetos* a little later, which is described as *belua monstrum ingens* in reminiscence of the *monstrum* Cacus (*Aen.* 8.198).[73]

We have established that Valerius' interpretation of the Hesione myth is based on tragic sources filtered through Ovid's *Metamorphoses*, and at the same time it engages dynamically with epic intertexts and conventions taken from the work of Vergil, in addition to those integrated already in the Ovidian model. The employment of tragedy at the expense of epic in the Ovidian Andromeda narrative and its combination with a mock-epic battle sequel, successfully reinvents epic. In his effort to cut his own original footprint in the epic tradition, Valerius reinvents epic "dualism": he nods to the intercrossing of epic and tragedy at the core of his two great epic predecessors, as he reaches back to Ovid's Andromeda in the first part of his Hesione narrative. Still, he replaces the mock-epic fighting of Perseus (first invisible against the *cetos*, then a priori invincible, being in possession of a miraculous weapon of mass destruction, Medusa's head, that turns to stone all who gaze at it) with recollections of the epic (indeed gigantomachic) fighting of the Vergilian Hercules.

3.2 Io

"Why should I mention Io? Why indeed? I have no notion why." These words from A.E. Housman's poem, *Fragment of a Greek Tragedy* (orig. published 1883), a paradigm of a tragic burlesque, fittingly describe the reaction to Orpheus' decision to sing of Io's travails. The Argonauts have just completed their adventure in Bebrycia and their victory over Amycus (*Arg.* 4.324–343), and they continue their

---

71 Harper Smith 1987, 199 observes that the Vergilian echo considers the comparison of Hesione to a bellowing bull "inappropriate to the situation." Keith 2013, 290 also identifies the two Vergilian subtexts and, based on the erotic context surrounding them in the original, argues for a clever play on behalf of Valerius with the amatory theme that typically distinguishes a paradigmatic version of the hero-saves-maiden-in-distress story.

72 Galinsky 1968.

73 Harper Smith 1987, 214–219, sees many parallels between Valerius' *belua monstrum ingens* and the monstrous snakes that attack Laocoon in *Aeneid* 2. The *Aeneid* abounds in creatures described as *monstra*, including Cacus, Hercules' opponent in *Aeneid* 8, in the mythos set at the core of the Evander episode, a narrative repeatedly evoked in Valerius as already noted.

voyage to Colchis through Bosporus (344–350). Orpheus sings to his companions the story of Io, a nymph originally who was transformed into a heifer and then back to a nymph more than once; who was raped by Jupiter, persecuted by Juno, maltreated by Argus who drove her on and on in a long and arduous journey. Mercury enchanted and killed Argus; then Tisiphone at the orders of Juno appeared and struck the maiden/heifer with panic forcing her to wander anew all over the world until finally she reached Egypt where she found salvation only after the Nile attacked Tisiphone; finally at Jupiter's intervention she was deified and became the goddess Isis (*Arg.* 4.351–421).

At first reading, the recollection of Io's plight explains the etymology of Bosporus ('the cow's passage') at the moment the Argo crosses the very waters, and strongly suggests the identification of Jason's expedition with the peregrinations of Io, thus anticipating the hardships laying ahead for the Greek crew. Soon afterwards the Argonauts reach Thynia and encounter the blind seer Phineus, whose prolonged suffering mirrors Io's own. The Argonauts rid him of the Harpies (*Arg.* 4.422–529) and Phineus discloses prophetic information, including a series of labours, concerning their mission (530–625).[74] The ready acknowledgement of the Ovidian account of Io (established by the use of common, rare vocabulary, phrases and distinct language structure), primarily the version in *Metamorphoses* 1 enriched with elements of the second Ovidian treatment of the story in *Heroides* 14, as the obvious hypotext behind Valerius account, infuses with comedy (as it toys with his audience by reversing, contracting, and generally 'improving' on details of Ovid's model version) and even black humour an otherwise sober narrative.[75] Yet a distinct part of the elaborate structure of the story, Io's persecution by Tisiphone, is indebted partly to Vergil, while the emphasis on Io's wandering, which, for the first time in the Io tradition, has two phases, looks back to the significance of Io the wanderer in Greek tragedy.

Tisiphone, one of the Furies, is a denizen of the netherworld, and she is solicited by Juno to renew the persecution of Io-cow in the second half of Orpheus' song (*Arg.* 3.391 ff.). Even though Valerius does not explicitly attribute the appearance of Tisiphone to Juno's invitation, the Ovidian precedent (following Argus' death, Juno orders a Fury to hound Io) and the employment of a *cum-inversum* structure to describe Tisiphone's entrance, point to the *Aeneid*. There,

---

74 On Io's allusive interaction with other episodes of the *Argonautica* including the overarching theme of the Argonautic journey, see Murgatroyd 2009, 178 (with earlier bibliography).
75 See the observations in Murgatroyd 2009, 180–210, *passim*; also in Spaltenstein 2004, 293–309.

Allecto, Tisiphone's sister, is summoned by Juno to initiate a second set of labours for Aeneas, while the *cum-inversum* structure (3.391–394) employed at the opening of the *Aeneid* (*Aen.* 1.34–37) signals Juno's entrance into the plot and the imminent *peripeteia* (and the unravelling of the epic) as a result. Tisiphone takes the place of the anonymous Fury in Ovid's account, in order to add Vergil to the subtext and bolster the epic character of the narrative.[76] The engagement with the Vergilian text is complex. Firstly, by means of an interesting metaliterary comment, Valerius covertly expresses that Io's persecution by Tisiphone is an addition to the earlier accounts of the story: the cow the Fury chases now holds a different shape (*Arg.* 3.398, *qualis et a prima quantum mutata iuvenca*! 'How faring and how changed from that first heifer she was!'), a phrasing that echoes foremost the metapoetic opening line of the proem of Ovid's *Metamorphoses*: *In nova fert animus mutatas dicere formas / corpora*. With respect to the same line, moreover, critics have identified the allusion to *Aen.* 2.274 ff. (of Aeneas' impression on the appearance of the ghost of Hector): *ei mihi, qualis erat! Quantum mutatus ab illo / Hectore qui redit exuvias indutus Achilli* etc. ('Ah, how he looked! How changed he was from that Hector who returned wearing Achilles' armour...'),[77] another passage highly symbolic as it authorizes by means of a supernatural epiphany the transition from the Homeric epic mission to the Vergilian one.

More importantly, several scholars[78] have observed that *Arg.* 3.408, *praecipere et Pharia venientem pellere terra* ('to anticipate and repel the newcomer from the Pharian land'), the second line of the couplet that describes Tisiphone's effort to prevent Io's arrival in Egypt (another Valerian departure from the canonical account), is modelled on *Aen.* 10.277, *litora praecipere et venientis pellere terra* ('seizing the shore and driving the approaching [enemy] from land'), a phrase that describes Turnus, who, struck by Tisiphone's sister Allecto, is trying to ward off the Trojan fleet returning from Pallanteum. Turnus is closely linked to Io. As the ekphrases on his helmet and his shield reveal, his two emblems are a fire-breathing Chimaera and Io in her bovine form. Next to underscoring Turnus' origin (a descendant of Inachus; *Aen.* 7.372), the presence of Io on the shield suggests additional associations between the Rutulian hero and the Argive nymph.[79]

---

76 Murgatroyd 2009, 199 *ad* 392 identifies *Aen.* 7.544 (of Allecto, after she has stirred up fighting in Italy) *Iunonem victrix adfatur voce superba*, as the inspiration for Valerius' *Io victrix Iunonis* (*Arg.* 4.392); and the phrase *Tartareo ululatu* in *Arg.* 4.393 is, for Spaltenstein (2004, 303) "un calque explicite de Verg. *Aen.* 4.667 *femineo ululatu*," retaining also the hiatus, which is rare in Valerius' verse.

77 Murgatroyd 2009, 201 *ad* 398.

78 See Murgatroyd 2009, *ad loc*; Hurka 2003, 34 n. 139 listing earlier critics.

79 Discussed in detail in Hardie 1992, 63; Gale 1997; Horsfall 2000, 507–513.

The association between Vergil's Turnus and Valerius' Io is more distinct. Turnus is attacked, indeed transformed in character, by a Fury; the Io of Valerius undergoes her second transformation from maiden to cow as soon as she encounters Tisiphone. The fire-breathing Chimaera, a monster with the tail of a snake, on Turnus' helmet corresponds to Tisiphone, another monstrous creature, who appears before Io holding brands of fire and coiling snakes and yells in hellish fashion (*Arg.* 3.393).

In the Vergilian text the Fury's transformative attack on Turnus turns the Rutulian prince into a mortal embodiment of herself — a *furor*-driven, bloodthirsty monster, and this inevitably juxtaposes him to the innocent Io. Turnus loses his humanity, and his ties to Io are severed as the flames of the Chimaera eventually 'consume' Io.[80] Knowledge of the Vergilian model casts Io in the place of Turnus, a victim turned monster and eventually driven to death; in this respect the fate of the heroine becomes more tragic in Valerius' recollection of her story.

Greek tragedy, and specifically Aeschylean drama, is the leading source for the story of Io. As a matter of fact, with the exception of the two oldest tragedies, the *Persians* and the *Seven*, all other extant dramas of Aeschylus are distinguished by the motif of "the wanderer across the face of the earth," and Io serves to incarnate this motif. In all plays, she is used *paradigmatically*.[81] This paradigmatic identity of the tragedic Io has inspired Valerius who in turn uses the plight of Io as a mirror for the journey of the Argonauts. In the *Suppliants*, Io is reflected in the forced peregrination of the Danaids (Io's arduous journey is remembered by the Danaids in the central Stasimon of the play (524–599) and as the maidens are waiting for the decision of the Athenians on their plea. The analogy in the description of the two travelling routes is obvious: Io travelled against her will from her native Argos to Egypt and found refuge there; now her granddaughters are travelling against their will from their native Egypt to Argos and seek refuge).[82] In *Prometheus Bound*, she appears in person, on the stage, in the middle of her wandering. She offers a detailed account of her travails, while Prometheus prophesies for her a similarly long list of travails to come. The appearance of Io

---

80 Castelletti 2014, 63–66, commenting on the ambiguity of Turnus' character and fate (a monster like Chimaera or a victim of circumstances like Io), observes a boustrophedon acrostic at *Aen.* 7.790–792 starting with the letter A of *urna* at 792 and reading AACSSA = *ac assa* ('roasted, burned by fire'; or 'dried, thirsty'). Castelletti attributes the feminine adjective both to Inachus' *urna* and to Io, who as an image of Turnus' shield and so close to the spit-firing Chimaera "would be burned" by the flames of the monster (66).

81 See the discussion in Herington 1970, 85–86, upon which my discussion of Io's paradigmatic function in Aeschylus — and in Valerius at the imitation thereof — is founded.

82 The parallels are well illustrated in Rutherford 2007, 22–24.

in the legend of Prometheus is an innovation by Aeschylus, who combined the two previously independent traditions of Prometheus and Io[83] in order to pair the two heroes and underscore their common destiny and intense suffering as victims of Zeus' tyrannical authority. Prometheus' punishment and Io's wanderings further introduce before Aeschylus' audience a geographical overview of the known world while the two heroes themselves identify with its extremities. Io's plight invites Valerius' readers to recall Prometheus' detailed world map, and, once familiar with the earlier versions of the Argonautic legend, to look forward to the wanderings of the Argonauts, who in their return journey will virtually reach the ends of the world. Finally, the persecution of Io by Tisiphone and the long route the daughter of Inachus had to cover before her arrival in Egypt call to mind the persecution of Orestes by the Furies in the *Eumenides*, who likewise reportedly crosses (in 75–77, 238–240, 249–251) enormous tracts of land and sea with the Furies on his tail. The persecuted Orestes in turn leads back to Vergil, to Turnus but also to Aeneas.

In the *Aeneid* both Turnus and Aeneas are part of complex allusions that cast them in light of the persecuted Orestes. As Stefano Rebeggiani has rightly shown, the Orestes story in the *Aeneid* is linked to a number of key themes of the epic including that of madness and of taking revenge over a stolen wife.[84] Also, it is typical of Vergil to use his mythical paradigms in a way contrary to expectation: to associate a certain hero with a mythological figure and then gradually to move towards the association with a different hero, the antithesis of the former one. The Orestes story is a classic example of this technique. Introduced in *Aeneid* 3, where Andromache narrates to Aeneas the story of an Orestes possessed by *furor* over the loss of his promised bride to Neoptolemus and turning into an avenger, it becomes part of Aeneas' personal experience first in *Aeneid* 4, as the hero is unwillingly cast in the role of Orestes when he is persecuted by the *furor*-possessed Dido. In *Aeneid* 7, it is Turnus' turn to become Orestes, when he is attacked by Allecto. In the same episode, Allecto, disguised as an old hag, informs him that Aeneas has arrived to claim Lavinia, Turnus' own promised bride. The transformation of Turnus culminates in his description at the end of the Rutulian catalogue, and the emphasis therein on the ekphrases on his weapons affirm this in an impressive and emblematic way. By the end of the epic, however, it will be Aeneas who would claim the bride as promised to him, and along with it, the role of Orestes, though Turnus will not let go of the same claim so easily. His description as *furiis agitatus amor* ('love agitated by madness,' 12.668) aptly "condenses

---

83 See, e.g., Anderson 2008, 133.
84 Rebeggiani 2016, 61 ff., esp. 66–71.

in a sentence the two motivations of Orestes' madness from [*Aeneid*] 3: *furiae* and *amor*."[85] The fusion of the two (rightful) claims is confessed by Latinus at the opening of *Aeneid* 12 (19–44) and culminates in the poem's final scene, where, on the one hand, Turnus becomes the Orestes persecuted by the Furies, as the latter intervene for a second and final time against the Rutulian prince (*Aen.* 12.843–868), and, on the other, the description of Aeneas' killing of Turnus as a sacrifice (*immolate*, 12.949) and the qualification of Aeneas as 'burning with fury' (*furiis accensus*, 12.946) categorize the execution of the Rutulian alongside Orestes' execution of Pyrrhus upon the altar.

Io's cameo appearance on the shield of Turnus functions as a literary Ariadne's thread that guides the informed reader of Valerius' song of Mopsus through the dense intertextuality of the Vergilian model and the latter's elaborate tragic interface. As a result of this recollection, the reader of the *Argonautica* will be in a position to appreciate more thoroughly the approaching second half of the epic, which will revolve essentially around the same thematic nucleus as the second half of the *Aeneid*: the arrival of a foreign character who will claim by force a bride promised already to a different groom.

4 Conclusion

In the *Argonautica* Valerius defines his own epic voice through close dialogue with Vergil (and Ovid), based on the use of generic tension that is produced when he infuses epic narrative with tragic voice. By associating tragic elements with the forces of obstruction to Aeneas' mission, that is, Vergil's mission to compose the new epic of Rome, Vergil advanced the theme of tragedy as antithetical to epic, but also as a source for reading epic as a text of multiple levels and meanings. Valerius, who like his leading precedent, Apollonius, gives epic voices to celebrated tragic characters, embraces the tension between tragedy and epic as fundamental for properly appreciating generic exchange and poetic self-consciousness, and not least epic succession, a leading preoccupation of Imperial Latin epic composition.

---

85 Rebeggiani 2016, 69.

Gesine Manuwald
'Herculean Tragedy' in Valerius Flaccus' *Argonautica*

1 Introduction

That Valerius Flaccus' Flavian epic *Argonautica* is a highly intertextual poem, not only referring to Greek and Roman predecessors in the same genre (often by means of multiple or combinatorial imitation), but also by making use of other types of poetry (and prose) and even challenging the generic boundaries of epic,[1] is now widely acknowledged by scholars, in the wake of a re-evaluation of the epic poetry of the late first century CE in view of insights of modern literary theory.[2]

In relation to other poetic genres it has long been recognized that the structure of individual episodes can be seen as resembling a 'tragedy'[3] (similar to the Dido story in Vergil's *Aeneid*).[4] That there are individual verbal reminiscences of Senecan tragedy in Valerius Flaccus is also well known.[5] Tragic structures and tragic

---

1 On the play with generic tensions in Valerius Flaccus see Feeney 1991, 320–328; Blum 2019. On the relationship of scenes in Valerius Flaccus to love poetry see e.g. Heerink 2007.

2 For an early instance of this re-evaluation (particularly with respect to the relationship between the Flavian poets and Vergil) see Hardie 1993a; for an overview of the changing views in scholarship see Delz 1995.

3 Elements in an epic can only be identified as reminiscent of 'tragedy' on the basis of a definition of this dramatic genre, which is notoriously difficult. The discussion here will take its starting point from the description provided by Aristotle (*Poet.* ch. 6): it emphasizes the role of the plot and its effect on the feelings of audiences, for instance by reversals or recognitions (see also Bob Cowan in this volume). The relationship between epic and tragedy has also been explored with reference to other Flavian epics: on Statius and tragedy see e.g. Heslin 2008; Smolenaars 2008; Soerink 2014b; Augoustakis 2015.

4 See, e.g., on the Cyzicus episode in *Argonautica* 3, Garson 1964, 268–269: "The essential new feature of the Cyzicus episode is that, like Vergil's Dido story, it is cast in the tragic mould, and this is the aspect that deserves most emphasis. We should consider it under the following heads: (1) hybris; (2) peripeteia; (3) irony; (4) 'choric' interludes; (5) speeches."

5 For an overview of earlier secondary literature on this aspect (since 1871) see Grewe 1998, 173–174; Buckley 2014, 307–308. Owing to the fragmentary evidence, Valerius Flaccus' relationship to Roman Republican tragedy is almost impossible to describe (for an overview of a few potential references to Ennius' epic see Jocelyn 1988). The description of Hercules' fight with the sea monster to rescue Hesione (see below) might be reminiscent of Ennius' *Andromeda*; that the line *o domus, o freti nequiquam prole penates* (VF 1.721), spoken by Pelias, could be reminiscent of the line *o pater, o patria, o Priami domus* (Enn. *Trag.* 80 Ribbeck[2–3] = 101 Warmington = 87 Jocelyn = 23.10 Manuwald [*TrRF* v.2 / *FRL*]) in Ennius' *Andromacha* has been supposed (Ripoll 2008, 392).

https://doi.org/10.1515/9783110709841-006

colouring have been identified in the shape of scenes, character portrayals and foreshadowings in Valerius Flaccus, while the presence of such elements may lead to generic tensions.[6] A prime example is Medea, a tragic heroine par excellence and featured in numerous Greek and Roman tragedies; her interaction with Jason in the second half of the epic has been a major focus of such studies.[7]

What has been studied less is whether — apart from Medea (and Jason) — there are elements of tragedy in the stories of other characters in Valerius Flaccus' *Argonautica* and how existing tragic dramas about them might have influenced features throughout the epic.[8] The most prominent Argonaut after Jason is Hercules,[9] and it is understood that, in Valerius Flaccus' version, the scenes devoted

---

Possible connections between Republican tragedy, especially Accius' *Amphitruo* and Seneca's *Hercules furens*, have been considered, but the remaining fragments of Accius' play are too few to enable clear conclusions (see Fitch 1987, 48–49; Billerbeck 1999, 23–24).

6 See e.g. Ripoll 2003b; 2004; 2008; Buckley 2013; 2014; Blum 2019; cf. also Liberman 1996.

7 See e.g. Grewe 1998; Ripoll 2003b; 2004.

8 On the approaches taken in scholarship so far see Ripoll 2008, 383–384: "Mais ces travaux n'envisagent que l'emprunt de motifs ponctuels de telle ou telle tragédie dans tel ou tel épisode de l'épopée de Valérius: c'est davantage de l'influence des tragédies (et plus précisément, de certaines d'entre elles) que de la présence du tragique qu'il est question. Or certain critiques ont reconnu à cette épopée une couleur tragique que ne se réduit pas à l'influence ponctuelle de quelques intertextes, mais peut englober celle-ci. Il est donc pertinent de poser le problème du tragique sous un angle plus large, en ne s'en tenant pas exclusivement à une intertextualité «directe», mais ne élargissant l'investigation à des ressorts dramatiques ou à des elements thématiques plus larges qui contribuent à cette «ambiance tragique» ressentie par certains critiques de façon semi-intuitive. Il convient aussi de préciser la place exacte de cette couleur tragique dans le projet poétique d'ensemble de l'œuvre. Quant on parle de la présence du tragique dans l'épopée de Valérius Flaccus, c'est en général aux derniers chants, ceux où apparait Médée, que l'on pense. En dehors des chants VII et VIII, la critique s'est peu intéressée à cette problématique: citons simplement un article de R. Garson partiellement consacré à l'influence tragique dans l'épisode de Cyzique au chant III, dans lequel l'auteur met très bien en lumière le travail de réélaboration dramatique et tragique effectué par le poète flavien à partir du récit d'Apollonios de Rhodes. C'est dans le prolongement de cette analyse que je voudrais me pencher à present sur la série d'épisodes du chant I mettant enjeu le destin d'Éson, le père de Jason: des passages souvent étudiés séparément, notamment sous l'angle de l'intertextualité, mais que l'on n'a jamais vraiment tenté de mettre en relation les un avec les autres pour fair apparaître la coherence qui se dégage de cet ensemble. Je voudrais montrer que cette série d'épisodes a été délibérément conçue par le poète comme une veritable tragédie qui se développe en contrepoint de ce que j'appellerai «l'axe épique» du chant I (c'est-à-dire les préliminaires de l'expédition argonautique); les reminiscences sénéquiennes relevées par les commentateurs ne sont donc qu'un élément d'un dispositif plus vaste. Je voudrais aussi suggérer que cette couleur tragique ne relève pas d'un effet pathétique ponctuel, mais s'intègre dans le projet poétique d'ensemble de l'œuvre."

9 On Hercules in the literature of the first century CE see Piot 1965; Ripoll 1998a, 86–163. The studies of Schütz (1950) and Zwierlein (1984) do not include Valerius Flaccus.

to him form a narrative thread of their own.[10] While there are studies on Hercules' character (and his relationship to Jason),[11] it is surprising that the ways in which the presentation of his story in the *Argonautica* might bear resemblances to tragic narratives has not been studied in detail,[12] especially in view of the fact that Greek and Roman tragedies featuring Hercules among the protagonists survive in full (Sophocles, *Philoctetes* and *Trachiniae*; Euripides, *Alcestis, Heracles*, and *Heraclidae*; Seneca, *Hercules furens* and *Hercules Oetaeus*[13]).[14] The reduced attention to the role of tragedy, that of Seneca in particular, in comparison to that of Homer or Vergil may be connected with the fact that scholars have only recently started

---

10 See esp. Adamietz 1970; also Adamietz 1976, *passim*. They are therefore more than 'self-contained tableaux' (thus Galinsky 1972a, 164 n. 20 [p. 166]).

11 See e.g. Adamietz 1970; Galinsky 1972a, 163–164; Gärtner 1994, 100–101, 289–291; Billerbeck 1986, 3130–3134; Ripoll 1998a, 88–112 (who, among other details, notes the general influence of the mythological tradition and a Stoic presentation as in Seneca); Edwards 1999 (argues that a 'Herculean epic' is impossible and Hercules was eclipsed in Latin poetry with the exception of Senecan tragedy); Zissos 2014, 272–275.

12 See Buckley 2014, 307: "The linguistic influence of Valerius' most immediate tragic precursor, Seneca, on the Flavian epic has also been long recognised – in 1871 Karl Schenkl noted that Valerius was a diligent reader of Senecan tragedy – but the significance of the role Senecan tragedy plays within the *Argonautica* has not been explored in much depth." Buckley (2014, 319–324) provides a brief comparison between Valerius Flaccus' Hercules and the Senecan Hercules tragedies, focusing on the presentation of characters and the impact on the epic as a whole. Some more general considerations on the role of Hercules in the generic tensions at work in the *Argonautica* can be found in Blum's study (2019, 72–87).

13 The question of this drama's authenticity is irrelevant in this context (on this problem cf. e.g. Walde 1992, *passim*). Views on the poet do, however, affect assumptions on the date of the play and the question of whether it was written before Valerius Flaccus' *Argonautica*. For comparison of motifs, if no direct influence is postulated, this can largely be ignored too. For comments on Hercules in Seneca see also Sen. *Ben.* 1.13.3: *Hercules nihil sibi vicit; orbem terrarum transivit non concupiscendo, sed iudicando, quid vinceret, malorum hostis, bonorum vindex, terrarum marisque pacator; Constant.* 2.1: *pro ipso quidem Catone securum te esse iussi; nullam enim sapientem nec iniuriam accipere nec contumeliam posse, Catonem autem certius exemplar sapientis viri nobis deos inmortalis dedisse quam Ulixem et Herculem prioribus saeculis. hos enim Stoici nostri sapientes pronuntiaverunt, invictos laboribus et contemptores voluptatis et victores omnium terrorum; Ag.* 808–866; *Apocol.* 5–7. On Seneca's Hercules see Galinsky 1972a, 167–184; for recent overviews of *Hercules furens* and *Hercules Oetaeus* see Billerbeck 2014 and Littlewood 2014 respectively.

14 On Hercules in Greek tragedy see e.g. Galinsky 1972a, 40–80. No Roman tragedy named after Hercules is known from the Republican period (see also Galinsky 1972b, 128–129). Hercules does not appear in comic roles in Rome (see Galinsky 1972b, 128).

to explore the influence of Neronian literature on Valerius Flaccus in greater detail.[15] While the focus of the present study is on the direct relationship between Valerius Flaccus and tragedy, one must bear in mind that there is indirect influence too, as his model Apollonius Rhodius already reacted to classical Greek tragedy.[16] Further, Senecan tragedy is not the only intertextual reference or parallel; often there is also a connection to earlier epics, especially Vergil's *Aeneid*, with which Seneca may have also interacted. In order to illustrate the role of tragedy, possible connections to other literary genres will be disregarded here.

As a contribution to a more detailed analysis of intertextual connections between epic and tragedy, this essay will first look at the Hercules thread in the *Argonautica* as a potential 'tragedy' and then consider whether motifs in Valerius Flaccus' epic might bear similarities to existing Hercules tragedies.[17] Compiling this evidence will make it possible to draw conclusions on the relationship of Valerius Flaccus' poem to 'Herculean tragedies' and to tragic structures more generally and then on the effect of these connections on the epic's outlook.[18]

2 The Hercules story in Valerius Flaccus as a 'mini-tragedy'

Within Valerius Flaccus' *Argonautica* the Hercules story is more elaborate than its presentation in his predecessor and thematic model Apollonius Rhodius since Valerius Flaccus adds extra scenes and modifies existing ones. In his version the Hercules story covers the following main steps: Hercules (along with his young companion Hylas) joins the expedition, causing Juno's displeasure (VF 1.108–119). Jupiter announces in the divine assembly that Hercules (like the sons of

---

15 On Lucan and Valerius Flaccus see Stover 2012, after only few preceding studies.

16 On Apollonius Rhodius and tragedy, see e.g. Hunter 1989, 18–19. The role of Hercules as a Stoic hero will be less relevant for this literary study (on the influence of Stoicism on Hercules in Valerius Flaccus see Billerbeck 1986, 3130; on 'Stoic' aspects in Valerius Flaccus' portrait of Hercules see Zissos 2014, 272–275; on the role of philosophy in Valerius Flaccus generally see Ferenczi 2014; Zissos 2014).

17 Similarly, Ripoll (2004) has argued that *Argonautica* 7 has a 'tragic structure,' that the 'two main characters reach the status of tragic heroes' and that 'there are verbal echoes of Seneca's *Medea*.

18 For Valerius Flaccus the Latin text in Ehlers' Teubner edition (1980) has been used, for Seneca that of Zwierlein's Oxford Classical Text (1986). English translations follow the Loeb editions, by Mozley (1934) and Fitch (2002/2004) respectively.

Leda) will eventually enter heaven (VF 1.561–573). Hercules wants to take action during the threatening sea storm that the Argonauts experience shortly after starting on their first sea voyage, but finds his club and quiver useless (VF 1.634–635). During the Argonauts' stay at Lemnos Hercules is the only Argonaut to remain on the ship and not to engage with the Lemnian women, so that his love of adventure makes him call his comrades back to their mission (VF 2.373–384). When the Argonauts stop near Troy, Hercules rescues Hesione, Laomedon's daughter, but does not receive the promised reward and escapes the snares of the treacherous king by moving on (VF 2.445–578). At Cyzicus Hercules participates successfully in the battle between the Argonauts and the local inhabitants, and his actions reveal to one of the victims that this is a fight between former hosts and guests (VF 3.124–137, 161–172). During the subsequent 'rowing contest' Hercules breaks his oar (VF 3.462–480). When the Argonauts land in Mysia, to enable Hercules to get a new oar, Hercules loses his friend Hylas on Juno's instigation, is devastated and is eventually left behind by the other Argonauts (VF 3.481–725). In pity for him and prompted by the entreaties of other gods, Jupiter arranges another task for Hercules, namely to free Prometheus (VF 4.1–81). Hercules' freeing of Prometheus is his last appearance in the epic (VF 5.154–176).

While the constraints of the epic plot and its form of presentation mean that there cannot be a one-to-one correspondence between a narrative sequence in epic and the structure of a tragedy, one might suggest that Valerius Flaccus' Hercules story could be read as an extended tragedy. In Valerius Flaccus Hercules is the strongest Argonaut, ready to take action at any time; yet simultaneously he appears as one of the most unfortunate. Even though on Lemnos Hercules is the only one to remind his fellow Argonauts of the purpose of their mission, he is unable to participate in the Argonauts' eventual success of reaching Colchis and obtaining the Golden Fleece. On the contrary, he not only loses his beloved Hylas, but is also left behind by the other Argonauts halfway through the journey. This catastrophe is the result of a sequence of events to which Hercules contributes unknowingly. The pitying intervention of his divine father Jupiter, which indicates the dimension of Hercules' suffering on earth, resembles the action of a *deus ex machina*. Therefore, the Hercules 'tragedy' in the epic ends with a positive outlook, rather than with utter devastation.

As in expositions in dramatic prologues, Valerius Flaccus adumbrates the fate awaiting Hercules at the beginning of the epic, when both parties of the gods, the antagonist (Juno) and the supporter (Jupiter), indicate their plans for him (VF 1.108–119; 1.561–573): it is thereby clear from the start that Hercules' path to heaven will be tough and wearisome, but that he will finally be honoured.[19] At the same time suspense is created as to how Hercules' fate will develop since Juno does not take immediate action after she has delivered the monologue indicating her plans. Moreover, while eventual reward after much toil is an expectation suggested for the Argonauts' voyage as whole (VF 1.234–238), it does not become evident to the characters in its application to Hercules. In particular, while the sons of Leda, for whom Jupiter announces a place in heaven in the same utterance (VF 1.561–573) in an appendix to his programmatic speech to the gods (VF 1.531–560), receive a divine light, which might indicate their exceptional status and the support from their divine father,[20] nothing of this sort happens to Hercules; therefore it is not obvious to characters in the epic that for Hercules too there is a positive expectation for the future.[21]

In an initial phase Hercules gradually accepts the requirements of the novel enterprise and proves himself successful. While he is unable to confront the sea storm on the Argonauts' first sea voyage with his traditional weapons (VF 1.634–635), he has made the mission's goal his own to such an extent that he cannot bear lingering at Lemnos and demands to be given back 'the perils of the Scythian sea' and the chance 'to stay the Cyanean rocks and to despoil one vigilant monster more' (VF 2.373–384). For readers this eagerness is full of tragic irony, since Hercules will leave the enterprise before he will have the opportunity to carry out these initiatives and to reach the river Phasis and king Aeetes in Colchis. Still, his wish to accomplish a heroic deed in connection with the sea voyage just with his friend Telamon, if nobody else is willing, is realized shortly afterwards (in a scene not included in Apollonius Rhodius): when the Argonauts land near Troy, Hercules and Telamon go off on their own and find Hesione besieged by a sea monster (VF 2.445–578). For Hercules this resembles a situation he has experienced before when completing his labours (VF 2.493–496), and he gets ready to fight the monster. The fighting raises special challenges because the opponent is a sea monster

---

19 That Jupiter foresees suffering even for his protégés and only initiates a resolution after much pain for individuals (see below) is in line with the portrayal of this god in Valerius Flaccus (cf. his intervention at the end of the battle on Cyzicus, VF 3.249–253).

20 Castor and Pollux are the sons of Tyndareus and Leda (Hom. *Od.* 11.298–304; VF 1.570–571; 5.367). At the same time, both of them were also seen as sons of Zeus (hence their other name Dioscuri, not used in Valerius Flaccus), or Castor was regarded as the son of Tyndareus and Pollux as the son of Zeus (VF 4.256; 4.312–313).

21 Billerbeck (1986, 3133) notes that in Jupiter's view simply participating in the voyage of the Argonauts is a step on the path to the stars. Still, although Valerius Flaccus has Jupiter make a comparison with Apollo and Bacchus, who travelled the world, with respect to Hercules and the Tyndaridae there is emphasis on toil.

in the water, and Hercules has to adapt his weapons; he uses rocks at hand and eventually kills the monster (VF 2.521–536).[22] This scene shows Hercules' readiness to take action as well as his flexibility and strength in fighting; while he feels pity for Hesione (VF 2.454–456; 2.493–496), the fact that she is an attractive young woman is not relevant for him. Thus, at this point Hercules appears successful and sure of victory, just as the traditional figure of Hercules completing the twelve labours. Accordingly, he retains the attitude shown at Lemnos: he is keen to move on and complete the real task (VF 2.574–576). This hurry enables him to escape the king's snares, which would have led to a change of mood and a different plot at an early point in the story; at the same time, the poet makes it clear that Hercules is being tricked without any responsibility on his part.

This successful phase full of action reaches its collective *peripeteia* at the Argonauts' next stopover: during the battle on Cyzicus Hercules continues to fight effectively with his traditional weapons, but this time his strength is directed against friends, of which he is unaware. This situation, which applies to all Argonauts, becomes obvious in a dramatic climax in the middle of the battle description, when Hercules vaunts his success: this makes his victim realize the enemy's identity and enables him to bring the true facts to the shades in the underworld (VF 3.168–172). Hercules' proudly expressed confidence and fighting spirit, which lead to his identification, make his guilt appear personalized, even though he does not realize what he is doing.[23] This battle also sees the first military successes of his companion Hylas, while their short duration and his subsequent fate are foreshadowed, again a dimension only available to readers (VF 3.182–185). Accordingly, for both Hercules and Hylas achievements in this battle are combined with problematic consequences for the future.

Prior to the impending catastrophe for Hercules, there is a comic interlude: during the rowing contest indicating the Argonauts' relief after the fight on Cyzicus and the subsequent purification and atonement ritual, Hercules, even spurring on to the contest, breaks his oar, falls over several of his companions and is reduced to inactivity until his oar is replaced (VF 3.462–480). The stopover that allows him to do so causes the catastrophe; thus, to some extent, Hercules is responsible for creating the circumstances of his downfall (as becomes apparent to

---

22 Structurally, Hercules' fight with this monster functions as a kind of replacement in his 'Argonautic journey,' since he will not get the chance to fight monsters at Colchis, as he envisages (VF 2.378–384).

23 In contrast to Jason (VF 3.290–313; 3.369–376) nothing is said about how Hercules deals with the situation afterwards in relation to potential feelings of guilt after the true conditions have become evident; he is a hero of action and less prone to reflections about events.

readers in terms of tragic irony). For when the Argonauts disembark at Mysia, Hercules' archenemy Juno spots a good opportunity for her revenge: while Hercules and Hylas are in the woods, she rouses a stag luring Hylas; Hylas follows the stag, even encouraged by Hercules (VF 3.550–551), and is then drawn into a pool by a nymph (VF 3.481–564). This version of Hylas' disappearance, with Juno's involvement, only appears in Valerius Flaccus: it turns this scene into a proper element of the Hercules story and links it with its other elements. Among Valerius Flaccus' other modifications in comparison with Apollonius Rhodius are the facts that Hercules and Hylas are together when Hylas disappears and Hercules even urges Hylas to pursue the stag (thus again contributing to the realization of Juno's plan and Hylas' loss in tragic irony) and that later Hercules is left in the dark about Hylas' fate. This elaboration increases the severity of the hero's downfall and the impression of its tragic nature: as a result of Hylas' loss, Hercules is completely devastated and helpless (VF 3.565–597; 3.726–740).[24]

The situation is resolved by the intervention of Jupiter as a kind of *deus ex machina*: in pity for his son he reproaches Juno and puts Hercules to sleep (VF 4.1–21). During this sleep Hylas appears to Hercules, tells him what happened and announces that Hercules will soon enter heaven (VF 4.22–57). This allows Hercules to get back on track, and he starts to complete unfinished business by turning his steps to Troy and claim his reward (VF 4.58–59). Here, in a second divine intervention, Jupiter, moved by the pleas of Latona, Diana, and Apollo, makes Hercules go off and free Prometheus (another incident not included in Apollonius Rhodius' version; cf. AR 2.1246–1259).[25] This is Hercules' last deed mentioned in the epic (VF 5.154–176), so that, although he is not able to accomplish what he signed up for as an Argonaut, his story ends in a positive and characteristic way, with Hercules removing a monster with great strength for the benefit of others. Moreover, the comparison with Jupiter and Neptune (VF 5.163–164) and the indication of an almost cosmic effect of his intervention may suggest that Hercules is near his deification, although his story is not pursued further, and the

---

24 This episode in itself can be seen as 'tragic' in character and structure. This is perhaps not a surprise in view of the fact that Ovid lists the Hylas story among the subject matter of tragedies (Ov. *Tr.* 2.381–408).

25 Described as "an innovative 'Prometheus Unbound' not present in his Hellenistic source" by Buckley 2014, 319. On this scene and its potential relationship to 'Aeschylus' see Liberman 1996; Tschiedel 1998. Liberman (1996) argues that the presentation of the delivery of Prometheus in Valerius Flaccus might have been influenced by a '*Prometheus Unbound*' and a version of the story as found on a red-figure vase (*LIMC* VII.1, s.v. Prometheus, p. 542 no. 72; *c.* 350–340 BCE). The intervention of a number of gods on Prometheus' behalf is unusual, and in the scene in Book 4 the emphasis is on the eagle, while at the actual freeing in Book 5 it is on the chains.

poet leaves it open what happens between this incident and his reaching the stars as promised by Jupiter. Still, such a framework created by the narrator, as is possible in the epic genre, provides a conclusion to the Hercules tragedy.

So, in the shape of a particular form of Euripidean tragedy, after ascent, *peripeteia*, and downfall, the tragic nature of the ending is limited, since suddenly a positive resolution is provided.[26] Even though Hercules stands out by his dominant characteristic of taking action for defence or rescue, at the same time, in line with the requirements in Aristotle's *Poetics*, he is not an entirely faultless hero. Additionally, as expressed by the conventions of epic narrative, his experiences are determined by divine influences and fate; his initiatives are therefore mainly responsive. Accordingly, despite his divine descent and his exceptional status as a hero, Hercules is a human being to be pitied, and his grief for Hylas completely derails him.

3 Valerius Flaccus' 'Herculean tragedy' and Senecan Hercules tragedies

Since the section of Hercules' life depicted by Valerius Flaccus is different from those dramatized in existing Greek and Roman tragedies, there is no direct correspondence to any of their plots, yet they exhibit motifs that re-occur in Valerius Flaccus in similar or contrastive form: in addition to the 'tragic' structure of the Hercules story in Valerius Flaccus, the epic narrative includes motifs also found in Hercules tragedies transmitted under Seneca's name. Some of these correspondences cannot be regarded as particularly telling since they are standard elements of the Hercules complex (such as his heroic deeds or his fighting prowess). Others, however, are more specific and display similarities.[27] Such correspondences are especially meaningful if they appear in sections that Valerius Flaccus has significantly modified in comparison with Apollonius Rhodius.

---

26 The ups and downs in the presentation of Hercules' career in Valerius Flaccus coincide with the different characters of individual books, which some scholars have identified (see esp. Lüthje 1971, e.g. 127, 130, 139, 182, 237–238), but for no other character is it shown to the same extent how their fate varies accordingly.

27 See Billerbeck 1986, 3134: "Tatsächlich steht unter allen flavischen Epikern der Hercules des Valerius Flaccus demjenigen Senecas am nächsten; denn sowohl in Silius' *Punica*, …, als auch besonders in der *Thebais* des Statius treten die asketischen Züge gegenüber dem Wohltätergedanken und dem konventionellen Heldenbild wieder stärker zurück" (though Valerius Flaccus is not mentioned as an example of reception in Billerbeck 2014, 432–433).

Then they might suggest an intertextual relationship, though for individual examples it often remains hard to tell.

Firstly, in contrast to Apollonius Rhodius (AR 1.128–132; 1.1317–1320; 1.1347–1348), Hercules is not in the middle of carrying out the labours for king Eurystheus, but has already completed them.[28] This chronology puts Hercules in Valerius Flaccus in the same position as the character in Seneca's *Hercules furens* and in *Hercules Oetaeus* (and also in Euripides' *Heracles*): he is an established hero who has shown his credentials, but, as readers know, is now near his end. At the same time this makes the impending deification seem plausible. The ending of the plot too bears similarities to one of the Hercules tragedies transmitted under Seneca's name: Seneca's *Hercules furens* also ends on a positive note as Hercules decides to leave and Theseus offers him a friendly reception in his country (Sen. *HF* 1314–1344).[29]

Further, Juno as an opponent to Hercules appears in both the tragedies and the epic; this mythical conflict is presupposed and therefore not introduced.[30] Both Seneca and Valerius Flaccus have enhanced Juno's role in relation to their Greek predecessors.[31] Yet, Juno's position is less straightforward in the epic since there is a tension between her hatred of Hercules and her support of the Argonauts. Therefore Valerius Flaccus has Juno only take action against Hercules once he is separated from the rest of the Argonauts, while he has changed the sequence so dramatically in relation to Apollonius Rhodius that Juno is responsible for all stages of Hercules' downfall (VF 3.481–740): she has the stag appear that leads Hylas to the pool, she instigates the nymph, and she sends favourable winds so that the Argonauts decide to continue their journey. Juno's two monologues concerning Hercules, in which she voices her feelings and her plans at Hercules' first appearance in the epic and before her final attack (VF 1.111–119; 3.509–520),[32] in particular the second one, display similarities with her opening monologue in Seneca's *Hercules furens* (Sen. *HF* 1–124): in both cases Juno complains that she cannot find any further measures to confront and overcome Hercules and that she is merely the sister of Jupiter (and not his wife and therefore must deal with illegitimate offspring). Then she devises a novel plan to challenge Hercules, according to which he will have to conquer himself, as he will lose

---

28 See e.g. Adamietz 1970, 34.

29 See Heldmann 1974, 52.

30 See Eigler 1988, 36–37. It is not highlighted in Apollonius Rhodius apart from a passing reference (AR 1.996–997).

31 See e.g. Heldmann 1974, 17–56; Billerbeck 1999, 32, 184–185.

32 On these monologues see Eigler 1988, 32–47, who focuses on their structure and role in the epic as well as their relationship to Vergil.

loved boys, and to manage his feelings. Although the situations are different, ultimately, in both tragedies and in the epic Hercules suffers not because of a fight with an external, present foe, but because of a fight with his (manipulated) emotions, which is described in detail.

In addition to structural similarities there are correspondences of individual motifs. For instance, to conquer Hercules the Senecan Juno calls on the Eumenides and the 'handmaids of Dis' (Sen. *HF* 86–88; 100–106; cf. 982–986). In Valerius Flaccus, when she sees Hercules leaving the ship and is planning her attack (VF 3.487–488), she intends to stir the Furies and Dis in future (VF 3.520). Valerius Flaccus elaborates on the motif when, slightly later, he has Jupiter envisage that Juno will call on the Furies to lead the Argonauts to victory, though he indicates that this will only be short-lived (VF 4.13–14). In Seneca these auxiliaries are shown to take action, while in Valerius Flaccus their potential support is merely envisaged; this characterizes Juno and the threat she causes, but it remains open how this might materialize.

Something similar may apply to the reference to the Sarmatians in Valerius Flaccus: in *Hercules furens* the Sarmatians are mentioned as a far-off people in a cold land where one can travel over frozen waters on horseback without ships (Sen. *HF* 533–539; cf. Hdt. 4.21; 4.110.2). In Valerius Flaccus it is not Hercules who has reached them; instead the Sarmatians appear in the host of fighters in Colchis and personify an unknown area far away. One of the other warriors involved in the battle, Gesander, claims that his people do not need ships, but can travel on horseback through seas and rivers (VF 6.231–238; 6.326–329). Again, the Sarmatians are characterized in a way that resembles their presentation in Seneca, but they appear in a context that is different and less relevant to the main narrative.

As regards the fate of Hercules, in *Hercules furens* the constellation of the Tyndaridae already sits in the sky (Sen. *HF* 14), while Hercules is still waiting to get his star, though this seems a certainty (Sen. *HF* 23); their journey to the stars is further compared to that of Bacchus (Sen. *HF* 66; 457–458) and Apollo (Sen. *HF* 451–455). Some of these comments form part of Juno's introductory monologue; she is apprehensive of Hercules seeking a way to the gods above by force (Sen. *HF* 66–74). Whereas Seneca's Hercules is aware that Jupiter has promised him the stars (Sen. *HF* 958–960), in Valerius Flaccus Hercules is unaware of such future developments for most of the time. The deification is part of Jupiter's plan only revealed to the other gods; when he promises rewards to the Tyndaridae and Hercules after much toil, he compares their fate with the examples of Bacchus and Apollo (VF 1.561–573). In the tragedy Seneca has Megara confirm that there is no easy way to the stars (Sen. *HF* 437), just as Valerius Flaccus has Jupiter announce this view. In *Hercules Oetaeus* too Hercules expects to enter heaven (*HO*

7–13), as does the chorus, who assume that Hercules will have a place among the stars (*HO* 1564–1575). After his death Hercules is seen joining the stars (*HO* 1940–1943; 1966–1972). In the tragedies the characters know that after much suffering for the benefit of mankind the hero will be rewarded;[33] in the epic there is more emphasis on the depiction of the condition of humans being in the dark about the future, including any eventual rewards, which increases the tragic character of the events shown.

After having slain Lycus in *Hercules furens*, Hercules prays to Pallas as his ally and helper, although it has not been made explicit in what way she may have helped him (Sen. *HF* 900–902); in his agony in *Hercules Oetaeus* he implores Pallas as his sister for help (*HO* 1314–1316). Evidently, in situations particularly meaningful for Hercules Seneca highlights the relationship between Hercules and Pallas Athene. This matches the fact that in Valerius Flaccus, when she is planning to attack Hercules decisively, Juno fears that Pallas may want to support her brother Hercules (VF 3.489–491) and therefore gives her a task to remove her from the scene before she launches her attack against Hercules. Valerius Flaccus comments that Pallas follows Juno's instructions although she sees through the intrigue of the 'stepmother' (VF 3.506–508). In developing the motif Valerius Flaccus thus demonstrates that Pallas too abandons Hercules and that Hercules is left without any divine support until the later intervention of his father.

As regards the newly inserted Hesione episode (without a model in Apollonius Rhodius), there is no direct parallel in the Senecan Hercules tragedies; there is only a brief reference to this well-known myth (cf. Hom. *Il.* 5.638–642; 20.145–148) in *Hercules Oetaeus*, commenting that Hercules loved Hesione, but passed her on to his companion Telamo (*HO* 363–364). When Valerius Flaccus introduces the story of Hesione's rescue in his Argonautic narrative (VF 2.451–578), he focuses on the heroic deed and ignores any personal relationship between Hercules and Hesione. In fact, in contrast to the tragedies (Sen. *HF* 465–471; *HO passim*), Hercules' interest in women is not a theme in Valerius Flaccus. On the contrary, he not only remains aloof during the Argonauts' stay in Lemnos (VF 2.373–374), as he does in Apollonius Rhodius (AR 1.855–856), but Valerius Flaccus also enhances Hercules' only close personal relationship, his friendship with Hylas. Therefore, the catastrophe of the latter's loss receives greater weight and resembles the loss of Hercules' family in Seneca's *Hercules furens*. Moreover, in both cases Hercules contributes to the disaster by his own initiatives: in Seneca he kills

---

33 On different interpretations of Seneca's *Hercules furens* and the respective roles of philosophy and literature see e.g. Billerbeck 1999, 25–38.

his wife and children during the madness caused by Juno, and in Valerius Flaccus he causes the stopover in Mysia and encourages Hylas to pursue the stag.

Hercules' 'fathers,' Amphitryon in Seneca and Jupiter in Valerius Flaccus, know that Juno is responsible for the catastrophe of 'their' son, but not even Jupiter is able or willing to take action to prevent it.[34] Hercules himself learns the reason for his misfortune retrospectively, but this does not make his situation easier (VF 4.1–14; 4.25–29; Sen. *HF* 1200–1201; 1237). Since Valerius Flaccus, like Seneca, informs readers from the start that Juno intends to destroy Hercules, their pity with Hercules' grief (VF 3.565–597; 3.726–740) as well as with Hercules' feelings of guilt in Seneca (Sen. *HF* 1159–1272) acquires a further dimension.

Elements of Juno's campaign in Seneca not only show correspondences with sequences connected with Hercules in Valerius Flaccus, but also with the scene setting the entire action in motion. On the human level Valerius Flaccus' story takes its starting point from the fact that the tyrant Pelias wishes to destroy his nephew Jason, in response to an oracle and because he fears Jason's *fama* and *virtus* (VF 1.26–30).[35] Since there are no monsters left on earth, he has difficulties in finding a means to execute this plan (VF 1.31–34). This is similar to the situation that Juno experiences at the opening of *Hercules furens*, when she has to realize that Hercules' *virtus* is honoured all over the world and there are no monsters left (Sen. *HF* 37–42); Hercules' world-wide *fama* is also stressed in *Hercules Oetaeus* (*HO* 315–317). In Valerius Flaccus a link to the Hercules story is made explicit since the poet states that the reason for the lack of monsters Pelias could confront Jason with is that Hercules has removed them (VF 1.34–36).[36] In both cases the notion of Hercules as the conqueror is illustrated by the fact that he now wears the spoils of the monsters he has overcome (Sen. *HF* 44–46; VF 1.34–35). Both opponents then come up with a novel challenge: Pelias has Jason confront the sea (VF 1.37; 1.59–66; 1.74), and Juno will make Hercules fight himself (Sen. *HF* 84–122). In *Hercules furens* Juno will be victorious. In *Hercules Oetaeus*, however, when Hercules succumbs, yet not owing to Juno's plans, he regards this as a victory over her, which should be shameful for her (*HO* 1179–1191). In Valerius Flaccus Pelias is unsuccessful since thanks to divine support Jason manages to travel over the seas and obtain the Golden Fleece.

---

34 Jason had learned of the impending loss of Hercules from an oracle at the start of the voyage, but was not given any details (VF 3.617–622). This suggests that Hercules' disappearance from the Argonautic voyage had long been predetermined.

35 On the influences of Senecan tragedy on the presentation of Pelias see Galli 2002 [2005]; Ripoll 2008; Buckley 2014, 310–311.

36 See also Zissos 2008, *ad loc.*

The sketch of Celaeneus' realm in Valerius Flaccus, which is located close to the underworld and where the seer Mopsus has learned the ritual for cleansing those who have killed unintentionally (VF 3.397–410), bears similarities (e.g. no seasons and thus no agriculture, no motion, darkness) to the description of the underworld, visited by Hercules and Theseus, in *Hercules furens* (Sen. *HF* 698–759). Despite their gloom, these are places where things are put right. In *Hercules furens* it is stressed that guilty souls are punished, according to their crime (Sen. *HF* 735–736); equally, good and merciful kings will be rewarded and enter Elysium (Sen. *HF* 739–747). These notions reappear in the presentation of the underworld in Valerius Flaccus in connection with the death of Jason's parents, a newly introduced section in comparison with Apollonius Rhodius, complementing the information about Celaeneus: there it is made clear that virtue is rewarded in the world below, and deserving individuals enter a blissful area (VF 1.841–850). One of the two gates through which the dead souls pass into the underworld in Valerius Flaccus is destined for individuals and kings other than outstanding ones and will also lead Pelias to his punishment (VF 1.832–850). This scenario in both authors is particularly significant, for punishment in the underworld is not a standard element of Stoic doctrine: it is only mentioned in Lactantius, where it is attributed to Zenon, maybe influenced by Vergil's *Aeneid* 6 and the commentary tradition on this passage (Lactant. *Div. inst.* 7.7.13; 7.20.8–10). Vergil's precedent is likely to have been relevant in Valerius Flaccus as well, but the political emphasis rather resembles the situation presented in Seneca.

4 Conclusion

The analysis of the presentation of the Hercules story in Valerius Flaccus suggests that this subplot may be regarded as a form of Euripidean tragedy, consisting of prologue, climactic development, comic interlude, catastrophe, and happy ending achieved by a *deus ex machina*, and that elements in the Hercules thread as well as in other parts of the narrative correspond to characteristic features in the Hercules tragedies transmitted under Seneca's name. This is most noticeable in Juno's prominent role from the start and the path to the hero's downfall, instigated by her. Such correspondences indicate that at least the Senecan Hercules tragedies might have been relevant for Valerius Flaccus, not in the sense that the same story is told (his narrative covers a different section of the myth), but rather in the way that structure and motifs are exploited (in addition to intertextual connections to other earlier texts).

For Valerius Flaccus' compositional techniques these correspondences demonstrate that he creatively engaged with earlier literature in genres beyond epic. Since Valerius Flaccus structures the Hercules story in a way resembling the sequence in Seneca's *Hercules furens*, i.e. introduces Juno as a driving force from the start and consequently modifies the Hylas episode so that she is the direct cause of Hercules' misfortune, the notion is reinforced (by means of the language and imagery of myth) that humans are exposed to influences beyond their control, when such a sad fate can even hit a hero such as Hercules who has not committed any obvious wrong. Thereby the arrangement of the Herculean tragedy in Valerius Flaccus, with its incorporation of elements also occurring in Seneca's *Hercules furens*, enhances the impact of the Hercules story and the epic's message.

This shaping of the Hercules story as a narrative resembling a tragedy, even though a satisfying resolution is reached by the intervention of a *deus ex machina*, has consequences for the juxtaposition of Jason and Hercules: it has long been acknowledged that the two men and their fates in Valerius Flaccus invite comparison and that Jason's position is affected by Hercules' presence. When Hercules' story is regarded as a tragedy with a balancing resolution at the end, it becomes apparent how much more 'tragic' Jason's circumstances are: he goes through a number of situations where he will be unhappy with any decision made; he will achieve the obvious goal and obtain the Golden Fleece, but he will have to suffer later for having accepted Medea's help and there will not be a happy ending (VF 1.224–226; 5.442–451). He never learns details about his own future and his role in the historical developments, whereas Hercules, at least after his most devastating experience, is given an indication of his ultimate ascent to heaven. Jason, as the leader of the expedition, is an instrument in Jupiter's plan of the world (VF 1.531–560), and for him a reward, like that promised for Hercules and the Tyndaridae, is never envisaged. This contrast between Hercules' 'tragedy,' which will ultimately end positively, and the situation of the other Argonauts endows the fate of Jason and his comrades with an even gloomier outlook.

Ruth Parkes
Finding the Tragic in the Epics of Statius

The manner in which Statian epic engages with tragedies has attracted growing in-terest.[1] Attention has, for instance, been paid to how the *Thebaid* exploits Euripi-des' *Hypsipyle*, which included an encounter between Hypsipyle and the Argive princes,[2] and the Theban plays of the Greek and Roman tradition, including Sen-eca's *Oedipus* where the necromantic evocation of Laius is rerun in a different genre and for the next generation.[3] The Scyrian interlude of the *Achilleid*, an episode which shows especial interest in spectacle,[4] has been discussed not only in light of its comic resonances (shades of a New Comedy plot involving rape, the discovery of an illicit child, and marriage)[5] but also its relationship with tragedies such as Euripides' *Scyrians*[6] or Seneca's *Troades*,[7] where the portrayal of Achilles hidden by Thetis looks to that of Astyanax concealed by Andromache.[8] Consideration has also been paid to tragedies such as Euripides' *Iphigenia at Aulis*, in which accounts of later parts of Achilles' life in subsequent, prospective portions of the unfinished poem have the possibility of engagement with.[9] Whilst this chapter includes dis-cussion of tragic intertexts, its main purpose is to address, through the medium of Statian epic, the broader question of how to identify the tragic mode in epic at any particular moment.[10] Attention will also be paid to the thematic implications of finding the tragic mode so marked up: so, for instance, how it can contribute to the *Thebaid*'s interest in the transmission of negative emotions among human charac-ters. Although there are clear differences between epic and tragedy, which were

---

1 Thanks to Magdalena Öhrman for advice on this piece, especially with regards to weaving.
2 For engagement with Euripides' *Hypsipyle*, see Brown 1994, 57–93; Soerink 2014b.
3 For use of the Greek Theban plays, see e.g. Heslin 2008; Marinis 2015. For engagement with Seneca's Theban plays, see e.g. Frings 1992; Delarue 2000, 143–159; Augoustakis 2015 (including discussion of Statius' use of the necromantic episode from Seneca's *Oedipus*).
4 See Heslin 2005, 145–149 for the way Achilles and Lycomedes' daughters are put on display.
5 See e.g. Newlands 2012, 69. Heslin (2005, 242) notes comic precedent for impregnation at a nighttime festival. Ripoll (2007, 56–57) looks at comic parallels for Achilles' disguise.
6 For the *Achilleid* and Euripides' *Scyrians*, see e.g. Aricò 1981; Heslin 2005, 195–198; Fantuzzi 2012, 31–35.
7 See e.g. Fantham 1979; Delarue 2000, 169–173; 205; McAuley 2016, 354–359.
8 Cf. Fantham 1979, 459–460; McAuley 2016, 357–359.
9 For Euripides' *Iphigenia at Aulis*, see Barchiesi 2005, 70, 31.
10 The term mode is used to denote a select group of features from a genre (Fowler 1982, 106–107). This limited group of features, which can be defined adjectivally (e.g. 'tragic'), may be pre-sent in another genre.

https://doi.org/10.1515/9783110709841-007

viewed in antiquity as distinct genres, there are also similarities. Close examination of literature written in the first century CE shows how literary cross-contamination and overlap in content and themes complicate the process of separating out the tragic and the epic. In identifying generic voices, use will be made of the idea that a text may, through the employment of signals, conjure a theoretical notion of genre. This enables discussion to encompass the *Achilleid*, a poem where different generic voices appear to fight for control over the narrative and where there is staged uncertainty over the direction of the poem.[11] For it is the case that one especially needs a sense of the rules in order to break them: a conjured theoretical view of what epic constitutes is necessary to create a sense of transgressiveness or divergence.

1 Differences between epic and tragedy

In the ancient world, tragedy differed from epic in a number of distinct ways: so, for instance, unlike epic it did not employ the dactylic hexameter metre. A number of differences can be linked to the fact that tragedy was tied (at least theoretically) to stage production. Hence its lack of the omniscient, third person voice found in epic. And hence the divergences in the genres' treatment of time and space. Both ancient drama and heroic epic normally had, in the words of Harrison, "plot and action directed teleologically towards a clear conclusion."[12] Nevertheless, significant differences pertained in the temporal and spatial movement to that conclusion. Ancient tragedy typically covered a time-scale of twenty-four hours or less and lasted the actual or theoretical duration of a performance; the practicalities of staging, combined with the time-scale, placed limitations on movement. Epic, by contrast, usually covered events over a considerable period of time[13] and a variety of places,[14] and was characterized by a lengthy narrative. Such factors were conducive to the enactment of a long journey, a common feature of Latin epics from the first century CE. And, indeed, we may find these epics mapping the spatial journey of the poem onto the textual journey of the narrative, as can be seen in the way the expedition of the Argive army in Books 4 to 7 of the *Thebaid* maps onto the drive

---

11 Cf. e.g. Newlands 2012, 69, and see Parkes 2008 on the placing of the *Achilleid* in an alternative epic tradition.
12 Harrison 2007, 27.
13 Cf. Hershkowitz 1998a, 25.
14 Curley 2013, 88 contrasts the single locus usually represented by tragic theatre with epic's sequence of often disparate loci.

towards depiction of fraternal warfare at Thebes.[15] The motif of journey *qua* epic narrative can also be detected in the way the *Achilleid*, which happens to break off after the propelling of Achilles from Thessaly to Scyros and thence towards Aulis, advertises its narrative thrust. Achilles is the passive agent borne onwards by a narrator who signals his desire to 'lead through' (*deducere, Ach.* 1.7) his hero to Troy, the site of his death, and the area of his final resting place (Cape Sigeum, 1.76). The journey is marked as an epic one by a combination of the scale (hinted at by play with the Greek for 'long' in the trumpet's epithet *Dulichia, Ach.* 1.6)[16] and the Homeric framing of the proem, which is flagged up through the epithet *Maeonio* (*Ach.* 1.4).[17] For all that it never gets there, the idea of moving on towards a distant goal lies behind the *Achilleid*. Epic, even truncated epic, has a sense of a lengthy movement onwards which is necessarily absent from tragedy.

This is not to suggest that movement forwards is straightforward in Statian epic. The appearance of onwards momentum is complicated by the flaunting of narrative delay, as we shall see, and also cyclicity. In the *Thebaid* this cyclicity takes the form of regressive (and typically nefarious) patterns identifiable in the characters' behaviour:[18] one might point to the repetition of Eteocles' vengeful withholding of burial rites at *Thebaid* 3.97–98 in Creon's refusal to allow Argive burial (*Theb.* 12.94–103)[19] or the kin-strife between the patricidal Oedipus and his father Laius (1.65–66), replayed in the familial conflict between Oedipus and his sons (1.76–87) and then in the fraternal animosity of these sons which results in mutual destruction (11.403–573). Such cyclicity is entrenched by a multiplicity of factors. These factors include revenge, which, though backwards-looking, is a typically self-perpetuating act: see, for example, the way Polynices and Eteocles' mistreatment of their blind father (*Theb.* 1.74–79) prompts Oedipus' invocation of the 'avenger' (*vindex*, 1.80) Tisiphone to stir up fraternal conflict (1.83–84) which in turn causes the self-styled 'avenger' (*ultorem*, 1.241) Jupiter to rouse brotherly strife through the

---

15 See Parkes 2013, 405–406.

16 Cf. Hinds 2020, 433, speaking of "the cross-linguistic metapoetic pun in *Dulichia... tuba* (6), whose island epithet trumpets an epic both 'long' (δολιχ-, δουλιχ-) and Odyssean."

17 See McNelis 2015, 578–579.

18 *Theb.* 1.2 *evolvere* suggests unrolling a scroll (OLD 6, s.v. *evolvo*). However, as McAuley (2016, 305) suggests, the unfurling of linear narrative at the beginning of *Thebaid* 1 is immediately complicated by the proemic material involving "the repetitions and regressions that characterize Theban familial history."

19 See e.g. Bernstein 2013a, 236. As Pollmann 2004, 112 observes, Creon shows a vindictive streak similar to Achilles in his treatment of Hector's corpse (on which, below).

means of the ghost of Laius (1.295–302). Such factors also include the sway of heredity,[20] as suggested by Oedipus' claim that Tisiphone will know Eteocles and Polynices are his own sons by their willingness to engage in kin-strife (*Theb.* 1.86–87). Critics like Newlands and Soerink[21] have justly detected affinities with the world of Senecan tragedy where nefarious history repeats itself,[22] in contrast with the teleological narrative of the *Aeneid* where the Trojans learn how to master the past by redoing it.[23] Nevertheless, set against this cyclicity, which is destined to continue in the form of the Epigoni (*ultoresque alii*, 'other avengers,' *Theb.* 7.220),[24] there is the possibility of moving out of a narratorial rut, as can be discerned in Theseus' resolution of the burial crisis in Book 12.[25] Furthermore, through the *Thebaid*'s length and geographical and chronological scope, the narrative provides a sense of moving forwards in time and space.

The generic differences in time and space may be illustrated by a comparison between Seneca's *Troades* and Statius' *Achilleid*. The former, which consists of 1179 lines, moves with no major time lapse from Hecuba's initial lament through to events involving the deaths of Astyanax and Polyxena, before ending with the messenger's orders for speedy embarkation of the Trojan women. In contrast, the *Achilleid* is cut off after 1127 lines and the Scyrian interlude alone extends at least the nine months of Deidamia's pregnancy. In the *Troades*, journeys are gestured to rather than shown on stage,[26] as is evident from the evocation of Achilles' travels from Scyros to and around the Troad in the context of the deeds done before fighting at Troy (*Tro.* 215–233),[27] and the Trojan women's forthcoming departure with the Greeks (1178–1179). Conversely, the Scyrian episode of the *Achilleid* is bookended

---

20 For the power of "genetic determinism" in the poem, see Davis 1994; Bernstein 2008, 64–85. Regressive behaviour is particularly evident in the Thebans with their tendency to return to place of origin (so Oedipus to his mother's womb and Amphiaraus to the mother Earth), and conditions of origin, such as the fraternal hostility of the Spartoi (so the warring royal brothers).

21 Cf. Newlands 2012, 4; Soerink 2014a, 23.

22 On the recursiveness, see Schiesaro 2003.

23 Cf. Quint 1993, 67 on repetition-as-mastery in the *Aeneid* describing "a teleological epic narrative that moves linearly to its final goal of victory." See e.g. Zissos 2009 for Seneca's upsetting of Vergilian teleology.

24 Cf. Davis 1994, 469.

25 Although Theseus is acting to avenge the unburied dead (cf. *Theb.* 12.570; 12.766), he does not vengefully deny Creon a tomb for his corpse (12.778–781) and thereby breaks the cycle.

26 There does appear to be limited geographical movement: see Marshall (2000, 40–41) for a reconstruction of the chorus' movements seawards.

27 At *Tro.* 229–233, Achilles' preparations for fighting against Troy are presented as a journey. In addition, we may think of Pyrrhus' own journey to Troy from Scyros, a way in which the emulous son has literally been "tracing" his father (cf. *Tro.* 237 *sequi*).

by the actual travels of Achilles from Thessaly to Scyros and from Scyros to Aulis, whither he is last seen sailing when the plot halts prematurely at *Ach.* 2.167. Aulis, which lies as a future possible locus of delay due to Diana's withholding of favourable winds until her appeasement through Iphigenia's sacrifice, is also one stage further along Achilles' land-hopping journey towards Troy.[28] Admittedly, the prospect of cyclic patterns is set up in the narrative future: so, for example, the epithet *Hecateia* applied to Aulis at *Ach.* 1.447 gestures beyond the military delay, which is provoked by the absence of Achilles, towards the delay at Aulis involving Achilles and the sacrifice of his "bride" Iphigenia.[29] However, there is a clear idea of narrative progression towards the far-off *telos* of Achilles' martial victories and death at Troy, in line with the movement towards that city. In the *Troades*, by contrast, there is a much less clear sense of geographical or narrative progression. Polyxena's sacrifice is a repeat of Iphigenia's[30] and for the majority of the characters, the Troad location is either the final end point (so Astyanax and Polyxena) or the place where the essence of their life has been spent (so the Trojan women).[31]

2 The problems of disentangling the epic and the tragic

Despite such differences between epic and tragedy, the task of identifying the tragic mode in epic by the first century CE is a far from straightforward one. Tragic and epic elements can be hard to disentangle. One of the difficulties stems from the issue of cross-contamination. By the time Statius was writing, epic's engagement with tragedy was well-established. The *Aeneid* and its epic successors had deployed

---

28 Pyrrhus' words at *Tro.* 215–228 stand as a possible prospectus of the route and geographical delays which could be encountered by the Statian Achilles before the fighting at Troy: cf. Delarue 2003, 4.
29 Rimell (2015, 283 n. 82) sees the goddess' delay of winds until the sacrifice of Iphigenia lurking behind *Ach.* 1.446. Note also the way a pattern of Achilles' relationships is hinted at by the reminiscence of the Senecan Helen's arguments concerning Polyxena's betrothal (apparently to Pyrrhus, in reality to the dead Achilles) in Achilles' outlining of his marriage credentials to Deidamia's father: cf. *Tro.* 879–882 and *Ach.* 1.898–899 with Fantham 1979, 458.
30 Boyle 2006, 200.
31 Cf. Marshall (2000, 41) on the chorus: "The journey to the sea is in no way hopeful: it is a journey from death, past death (tombs and scenes of battle), towards death, in the past, the present, and the immediate future."

sophisticated, and often sustained, allusion to Greek and Roman tragedies.[32] At the same time, the exploitation of works such as Vergil's *Aeneid* and Ovid's *Metamorphoses* in Seneca's tragedies[33] bestowed particular prominence upon the interaction of tragedy with epic.[34] A further difficulty, which is linked to the issue of cross-contamination, lies in the overlap in content. There is a generic cross-over in both human characters (the messenger and the nurse appear in epic as well as being stock figures of the tragic stage) and supernatural characters (the Furies are familiar tragic characters from Aeschylus' *Oresteia* on[35] but also an integral part of the epic world in the wake of the *Aeneid* where Vergil's depictions of Tisiphone and Allecto go on to impact subsequent epic).[36] There is also overlap in themes and motifs. So tragedy, which is of the world of the theatre, has clear associations with staging and spectacle, and metadrama is a key preoccupation[37] but spectatorship is also an important motif in epic, as shown by one of its earliest incarnations, the *Iliad*.[38] And so anger features in epic since the mention of Achilles' wrath at the opening of the *Iliad* but it is also a key emotion in tragedy, as suggested by Ovid's characterization at *Remedia amoris* 375: 'anger befits the tragic buskin' (*tragicos decet ira cothurnos*).

The cross-over of material is well illustrated by the motif of vengeance. Often associated with tragedy,[39] this is a recurring motif in epic since Homer's depiction of Achilles whose thirst to avenge Patroclus' death is revealed in his threat to give Hector's unburied corpse to dogs (*Il.* 23.182–183). In the *Thebaid*, it is notable as a powerful, thriving stimulus to action, as exemplified by Laius' ambiguous prophetic utterances, fuelled by his 'immortal hatred' (*Theb.* 4.609, *inmortale odium*), which serve to usher his grandson Eteocles towards his destruction.[40] For all Tiresias' placatory address at *Thebaid* 4.612–613 ('now enough avenged of your bloody destruction')[41] and suggestion that Oedipus has paid the ultimate price, a fate worse

---

32 For Vergil's *Aeneid*, see e.g. Panoussi 2009 and Horsfall 2016, 96–97, 104–105 (on signposting of the tragic mode in the *Aeneid*). For Ovid's *Metamorphoses*, see e.g. Curley 2013, and for Lucan's *Bellum Civile*, see Ambühl 2005. Buckley (2014) treats Senecan tragedy and Valerius Flaccus' *Argonautica*. For Silius Italicus' *Punica* and tragedy, see Bernstein in this volume.
33 See e.g. Trinacty 2014.
34 Tragedy had, of course, engaged with non-performative genres, including epic, right from its beginnings. For this "inter-generic reception," see Gildenhard and Revermann 2010, 3, 9–10.
35 Cf. Padel 1992, 170.
36 See Tisiphone at *Aen.* 6.555–556 and 6.670–672; Allecto at *Aen.* 7.323–405.
37 For Senecan use of metadrama, see e.g. Schiesaro 2003, and further below.
38 For spectatorship and the gaze in this and in later epic, see now Lovatt 2013a.
39 For the association of tragedy with vengeance, see e.g. Allen 2013.
40 On the ambiguity of Laius' words, see Parkes 2012, 279–280.
41 *Theb.* 4.612–613, *iam satis ulte cruentum / exitium.*

than death, in his act of self-blinding (4.614–617), it is clear that his vengeance is not satiated. As suggested by the present tense of *Theb.* 4.627–628, significantly changed from the perfect tense of the model lines uttered by Seneca's Laius at *Oed.* 638–639,[42] Laius perceives Oedipus' incestuous relationship with his mother as an ongoing insult and cannot move forwards. Furthermore, Statius also conjures the hallucinatory appearance of the vengeful ghostly Laius of Seneca's *Phoenissae* (Seneca's revisionist presentation of his *Oedipus'* Laius), who seems dissatisfied by the blinding (*Phoen.* 42–43) and after Oedipus' life (*Phoen.* 90–91): emphasis is thereby given to Laius' vengeance as a living, driving force.

Another cross-over theme is that of delay, typically thematized in connection with the question of plot progression. In Senecan tragedy *mora* is often used, in the words of Leigh: "to denote the principle which restrains the force necessary to unleash disaster and create the tragedy."[43] Thus, for example, the eponymous heroine of the *Medea* cries: 'now overcome sluggish delay' (*rumpe iam segnes moras, Med.* 54) as she urges herself to commit crime,[44] whilst in *Agamemnon*, the nurse urges Clytemnestra to allow delay before heeding her anger but this is rejected (*Ag.* 130–131). Delay is also a feature of epic. Indeed, by the time of Statian epic, there was self-conscious play with the way that, in practice, it acted to underpin the structure of epic narrative.[45] This is exemplified by the way the description of the army's stay in densely-thicketed Nemea,[46] and the extended flashback narrated by Hypsipyle within that interlude (*Theb.* 5.49–498), hinders the progression of the narrative towards the fighting until the soldiers are prompted to seize weapons (*arma, arma, Theb.* 7.135) and thence 'make up for delays' (*redimunt... moras, Theb.* 7.139). The

---

42 Cf. *Theb.* 4.627–628, *qui semet in ortus / vertit et indignae regerit sua pignora matri* ('who turns himself to his origins and brings back his own children to his undeserving mother') with *Oed.* 638–639, *egitque in ortus semet et matri impios / fetus regessit* ('and he drove himself to his origins and he brought back to his mother impious offspring'). The change in tense is noted by Augoustakis 2015, 385.

43 Leigh 1997, 187. Further, in the *Troades, mora* serves as one of the primary motifs (Trinacty 2014, 168 n. 147); cf. Balula 2015.

44 Cf. the words of Medea at *Med.* 988 as she hesitates before killing her sons: *quid nunc moraris, anime?* ('why do you now delay, my spirit?').

45 Cf. Parkes 2012, xvii.

46 The delayed progression of the army, enmeshed in Nemea's dense foliage (Parkes 2013, 411–412), matches up with the delay of the epic narrative. In the course of the episode, hindrances are overcome: trees are cut down (*Theb.* 6.84–106), and the journey made to Thebes in Book 7 involves crossing the Isthmus of Corinth which had been presented as a barrier separating the Peloponnese from mainland Greece (7.15–16, *omne quod Isthmius umbo / distinet*, 'all that the Isthmian prominence holds apart'). The army's freer movement ties in with movement towards Thebes.

Achilleid similarly flaunts narrative deferral linked to geographical delay. The sea-girt island of Scyros where Thetis places her son within a walled city (*Ach.* 1.287; 2.27) topographically holds up the young Achilles and hence the war narrative: the Argive army are waiting for Achilles at Aulis 'with poised standards' (*suspensis... signis, Ach.* 1.870). The departure of Achilles thence is only enabled by Ulysses' exposure trick (*Ach.* 1.721–725, 848–856, 874–877) and encouragement with words (*heia, abrumpe moras!*) which recall the Vergilian Mercury propelling the amorous Aeneas back onto his martial epic track.[47] Once he has persuaded his lover's father, who capitulates because he fears 'to delay the Argive war,'[48] Achilles can follow Aeneas[49] by leaving the island (although echoes of Seneca's *Troades* serve to remind us that, unlike his Vergilian model, he is going off to destroy Troy).[50] The hold-up at Scyros is in line with the *Achilleid*'s general mapping of narrative retardation onto physical barriers which check Achilles on his journey to Troy, although, at the same time, they also help drive him (and the story) onwards: for, as Rimell has noted, the lingering of the poem "in caves, valleys, homes, groves and wombs, shows how epic energy must ferment in enclosures."[51]

The difficulty of disentangling epic and tragic elements may be illustrated by the opening scene of *Thebaid* 8. Here Dis reacts to Amphiaraus' intrusion into Hades at *Thebaid* 8.31–83 as one invasion of his domain too many (*Theb.* 8.52–53, *anne profana tum totiens Chaos hospite vivo / perpetiar?* 'Shall I suffer Chaos to be so often violated by a living visitor?'). Angrily railing against the Olympians and summoning Tisiphone to 'avenge the seat of Tartarus' (*Tartareas ulciscere sedes, Theb.* 8.65), he acts to propel the poem along by issuing commands which the unfurling plot fulfils.[52] Dis' portrayal looks to that of the Vergilian Juno who has been hounding Aeneas and his men to atone for insults inflicted by the Trojan race (*Aen.* 1.26–28). In realisation that the action she stimulated in *Aeneid* 1 has now stalled,

---

47 *Ach.* 1.872 ('come on, break off delay'); cf. *Aen.* 4.569, *heia... rumpe moras* ('come on... break off delay).'

48 *Fatis Argivaque bella morari, Ach.* 1.915.

49 On Achilles as Aeneas (and Deidamia as Dido), see e.g. Feeney 2004, 89–90; Heslin 2005, 93–101; Rimell 2015, 283 n. 81; Augoustakis 2016b, 202.

50 The echo of Pyrrhus' boast that 'Troy was overthrown by [Achilles'] hand' (*manu / impulsa Troia, Tro.* 204–205) in Neptune's prophecy that Achilles will 'overthrow our walls with his hand' (*inpelletque manu nostros... muros, Ach.* 1.89) works to suggest the fulfilment of that prophecy. The recollection of Pyrrhus' assertion that after Achilles' death Troy stood 'uncertain which way to fall' (*dubia quo caderet, Tro.* 206) in Odysseus' claim that, at the prospect of Achilles, the walls of Troy are 'tottering' (*dubiis, Ach.* 1.871) gives weight to Odysseus' words. For the reminiscences, see Fantham 1979, 459.

51 Rimell 2015, 253.

52 Cf. Ganiban 2007, 119 on *Theb.* 8.65–79.

she decides to enlist the help of the underworld (*Aen.* 7.286–322), deploying the Fury Allecto whose infernal power splinters off into Turnus and Amata and Silvia's stag (*Aen.* 7.323–571) and propels the action further. There are a number of similarities between the two deities. As is clear from the way she sets herself against Mars and Diana who succeeded in securing retribution from their enemies (*Aen.* 7.304–307), Juno is spurred on by revenge, just like Dis. She employs a Fury to instigate action, as does the king of the underworld. Furthermore, Juno is akin to Dis in the way she acts as a poet-figure, driving along the plot with poetic energy drawn from chthonic sources.[53] That the Statian passage exploits the Vergilian section as an intertext is evident from verbal parallelisms, such as the echo of Juno's claim that if she cannot bend the higher powers, she will 'move Acheron' (*Acheronta movebo, Aen.* 7.312) in Dis' mention of 'disturbing Tartarus' (*movere / Tartara, Theb.* 8.78–79).[54]

However, the influence of the Vergilian scene was far-reaching on subsequent literature, perhaps a result of the metapoetic possibilities inherent in such a narrative stimulus, and we are faced with untangling a web of relationships which, to borrow Schiesaro's analogy: "resembles the stemma of a heavily contaminated textual tradition."[55] Not only did Statius draw widely on the *Aeneid* 7 scene,[56] notably in his description of Oedipus' prayer to Tisiphone (*Theb.* 1.56–87) and the Fury's appearance (1.88–122),[57] but so did Vergil's other successors working in the epic and tragic traditions. Thus Ovid had drawn on the Vergilian Juno's use of Allecto to instil furor in Amata and Turnus in his depiction of Juno's deployment of Tisiphone to rouse madness in Athamas and Ino (*Met.* 4.432–530).[58] And thus Seneca was inspired by the scene, as we can see in the way elements of *Aeneid* 7 are reworked in the Fury's dispatch of Tantalus to infect the household (*Thy.* 1–121).[59] Similarly, another instance of a tragedy in which Seneca had exploited the Vergilian scene (alongside *Met.* 4.432–530, one of its legacy episodes),[60] is *Hercules furens*. When

---

53 For the Vergilian Juno as a creator of the narrative, see e.g. Hershkowitz 1998a, 101–102. For Dis, see e.g. Lovatt 2015, 424 on the god in Book 8 as 'a new figure of the poet, creating his own proem.'

54 Cf. the echo of Juno's *ast ego* from *Aen.* 7.308 (and 1.46) at *Theb.* 8.61 (Augoustakis 2016a, 91).

55 Schiesaro 2003, 84, speaking of Seneca's *Thyestes*.

56 Cf. Ganiban 2007, 30 n. 23.

57 Ganiban 2007, 30–32; further bibliographical references at Ganiban 2007, 30 n. 23. For the Vergilian Allecto as a model for the Statian Tisiphone, see e.g. Hershkowitz 1998a, 54.

58 Cf. Hershkowitz 1998a, 161–162.

59 Cf. Schiesaro 2003, 32–34.

60 Cf. Fitch 1987, 116, 146, 150.

the vengeful Juno harnesses infernal powers by summoning Megaera to madden Hercules in this play, she recalls both her behind-the-scenes Euripidean counterpart, Hera,[61] and the Allecto-rousing Juno of *Aeneid* 7[62] (whose actions in *Aeneid* 7 are partly patterned on the Euripidean Hera's deployment of Lyssa to enrage Heracles).[63]

A key model for the Statian Dis, alongside the Vergilian Juno, is, in fact, the Juno who opens Seneca's *Hercules furens* (*HF* 1–124). Like Dis, this deity is spurred on by vengeance and, just as Dis is enraged by Amphiaraus' irruption into Hades, Juno's passions are partly roused by Hercules' violation of the underworld, as evidenced by her order to the Furies: 'seek revenge for the desecrated Styx' (*poenas petite vitiatae Stygis*, *HF* 104).[64] Like Dis, Juno, who herself is something of an infernal power in the play,[65] makes use of chthonic energy. She calls on the Furies (*HF* 86–88; 100–111), specifically Megaera (101–103), and also asks for Titans and a giant to be released (79–82), a request which is picked up in the maddened Hercules' threats to set Saturn and the Titans against Jupiter at *HF* 965–968: *vincla Saturno exuam, / contraque patris impii regnum impotens / avum resolvam; bella Titanes parent, / me duce furentes* ('I shall strip Saturn of his chains, and against my unfilial father's unbridled rule, I shall loose my grandfather. Let the Titans in rage prepare war, with me as leader'). Dis similarly calls on a Fury, Tisiphone (*Theb.* 8.65–79), and, in words reminiscent of those of Hercules at *HF* 965–968,[66] notes menacingly that he already has 'the chains of the Giants shaken and the Titans eager to come out to the heavenly sky and our wretched father' (*Theb.* 8.42–44, *quassa Gigantum / vincula et aetherium cupidos exire sub axem / Titanas miserumque patrem*). The outburst of the "dramaturge" Juno[67] sets plot lines in motion, in the manner of the poet-figure Dis, although in both cases events do not progress in the order in which they are conceived.[68]

We have thus seen that the *Thebaid* 8 passage demonstrates an intertwining of tragic and epic intertexts. Furthermore, it contains matter, such as vengeance, and

---

61 Iris and Lyssa are the deities directly involved (Eur. *Her.* 822–874): see *Her.* 831 for the involvement of Hera.
62 Cf. Fitch 1987, 116–117, 146, 151, 153; Littlewood 2004, 6, 116 n. 31; Trinacty 2014, 129–137.
63 See e.g. Wigodsky 1972, 93–94; Galinsky 1972a, 132.
64 Bessone 2011, 99 n. 3 well compares *Theb.* 8.52–53.
65 So Fitch 1987, 117.
66 Augoustakis 2016a, 82.
67 For the Senecan Juno as a dramaturge figure, see Schiesaro 2003, 186; Littlewood 2004, 120.
68 Ganiban 2007, 119 n. 8 notes the fact that events do not follow in the sequence given in Dis' words.

characters, such as the Furies, which occur in both epic and tragedy. Do we recognize a tragic moment in Dis' outburst? Does the text foreground the *Hercules furens* intertext as belonging to Senecan tragedy or does it assimilate it as a legacy passage of *Aeneid* 7, rendering it, we might say, "genre-neutral"?[69] The opening section of Book 2 (*Theb.* 2.1–133) poses a similar dilemma. Here Eteocles is left 'roused by wrath' (*Theb.* 2.132 *excitus ira*) after a ghostly visitation from Laius who is still suffering in anger the effects of Oedipus' sword said to have driven home 'the first wrath of the Furies' (*Theb.* 2.10 *primas Furiarum... iras*).[70] Like the *Thebaid* 8 passage, this scene is a complex blend of epic and tragic intertexts. The shade is conveyed by Mercury to Eteocles' bedchamber on Jupiter's orders (*Theb.* 1.292–302; 2.1–2, 115–116). Mercury evokes his Vergilian counterpart from *Aen.* 4.238–278 who calls on a sleeping Aeneas at Jupiter's bequest.[71] In addition, this 'god' (*deus*, *Theb.* 2.55), who is 'enveloped in dark shadow' (*fusca... obsitus umbra*, *Theb.* 2.55), carries out his orders by visiting the sleeping Laius, like the goddess (*dea*, *Aen.* 7.408) Allecto who goes to fulfil Juno's commands by rising on 'dark wings' (*fuscis... alis*, 7.408) on a nocturnal trip to Turnus.[72] The Vergilian Allecto serves additionally as a model for Laius. Both underworld characters come upon their victims as they sleep, and as Allecto appears in the form of the priestess Calybe, so Laius is disguised as the seer Tiresias.[73] Yet, alongside epic, there is also engagement with tragedy. In its use of a vision of a shade, Statius' scene looks not only to Vergil's depiction of the ghostly Hector's visit,[74] but also to Senecan practice. The shade Laius appears to his grandson Eteocles in order to rouse him against his brother Polynices. It is clear[75] that this looks to the ghost of Tantalus, brought up by a Fury at the beginning of the *Thyestes* to instigate fraternal conflict among his grandsons, and

---

69 This classification of the *Aeneid* 7 section as epic necessarily simplifies Vergil's complex generic engagement, as suggested by evocation of Euripides' *Heracles* or the address to the erotic muse Erato at 7.37–38.

70 The sense is surely both of internal fury as well as an external Fury. The scene illustrates the transmission of anger. For the connection, cf. Coffee 2009, 248: "distilled in... [Eteocles'] blood is the desire for violence of the line of the Theban rulers, the same desire that had lead Eteocles' father, Oedipus, to commit his rash killing at the crossroads."

71 See e.g. Hardie 2012, 204. Cf. *Theb.* 2.115–116 with *Aen.* 4.268–269.

72 Cf. Gervais 2013, 67.

73 Both Allecto and Laius add a fillet (*vitta*, *Aen.* 7.41; *infula*, *Theb.* 2.99) and have an olive spray entwined (*Aen.* 7.418, *tum ramum innectit olivae*, 'then she entwines a twig of olive'; *Theb.* 2.99–100, *glaucaeque innexus olivae / vittarum provenit honos*, 'the honour of the fillets entwined with grey olive emerged to view'). See Gervais 2013, 87, 90.

74 Cf. Gervais 2013, 87.

75 See e.g. Gervais 2013, xlii.

the ghost of Thyestes whose appearance at the start of the *Agamemnon* heralds further familial dysfunction.[76] Even here, however, the cross-contamination between epic and tragedy might make us query how much of a 'tragic' charge the Senecan intertexts carry. The opening of Book 2 looks to Book 1 in the choice of Taenarus as a route between the underworld and Thebes[77] and in the use of both *Aeneid* 7 and *Thyestes* as intertexts.[78] There is thus a sense in which the Senecan *Thyestes* has already been absorbed as part of the intertextual fabric of this epic. In light of the interwoven literary tradition and the shared generic content (anger) and cast (the ghost figure), is there anything to encourage us to read the scene as 'tragic'?

3 Marking up the tragic

In the face of such overlap and cross-contamination, how can we identify the tragic mode in epic? One way is through searching for passages where the tragic is actively flagged up.[79] This may be done when the text evokes tragic intertexts at the same time as marking the narrative as anomalous in some way. Take, for example, the case of Phegeus whom Theseus uses to pass on to Creon his ultimatum of burial rites or war (*Theb.* 12.596–598). We have seen that the character of the herald straddles epic and tragedy. Here, however, the text conjures a theoretical view of tragedy in which the messenger figure is key and nudges the reader towards recognizing the passage in this generic light. For, as Heslin has argued, the apparent redundancy of Phegeus' sudden and brief cameo at 12.681–686 bearing the words of Theseus (*dicta ferens Theseia*, 12.681) shortly ahead of that leader's appearance, helps guide us to see this narrative moment as tragic, starring a messenger *qua* tragic figure and set within a nexus of tragic allusions (for Phegeus' interruption of Creon's execution of Antigone and Argia evokes Sophocles' *Antigone* in the threat to Antigone's life and the sudden appearance of a messenger with surprising news, and

---

76 Damningly, Laius, who undergoes only a momentary hesitation upon his return to Thebes, displays a readiness not shown by the Senecan shades: see Bernstein 2003, 358. Bernstein (2003, 358 n. 9) well contrasts the lack of force needed in the case of Laius with the compulsion required in the case of Tantalus (Sen. *Thy.* 86–100). For the unwillingness of Thyestes, cf. *Ag.* 12–14.

77 Cf. Gervais 2013, xxi.

78 For Thyestes behind the depiction of Tisiphone's appearance in *Thebaid* 1, see e.g. Feeney 1991, 347–348 n. 116.

79 Cowan in this volume takes a similar approach, with a focus on *anagnorisis* alongside other generic markers of tragedy (intertextual, contextual, thematic).

Euripides' *Suppliant Women* in Theseus' dispatch of a herald).[80] In the words of Heslin (2008, 119), "[the messenger's] appearance here in epic is a signal of crossing genres... the sudden appearance of a messenger here is an acknowledgement to us that this Theban tableau is paradigmatically tragic." A similar example occurs in the *Achilleid*. As Heslin (2005, 195–196) observes, in one passage, and one passage only (*Ach.* 1.669–674), we hear of a nurse who helps Deidamia hide the pregnancy and birth. The oddity of having such a brief and fleeting reference to a character who is not heard of again helps signpost the moment as a tragic one. In spite of the difficulties involved in treating the fragmentary *Scyrians* as an intertext, Heslin is surely right to see Statius as gesturing towards the nurse character in Euripides' play, who was involved with hiding Deidamia's pregnancy: "While nurses may sometimes be found in epic, the sudden and superfluous presence here of a nurse, tragic and Euripidean figure *par excellence*, should alert us to the possibility of an interloper from that genre" (2005, 196).[81] The narrative oddity causes us to ponder on the nurse character and we are nudged, in conjunction with the Euripidean intertext, towards seeing the figure here as of the tragic world.

Another means of flagging a passage up as tragic is through using metageneric markers, self-reflexive moments within works wherein there is evocation of an element (or elements) associated with a genre.[82] If an epic text wants to flag up a moment as tragic, it might conjure a feature associated with the tragic stage. This is shown by the Ovidian simile of *Metamorphoses* 3.111–114 in which Sown men rising from the earth are likened to figures on the rising *aulaea* of the theatre, a comparison which, Hardie well suggests, may signpost "entry into a stagey, tragic world" as evoked by Ovid's Theban narrative.[83] Aspects of the theatre-set can also involve props, as Buckley's reading of Valerius Flaccus' *Argonautica* 2.211–212 illustrates. Here the dramaturge-cum-actor Venus, who is staging a dramatic illusion to encourage the women towards massacre, accompanies her production of groaning sound effects (VF 2.210) with a theatrical prop in the form of a 'gasping head' (*singultantia ... / ora*, 2.211–212). Such flaunting of theatrical elements is combined with the replay of tragic plot (Agave displaying Pentheus' severed head) and tragic script (reminiscences of Agave's boast of achieving greater things at Euripides' *Bacchae*

---

80 Heslin 2008, 119–120.
81 Heslin 2005, 196.
82 Cf. Harrison 2007, 27–33.
83 Hardie 1990, 226 n. 14. See Keith 2010, 193 for tragic intertextuality at *Met.* 3.97–98 prior to this signalling. Cf. Cowan in this volume for theatrical imagery as a generic marker for tragedy.

1237 in Venus' 'greater crime,' VF 2.209–210) to create "an essentially artificial spectacle, an elaborately mannered and clearly self-aware representation of tragedy."[84]

Another theatrical feature which could thus be deployed is tragic costume, the association of which with the tragic genre can be shown from Senecan drama where it is used as a means to flaunt the plays' metatheatricality. So, for instance, in his account of necromancy spectacle, Creon comments of Tiresias that 'a gloomy robe flows down to his feet' (*lugubris imos palla perfundit pedes*, *Oed.* 553). As Boyle has suggested, the idea of a *palla* sweeping down to the feet of the "metatragic figure"[85] of Tiresias in such a context gestures to the use of *palla* as a technical term for the full-length costume worn by the tragic actor.[86] Similarly, to take another example discussed by Boyle, the declaration of the newly blinded Oedipus that this 'face' (*vultus*, *Oed.* 1003) 'suits Oedipus' (*Oedipodam... decet*, *Oed.* 1003) evokes the 'mask' (*vultus*) which the actor playing that role on stage would have just adopted.[87]

Epic can similarly deploy tragic costume as a signal of tragedy, as evidenced by the well-known example of Venus in buskins at *Aen.* 1.337 (*coturno*). This choice of footwear worn by actors in tragedy (*OLD* 1b, s.v. *cot(h)urnus*) in tandem with the goddess' delivery of an expository tragic prologue, flags the tragic nature of the forthcoming Dido episode.[88] A further instance might be drawn from the *Metamorphoses*, a text known to use costume to mark up generic play as we can see in the case of Mercury's *virga* which is adapted according to the literary context.[89] It is surely no coincidence that we are told at *Met.* 4.483 that, when preparing to infect Athamas and Ino, the Ovidian Tisiphone 'puts on' (*induitur*, *Met.* 4.483) a 'robe red with dripping blood' (*fluidoque cruore rubentem... / pallam*, *Met.* 4.482–483), a detail absent from Vergil's description of Tisiphone's *palla... cruenta*[90] which lies as a model. The very act of donning costume is evocative of drama, which is based on such role playing. More specifically, Tisiphone is putting on a costume (*palla*)

---

84 So Buckley 2013, 89.

85 Boyle 2011, 243.

86 Also known as the syrma: cf. Brink 1971, 270. So Boyle 2011, 243.

87 Cf. Boyle 2011, 343. See e.g. Suet. *Nero* 21 for evidence for mask use in the Neronian period. Even if Senecan plays were not acted out in theatres, their scripting was conditioned by theatrical conventions and the option lay open for readers and listeners to envisage them as staged.

88 Cf. Harrison 1972–3, 20; Curley 2013, 55.

89 Mercury's *virga*, with which the god was iconographically associated, is retained as a shepherd's staff at *Met.* 1.674 (cf. *Met.* 1.671–672), heralding a move to a pastoral section (cf. Conte 1992, 107–108; Barchiesi 2006, 411) and polished up (*Met.* 2.735–736) as the god moves into the urbane world of elegiac-didactic (cf. Griffin 1992, 125).

90 'bloody mantle' (*Aen.* 6.555).

which had associations with tragedy. This signals the generic colouring of the forth-coming section (*Met.* 4.481–511) in which the Fury's victims, Ino and Athamas, re-play their tragic past.[91]

The presence of metageneric signposting can help in the identification of tragic mode. The description of Laius' apparition in *Thebaid* 2 involves a mixture of inter-texts from both literary traditions and characters and subject matter common to both genres. The 'tragic' nature of this narrative moment is flagged up by the com-bination of Senecan intertextuality and reference to dramatic practice. Laius adopts a disguise, which, as we have seen, nods to the Vergilian Allecto's imitation of the priestess Calybe. Yet the Statian passage lays considerable stress on Laius' imper-sonation of Tiresias. While Allecto 'puts on' (*induit, Aen.* 7.417) 'white locks and a fillet' (*albos / cum vitta crinis*, 7.417–418), Laius 'puts on' (*induitur, Theb.* 2.97) the seer's 'woolen fillets' (*vellera, Theb.* 2.96) and 'voice' (*Theb.* 2.96). His disguise en-compasses mimicry of Tiresias himself as well as seer costume, role-playing which is evocative of the theatrical world.[92] Of further significance is the fact that Laius takes on the appearance of Tiresias, a well-known figure on the tragic stage:[93] in-deed, the reference to the fillets being 'familiar' (*nota, Theb.* 2.96) surely points both to Allecto's adoption of priestly headgear and to the wearing of such costume by the character Tiresias on the tragic stage.[94] Moreover, we may detect play with the-atrical terminology. With the application of the verb *induitur* to Laius' assumption of Tiresias' *opacos /... vultus* (*Theb.* 2.95–96), we are fleetingly guided to think be-yond Laius' impersonation of the seer's 'blind expression' to the blind mask worn by Tiresias in his appearances in tragedy.[95] The tragic resonances of the moment are thus pointed up. Attention is directed to the *Thebaid*'s deployment of Seneca's two Tantalid plays, the *Agamemnon* and *Thyestes*, and the wider ethos of Senecan

---

91 See Gildenhard and Zissos 1999, 174–176 for the tragic elements in this section within the over-archingly epic episode.

92 There is precedent for a disguise involving voice in Juno's impersonation of Beroe (*Met.* 3.277). One might wonder whether the Ovidian scene itself gestures to a tragic scene from Aes-chylus' *Semele* (fr. 168 Radt) involving Hera disguised as a begging priestess.

93 For the seer in Greek tragedy, cf. Ugolini 1995, 117–150.

94 Seo (2013, 152) sees the phrase *vellera nota* as looking to the familiarity of Tiresias as a tragic figure.

95 The reference to 'his own pallor' (*pallorque suus*) at *Theb.* 2.98 returns us to thinking of Laius' face. Mercury has already provided the acting Laius with a staff (2.11), the kind appropriate for a blind character on stage, by giving him the wand he had conspicuously adopted at *Theb.* 1.306–308. Like the Ovidian Mercury (upon whom he is mapped at *Theb.* 1.303–311; cf. *Met.* 1.671–674), he has an adaptable *virga*.

tragedy conjured. The engagement evokes a world of cyclic crime where negative passions are transmitted through the generations.

As well as exploiting reference to physical features of the stage to flag up the tragic mode, epic can also use theatrical language. At *Thebaid* 5.658, after learning of Hypsipyle's negligence, Lycurgus angrily cries that he will make Hypsipyle forget 'all her tale of Lemnos' (*omnis fabula Lemni*). The word *fabula* primarily works to suggest the nonsense that Lycurgus deems Hypsipyle's stories to be.[96] Yet Soerink is surely also right to see a meta-poetic gesture here to *fabula*'s sense of 'tragedy.'[97] Events on Lemnos provided rich fodder for tragedians[98] and, indeed, in his *Hypsipyle*, which is being reworked by Statius in this part of the poem, Euripides presents Hypsipyle's back-story on Lemnos as a topic of her subject-matter.[99] Another instance occurs at *Thebaid* 4.379, where the leader of the Bacchantes who utters an address to Bacchus (4.383–404) is termed *regina chori* ('queen of the band'). She starts off by praising Bacchus (*Theb.* 4.383–389), in a way that could recall a tragic chorus' hymn to the god of drama[100] and then moves on to a sentiment which is familiar from tragic choruses: the wish she was elsewhere, far from her troubles.[101] In tandem with such tragic material, the use of the word *chorus* can guide us to seeing this figure as a *coryphaeus* from tragedy.[102] Evocation of the tragic mode poignantly underscores the ominous fate of those soon to be embroiled in war at Thebes. Bacchus, the patron god of tragedy,[103] will soon enter the action, orchestrating at first the drought (4.680–696) and later, in a nod to his *deus ex machina* role in Euripides' *Hypsipyle*, the reunion of Hypsipyle and her sons (5.710–730).[104] However, at Thebes he will conspicuously fail to reprise his role of a god intervening to reunite family, and the part of *deus ex machina* is left to Theseus, who brings resolution only after the armies have fought.

A further example of the exploitation of tragic language can be drawn from the beginning of *Thebaid* 8. We have seen that the opening scene looks to epic and tragic passages and contains characters and material common to the two genres. The text, however, does not discreetly assimilate the *Hercules furens* intertext into an epic whole but marks up the tragic moment. At *Theb.* 8.68 Dis orders Tisiphone

---

96 Cf. Soerink 2014a, 203.

97 Soerink 2014a, 203. For *fabula* to indicate tragedy, see Boyle 2006, 246 n. 7.

98 Cf. Hutchinson 2013, 350.

99 Cf. Soerink 2014b, 184–185.

100 Cf. Eur. *Ba.* 71; Sen. *Oed.* 403–508.

101 Cf. Parkes 2012, 210.

102 Cf. *OLD* 3, s.v.: "the performers in a chorus."

103 Soerink 2014b, 178.

104 Cf. Soerink 2014b, 178–179.

to 'produce' (*ede*) an 'abomination' (*nefas*). He deploys a verb used for putting on shows at Rome[105] and the idea of staging a production is further brought out by the language of spectatorship found at *Theb.* 8.74: 'may it please the brutal Thunderer to look on those things' (*iuvet ista ferum spectare Tonantem*). Although spectacle can be a feature of epic, its conjunction here with Senecan intertextuality suggests a theoretical conjuring of tragedy as a genre with staging at its heart. The mutual reinforcement of the language of performance and presence of the Senecan intertext encourages us to see Dis as dramaturge and to detect the presence of the tragic mode. One result is that we are thereby encouraged to pursue the implications of engagement with the play as a whole, rather than confining ourselves to a single passage. As the vengeful Juno's machinations lead to the madness of Hercules, so one outcome of the vengeful Dis' intervention is the frenzied Capaneus' gigantomachic climb towards the Olympians at *Thebaid* 10.837–939, the fulfilment of his curse (8.76–77). There are resonances here with the depiction of Hercules' ambition to attain heaven (*HF* 958–959), by force if necessary (965–968). We realize that both deities work on characteristics and feelings latent in the humans: Hercules' confidence is tipped over into hubris by Juno's involvement[106] just as Dis' curse pushes the over-confident, blasphemous Capaneus towards his theomachic actions. The *Thebaid* exploits the Senecan play's depiction of human and divine forces working in combination in its exploration of the internal and external motivations that drive characters such as Capaneus.

Yet another way for an epic poem to mark up the tragic mode is, somewhat paradoxically, to advertise its epicness: epic identity is often asserted in reaction to the presence of another genre, a process which in turn flags up that generic intrusion. Although it lacks the distinctive performative markers of tragedy, epic is nevertheless able to conjure a stereotypical picture of its generic essence[107] by, for instance, means of imagery. In view of the strong nexus of associations between the ocean and a genre whose founder, Homer, was frequently represented as such a body of water, this could involve sea imagery.[108] Statius' figuring of his completed epic as a ship now anchored after its journey on the 'vast sea' (*longo... aequore*, *Theb.* 12.809) provides one illustration of the link between epic and the ocean. The connotations of the image had previously been conjured in two interlinked com-

---

105 See Lovatt 2005, 274; Ganiban 2007, 182.

106 See Riley 2008, 80 for Juno's exacerbation of Hercules' semi-latent mania.

107 See Hinds 2000.

108 See Myers 2009, 54. See Morgan 1999, 32–33 for Homer and the ocean.

parisons: firstly, the simile of *Thebaid* 4.24–30 which marks up the apparent beginning of the poem's martial themes[109] by likening the departing warriors to sailors about to go over the 'vast sea' (*longum... aequor*, *Theb.* 4.24) and, secondly, the simile of *Thebaid* 7.139–143 where the newly roused Argive soldiers are compared to men setting sail from the harbour. In the intervening lines, the expectations aroused by the first departure simile are left largely unfulfilled. Whilst the soldiers do leave Argos they only progress to nearby Nemea where an encounter with Hypsipyle causes them to stray from their military goal. The Nemean episode (*Theb.* 4.4.646–7.104) sees a diversion into non-epic genres, not least tragedy,[110] and it is only at 7.135 ff. that the army resumes its expedition and the poem resumes its martial epic course. The sense of moving back after generic derailment is reinforced by the sea simile of *Theb.* 7.139–143. The poem is, at least momentarily, back on its 'epic' track, the ultimate success of the journey suggested by the poem-as-ship metaphor of *Theb.* 12.809.

The generic associations of the ocean are similarly evoked in the *Achilleid*. Achilles declares that he is going, as one 'sought' (*quaesitus*, *Ach.* 2.19), to 'Trojan war and Argive ships' (*bella... Troiana ratesque / Argolicas*, 2.18–19). Presumably heading first to Aulis, where he is awaited by the army,[111] his ship sets sail and Scyros, focalized from the perspective of the departing vessel, 'begins to move away from the vast sea' (*incipit et longo Scyros discedere ponto*, *Ach.* 2.22). The epithet *longus* contains the idea of time taken to cross the stretch of space.[112] The term thus does not only provide a contrast between the expanse of ocean and overcrowded land- and seascapes previously encountered,[113] it is also suggestive of the lengthiness of the voyage ahead. The epic connotations of the sea image are surely played on at this very juncture.[114] As the ship carrying Achilles to war moves out to the vast

---

109 See McNelis 2007, 82.

110 See e.g. Augoustakis 2010, 45–46 for elegiac colouring and Parkes (forthcoming) for pastoral.

111 References to winds do not necessarily indicate immediate movement towards the Troad. Notus (cf. *Ach* 1.20) can stand for any wind (*OLD* 1b, s.v.) while Zephyrus (cf. *Ach.* 1.46) can be used for the gentle breezes that make up ideal sailing conditions (Zissos 2008, 242).

112 *OLD* 4a, s.v. *longus*.

113 So the narrow strait of the Hellespont chock-full with nymphs or ships (*Ach.* 1.28–29; 1.203–204; cf. Newlands 2012, 71), the island of Scyros in the 'close-packed Cyclades' (*artas / Cycladas*, *Ach.* 1.204–205), and the seas of Greece thronged by ships mustering for war (*Ach.* 1.445–446; 1.790). See Feeney 2004, 88 for a discussion of the crowded waters in terms of literary belatedness.

114 Newlands 2012, 70–71 rejects the interpretation, preferring to see an open generic direction.

sea, so the poem moves closer towards fulfilling the epic criteria of length and to-wards telling an 'epic' martial story-line which is forecast to include elements, like the dragging of Hector's body (*Ach.* 1.6), found in the *Iliad*. The poem's confident assertion of its epic direction is admittedly short-lived. The sight of Deidamia 'left behind' (*relictae*, *Ach.* 2.28), narrated in a passage of elegiac resonance (2.23–30),[115] prompts Achilles to hesitate and the course of the narrative to waver. Nevertheless, in being afforded a glimpse of the long journey ahead, we are given a sense that the narrative goes beyond the limitations (be they temporal, geographical, or chrono-logical) of, say, a tragic plot.[116] Once the ship has sailed away from the shores of Scyros, the narrative has gone beyond Euripides' *Scyrians*. It promises a future that goes towards and beyond other tragic intertexts like Euripides' *Iphigenia at Aulis*. By the start of Book 2, Achilles has, at least temporarily, overcome the threat posed in the Scyros episode by his doomed intertextual model, Astyanax. His death at Troy, and perhaps the aftermath of his death, offer opportunities for encounters with tragic material,[117] but this is in the future that the poem is working towards.

An essentialist picture of epic might alternatively be conjured through diction, as can be seen in the case of *arma* ('arms'). Although, in practice, war has a pres-ence in a variety of genres, in Latin poetry it becomes theoretically tied to epic. The word *arma* could be used to conjure epic associations since at least the *Aeneid*, which deployed it as an opening in reference to the martial content of its epic pre-decessor, the *Iliad*.[118] And even in the *Aeneid*, the term can be seen to act as short-hand for epic.[119] In her consideration of the tragic resonances of the scene in which Aeneas, in his tragic messenger-like rhesis, relates the death of Priam,[120] Rossi has seen significance in the way that at *Aeneid* 2.509 Priam is said to adopt *arma*: "The reappearance of the key word *arma* at this point of the narration and in the initial position of the hexameter gives Priam's action a symbolic connotation. By wearing his *arma*, Priam attempts, futilely, to regain an epic dimension and to break away from tragic space."[121] The epic language works to mark up Priam's move from trag-edy (we have heard of his death at the altar, *Aen.* 2.501–502) to epic (armed warrior, about to adopt the protocol of Homeric-style duelling warriors until the pattern is broken by slaughter at the altar). At the moment when the protagonist/narrative is

---

115 Cf. Rosati 2005, 146–147, drawing attention at 147 to the link with the abandoned women of the *Heroides*.

116 The *Achilleid* is likewise propelled beyond the threat of closure posed by comic colouring.

117 So, perhaps, in the lamentation of Thetis or the sacrifice of Polyxena.

118 Cf. e.g. Harrison 2007, 31.

119 See Barchiesi 1997, 16–17.

120 Rossi 2004, 44–49.

121 Rossi 2004, 48.

transitioning from tragic to epic (and thence back to tragedy), there is a self-reflexive gesture back to the *Aeneid*'s initial allegiance to martial epic.

Following the *Aeneid*, *arma* becomes even more a way of conjuring martial epic.[122] The seizure of 'arms, arms' (*arma, arma*) by soldiers at *Thebaid* 7.135 surely gestures to the poem's movement back onto its "epic" path after it had wandered in the Nemean interlude. There has previously been play on the generic associations of *arma* in Hypsipyle's words to Adrastus at *Thebaid* 5.29–39 in response to his request for her history. Seemingly about to retell the story of her Lemnian past, Hypsipyle starts her narration in a way that looks to epic and tragedy.[123] For her claim to Adrastus that 'ruler, you order me to renew savage wounds' (*inmania vulnera, rector, / integrare iubes*, *Theb.* 5.29–30) looks to the opening of Aeneas' tragic-style rhesis to Dido: 'Queen, you order me to revive an unspeakable grief' (*infandum, regina, iubes renovare dolorem*, *Aen.* 2.3).[124] The reference to Furies (*Furias*, *Theb.* 5.30) could indicate a tragic or epic direction, as could the reference to the Lemnian massacre (5.30–32) which had been treated in epics such as the Argonautic poems of Apollonius and Valerius Flaccus as well as in numerous tragedies. However, a notable cluster of tragic elements occurs in lines 5.33–34: a reference to a Fury (*Eumenis*, 5.33), a triple address (5.33–34),[125] and a salute to night (*o nox!*, 5.33) such as is found in tragedy.[126] Even the weaving metaphor contained in Hypsipyle's question 'why do I weave a long preface to my troubles?' (*quid longa malis exordia necto?*, *Theb.* 5.36) contains a tragic slant in its evocation of a weaving metaphor from Euripides' *Hypsipyle*.[127] The threat to the specifically 'epic' nature of the narrative, its potential derailment by tragic matter, is pointed up through Hypsipyle's comment at 5.37: 'arms call you' (*vos arma vocant*).[128] But such a warning is

---

122 A range of examples is provided by Barchiesi 1997, 17–23.

123 For Hypsipyle as an epic narrator, see Walter 2014, 222–224.

124 See Ganiban 2007, 73 with bibliographical references.

125 Cf. Hutchinson 2013, 351 n. 48.

126 Cf. Eur. *Androm.* 114.1 Kannicht; Hutchinson 2013, 351 n. 48. There may be specific recollection of a similar address by a daughter at Sophocles' *Electra* 203 (ὦ νύξ): see Hutchinson 2013, 350–351.

127 See Newlands 2012, 42 for connections with the metaphor of weaving in Euripides' *Hypsipyle* Collard and Cropp fr. 752 f. 11 κρέκειν. The word exordium indicates the warp set up on a loom before the web is started (*OLD* 1, s.v.). The weave, which was planned from the beginning through to its conclusion, was set up using a starting border, to be met at the end of the weave with another finishing border (cf. the use of *exordiri* at Plautus, *Pseud.* 399–400). The metaphor itself thus aptly hints at a bracketed-off object, a mini-weave of tragic matter, a finite part within a greater whole.

128 Cf. Hutchinson 2013, 351 (seeing Furies as a typically tragic phenomenon): "A tension between tragic and hexametric preoccupations at first seems to appear when Hypsipyle seeks to

disregarded and, following encouragement from Adrastus, Hypsipyle goes on to tell the Lemnian massacre story. The Argive princes listen to a story familiar from tragedy and rework their role as bit characters in Euripides' *Hypsipyle*. In doing so they can, however, only postpone, rather than avoid, their entrance as star players in the world of Theban tragedies. The tragic colouring of the Nemean episode poignantly draws attention to the futility of the princes' attempt to stave off their active participation in the 'tragic' events of the Argive-Theban war and its aftermath.

The case of Hypsipyle prompts one further example involving the identification of tragic mode. Hypsipyle's involvement retards the narrative, as is emphasised by the allusion to her 'delaying awhile in modest tears' (*paulum fletu cunctata modesto, Theb.* 5.28) before speaking. Such reference to delay draws attention to the heinous nature of the expedition (better to listen to Hypsipyle's story of familial slaughter then move on to kin-civil war) but also links to generic play. It has been established that delay is found in both epic and tragedy. However, here the narrative nudges us to see it as a feature of the latter genre, for it is linked to the intrusion of tragic material and appears to halt the onward momentum of the 'epic' narrative. When Hypsipyle breaks off at *Thebaid* 5.36 in a way that flags up digressiveness (*quid longa malis exordia necto?*), she does so, as we have seen, while drawing upon a weaving metaphor deployed by her Euripidean counterpart. Hypsipyle has previously upset an epic drive onwards whilst appearing in a scene containing tragic elements at *Theb.* 4.776 ff. After Adrastus, who seeks water to replenish 'hearts listless for war' (*pectora bellis / exanimate, Theb.* 4.766–767), expresses uncertainty over her identity, Hypsipyle gives some details of her background (4.776–780). Her speech is reminiscent of a tragic prologue in its expository function.[129] Furthermore, the content, such as reference to her 'divine descent' (*caelestis origo, Theb.* 4.776) engages with the words of her Euripidean incarnation in the prologue to the *Hypsipyle*.[130] However at 4.781 she breaks off: 'but why am I saying this and delaying you in your exhaustion from the waters you desire?' (*sed quid ego haec, fessosque optatis demoror undis?*). Hypsipyle goes on to take the warriors to a water-source which reinvigorates their drive onwards to war (*Theb.* 5.2–6), thereby restoring the narrative onto its epic path for a brief while until Adrastus once again questions

---

break off her account: *et vos arma vocant magnique in corde paratus* (37). This contrasts with her *redit... cordi / Eumenis* (32-3)."

129 The Vergilian Venus of *Aeneid* 1, one of Hypsipyle's literary models (cf. Parkes 2012, 281, 306) similarly gives background material in tragic prologue-style.

130 Cf. Brown 1994, 94; Eur. *Hyps.* fr. 752a Kannicht.

Hypsipyle on her background. There is tension between the narrative's epic momentum and the tragic feel of these two scenes concerned with delay. In the passage from Book 4, Hypsipyle herself instigates the "tragic" digression. In the passage from Book 5, it is prompted by Adrastus, who appears reluctant to press on with the nefarious expedition. Here again a sense is created that the Argives would prefer to be in the audience of tragedy than face their future "tragic" destiny in the forthcoming war and its aftermath.

Thus, in spite of the overlap in generic features and the commingling of literary traditions, it is possible for Statius' epic poems to advertise their evocation of a tragic mode. Mutual reinforcement of allusion to tragic texts and the inclusion of metageneric signals, such as reference to theatrical terminology, means that the reader may be alerted to the presence of a tragic voice at that given moment. This impacts on interpretation of intertextual passages which might be at risk of passing unnoticed, viewed in isolation, or perceived as being absorbed in a dominant epic tradition. Instead, the reader is encouraged to pursue the wider implications of engagement with a specific tragedy or with the ethos of tragedy as evoked.

Kyle Gervais
Senecan Heroes and Tyrants in Statius, *Thebaid* 2

1 Introduction

Intertextual studies of Senecan tragedy and Statius' *Thebaid* encounter special challenges. Seneca has long been recognized as an important influence on Statius' epic, and broad similarities are immediately recognizable – the shared Theban subject matter in Seneca's *Oedipus* and *Phoenissae*, for instance, or the theme of fraternal conflict in *Thyestes*. Nevertheless, the poetic idioms of Statius and Seneca are sufficiently different (due in part to the differing metrical demands of dactylic hexameter and iambic trimeter) that the most common and successful strategy for intertextual analysis of Flavian epic, relying on verbal similarities, must be used cautiously and in combination with similarities of theme, structure, and character.[1] Furthermore, despite working in the tragic genre, Seneca regularly alludes to works in other genres, especially Latin epic. Thus, when a verbal link between Statius and Seneca is found, it typically must be incorporated into a wider range of resonances with other texts.

A convenient example may be found in Laius' epiphany to Eteocles in *Thebaid* 2, where he warns his grandson of the preparations that Polynices is making to return to Thebes and regain his throne. The epiphany engages with a dizzying array of intertextual models, including Agamemnon's dream in *Iliad* 2, half a dozen epiphanies in the *Aeneid*, several scenes in the *Metamorphoses* and *Bellum Civile*, and (as we will see) the openings of Seneca's *Agamemnon* and *Thyestes*.[2] The last words of Statius' scene, closing out the first section of the book, effect a complex verbal allusion to several predecessors. Troubled and confused by his grandfather's visitation, Eteocles looks around for signs of his brother Polynices (*Theb.* 2.132–133):

---

1 This was recognized as early as Helm 1892, 35, who nevertheless offered more than 20 pages of analysis built primarily on verbal links between the *Thebaid* and Senecan and Attic tragedy. A recent example of a successful intertextual analysis is Augoustakis 2015, with a brief bibliography of scholarship on Statius and Seneca, to which add especially: Frings 1992; Delarue 2000, 141–176; Parkes 2012, xxx n. 71; Augoustakis 2016a, *passim*; and Rebeggiani 2018, *passim*, whose important monograph appeared too late to be incorporated fully in my work.
2 See further Gervais 2017, 97–98.

https://doi.org/10.1515/9783110709841-008

> *Excitus ira*
> *ductor in absentem consumit **proelia fratrem.***

Thus stirred by rage the commander wastes **battle** on his absent **brother.**[3]

The clausula *proelia fratr-* is a Statian favourite (cf. *Theb.* 4.308, 8.36, 11.306); readers steeped in the *Aeneid*, the *Thebaid*'s most salient intertextual model, will recognize the words as a reference to Juno's prayer to Allecto (*Aen.* 7.335):[4]

> *tu potes unanimos armare in **proelia fratres.***

You can make harmonious **brothers** arm for **battle.**

And indeed, Allecto's epiphany to Turnus is a prominent intertext for Laius' epiphany to Eteocles.[5] Ovid subsequently uses the clausula in his "little *Aeneid*" to describe the winds that break the Trojan ships from their moorings before they are transformed into nymphs (*Astraei... eunt in **proelia fratres**,* 'the Astraean brothers join battle,' *Met.* 14.545). Finally, Seneca deploys the words in a Theban context for the first time in his *Oedipus*, referring to the battle between the Theban Spartoi (*Oed.* 749–750):

> *Illa Herculeae norint Thebae /* ***proelia fratrum.***

May Herculean Thebes have known that **battle** between **brothers** [sc. and no others].

This is, as Boyle notes, "conspicuously vain appeal,"[6] since the sons of Oedipus will soon replay in spectacular fashion this original fraternal warfare — Statian *fraternas acies*, describing the sons of Oedipus (*Theb.* 1.1) *and* the Spartoi (*Theb.* 1.184). A broader intertextual analysis of this single phrase thus shows Statius positioning his work as a successor to both Vergilian epic and Senecan tragedy, here supplying the *proelia fratrum* that Seneca's chorus seeks to elide. Furthermore, Seneca's chorus refers to Thebes as 'Herculean,' a bold formulation for a city currently suffering under the rule of Oedipus, who is a distinctly non-Herculean hero. The epithet is proleptic, referring to Hercules' time at Thebes married to Megara, daughter of Creon, the successor to the warring sons of Oedipus that the chorus tries to wish out of existence. But to get to this point, Thebes must —

---

3 All translations are my own (translations from *Thebaid* 2 have been adapted from Gervais 2017).

4 This formulation is itself evocative of the Theban brothers' fratricidal war: Hardie 1990, 230.

5 Gervais 2017, xxxix.

6 Boyle 2011, 285.

from a Statian perspective — go through the *Thebaid*, an Oedipal epic which firmly rejects Herculean heroism (as we will see).

It is with these complexities in mind that I present a survey of Senecan intertexts in *Thebaid* 2, a book for which I have produced an edition and commentary, but also one particularly promising for analysis through a Senecan lens. The book opens in the underworld with the ghost of Laius, whose links to the ghosts in *Agamemnon* and *Thyestes* have long been acknowledged (but the influence of Seneca's *Hercules furens* on Statius' underworld landscape is less recognized). It continues with the wedding of Polynices and Tydeus to the daughters of Adrastus, which offers ominous foreshadowing of the Theban war to come,[7] and a survey of Thebes' tragic past in the ekphrasis of Harmonia's necklace. Tydeus' embassy to Eteocles centres on issues of power and perfidy which look to similar discussions in Seneca's *Phoenissae*. Finally, the ambush of Tydeus by fifty Theban warriors is fought on the site of the Sphinx's lair (whose defeat is described with reference to Seneca's *Oedipus*), and features allusions to *Thyestes* that hint at Tydeus' tragic end as a cannibal in *Thebaid 8*.

2 *Oedipus* and *Hercules Furens*

The general influence of Seneca's *Oedipus* on Statius' epic has been discussed by Boyle (2011, xc–xciii); Augoustakis (2015) has explored in particular the links between the necromancies of Laius in *Oedipus* and *Thebaid* 4. The influence of *Hercules furens* has not to my knowledge been much explored. In *Thebaid* 2, Seneca's *Oedipus* offers a model for Statius' description of Oedipus and the Sphinx, while details from *Hercules furens* shape Statius' description of underworld through which Laius and Mercury travel. Although the links with these two plays in *Thebaid* 2 are confined to short individual passages, they may be interpreted within a larger context of models for heroism in the epic, which I will briefly outline.

After Tydeus' failed embassy to Eteocles, the tyrant sets an ambush for him at the site of Oedipus' victory over the Sphinx, which Statius describes (*Theb.* 2.504–518). The most prominent Latin model for Oedipus' feat is a short passage from the first act of Seneca's *Oedipus*, in which the king of the plague-ridden

---

7 See my notes *ad loc.* in Gervais 2017.

Thebes recalls his encounter with the Sphinx (*Oed.* 92–102).[8] As is typical of Senecan intertexts, Statius' engagement with Seneca here is signalled primarily by shared details rather than exact verbal echoes. Thus, both passages feature: the bones of the Sphinx's former victims (*semesaque nudis / pectoribus... ossa, Theb.* 2.508–509; *albens ossibus sparsis solum, Oed.* 94), the monster's riddling words (*dictis... inexplicitis... dirae commercia... linguae,* 510–512, *doli,* 516; *nodosa sortis verba et implexos dolos / ac triste carmen,* 101–102), and three lines (513–515; 98–100) that describe the Sphinx's impatience to attack (*nec mora; impatiens morae*), the readying of its claws and mouth (*ungues... dentes; malae... unguis*), and the horrible sounds it makes (*terribili applausu; sonuit horrendum*). Surrounding these shared details are more explicit verbal links. The opening and closing lines of Statius' passage feature words found in the final line of Seneca's passage:[9]

> *contra importuna crepido,*
> *Oedipodioniae domus* **alitis**; *hic* **fera** *quondam...*
> ...
> **Tristis** *inexpletam scopulis adfligeret alvum.* (*Theb.* 2.504–505, 518)

An evil ledge lies opposite, the home of the Oedipodian **bird**. Here the **savage beast** once.... She **grimly** dashed her insatiate belly against the crags.

> *ac* **triste** *carmen* **alitis** *solvi* **ferae**. (*Oed.* 102)

And I solved the **grim** riddle of the **savage bird**.

Furthermore, the impressive and rare[10] epithet *Oedipodioniae* at the beginning of Statius' passage highlights not only the importance of Oedipus in the epic and the troubling link between the hero and the monster that he kills (see below), but also may be read metapoetically: the Sphinx that Statius describes in this passage is 'Oedipus' bird,' that is, drawn from Seneca's *Oedipus.*

Seneca's *Oedipus* is, of course, far from the only intertext for Statius' passage. The intertextual resonances in lines 506–507 are particularly rich, for instance,[11] but here I will highlight Statius' description of the bones in the Sphinx's lair (*semesaque nudis / pectoribus stetit ossa premens,* 'she stood with naked breasts

---

8 Smolenaars (2004) cites several verbal echoes of Seneca's *Oedipus* in his intertextual analysis of Statius' Sphinx passage.

9 I have found other examples in *Thebaid* 2 of verbal links between the end of a predecessor's passage and the beginning of a Statian passage (e.g., Gervais 2015, 69; 2017, 162).

10 Found elsewhere only at Ov. *Met.* 15.249 and Luc. *BC* 8.407 (*Thebae*), and Stat. *Theb.* 10.801 (*fratres*).

11 Cf. Gervais 2017, 248–249.

pressed onto half-eaten bones,' *Theb.* 2.508–509). This detail is found in Seneca's passage, but the precise wording owes more to Vergil's description of Cerberus in the hymn to Hercules at *Aen.* 8.296–297 (*te [tremuit] ianitor Orci / ossa super recubans antro semesa cruento*, 'the guardian of Orcus, lying above half-eaten bones in his bloody cave, trembled before you'). This would seem to align Statius' Oedipus with Vergil's Hercules as a monster slayer and civilizing force.[12] But by the end of the passage, Statius has instead followed Seneca by aligning his Oedipus with the very monster that he slays (*heu simili deprensa viro!*, 'she was caught out by a hero (alas!) like her,' *Theb.* 2.516; *implicitum malum / magisque monstrum Sphinge perplexum sua*, 'an entangled evil and the monster more confused than his Sphinx,' *Oed.* 640–641; cf. *Phoen.* 122). We will return to this conflict between Oedipal and Herculean models of heroism, but first I turn to the traces of Seneca's *Hercules furens* in *Thebaid 2*.

The account of Laius' ascent from the underworld draws various details from Theseus' description of Hercules in the underworld at *HF* 658–827. Statius' passage starts with a sluggish and sterile infernal landscape, which adapts a similar Senecan passage, borrowing much of its distinctive vocabulary:[13]

> *Undique **pigrae***
> *ire vetant nubes et turbidus*[14] *implicat **aer**,*
> ***nec Zephyri** rapuere gradum, sed **foeda** silentis*
> *aura poli. ...*
> ...
> *tum **steriles** luci possessaque manibus arva ...* (*Theb.* 2.2–5, 12)

On every side **stagnant** clouds forbid his advance and murky **air** enwraps him. **Nor** have **Zephyrs** sped his pace, but the **foul** breeze of the silent region. ... Then the **barren** groves and the fields held by ghosts ...

> ***nec** adulta leni fluctuat **Zephyro** seges ...*
> ***sterilis** profundi vastitas squalet soli*
> *et **foeda** tellus torpet aeterno situ ...*
> *immotus **aer** haeret et **pigro** sedet*
> *nox atra mundo.* (*HF* 699, 701–702, 704–705)

---

12 Here I pass over the complexities of the portrayal of Hercules in *Aeneid* 8, which encompasses monstrous elements (cf., e.g., Feeney 1991, 158–161).

13 None of the bolded words (or their cognates) in these passages are found, for instance, in descriptions of the underworld in *Aeneid* 6 or *Metamorphoses* 4.

14 Shackleton Bailey (2003) prints Baehrens's conjecture, *torpidus*, in his edition (the nonsensical *turpidus* is a minor variant in the manuscripts). This would provide a further verbal link to Seneca (cf. *torpet, Oed.* 702).

> **Nor** do mature crops wave in the **Zephyr**. ... The infernal soil is covered with a squalid, **barren** desolation and the **foul** earth languishes in eternal neglect. ... The **air** hangs motionless and black night sits over the **stagnant** world.

Through Statius' landscape run the twin rivers Styx and Acheron (*Theb.* 2.5–6), a pairing also distinctively Senecan (*HF* 711–717).[15] The earth is described as 'opening up backwards' for Laius' ascent (*patuisse retro, Theb.* 2.14), a detail found at the beginning of *Hercules furens* (*patefacta ab imis manibus retro via est*, 55; cf. a description of Hercules in the underworld in *Troades: retro patefecit iter*, 724). Finally, the entrance to the underworld in both passages is located at Taenarus (*Theb.* 2.32, *HF* 663; this is one of the standard entrances to the underworld).

Hercules' journey to the underworld culminates in his encounter with Cerberus; Laius too meets Cerberus, but the guard dog is soothed to sleep by the magic staff of Laius' guide, Mercury (*Theb.* 2.26–31). This of course recalls Aeneas' encounter with Cerberus in *Aeneid* 6, where the Sibyl feeds it a soporific treat (6.417–423). Statius even seeks to outdo Vergil's scene by suggesting that Cerberus is more dangerous to those leaving the underworld (as Laius is) than entering (as Aeneas was).[16] But other details of Statius' passage point instead to Seneca. Each individual similarity is perhaps unsurprising: Cerberus is habitually *saevus* (*saevus et intranti populo, Theb.* 2.28; *hic saevus umbras territat, HF* 783), he 'bristles' when provoked (*horrentem, Theb.* 2.30; *viperis horrent iubae, HF* 786), his snakes are 'threatening' (*minax, Theb.* 2.29 and *HF* 794), and both Mercury and Hercules 'soothe' and 'tame' the guard dog (*mulcens* and *domuisset, Theb.* 2.30, 31; *domitus* and *permulcens, HF* 802, 807). Cumulatively, however, they effect a sustained engagement between the two passages. Furthermore, and as he did for the Sphinx intertext, Statius signals this engagement with verbal echoes at the outset:

> *Illos* **ut** *caeco recubans in limine* **sensit**
> *Cerberus, atque*[17] *omnes capitum* **subrexit** *hiatus,*
> *saevus* **et** *intranti populo* ... (*Theb.* 2.26–28)

> **When** Cerberus **sensed** them as he lay on the hidden threshold, and he **raised** all his heads with their gaping jaws, fierce as he was **even** to people entering...

---

15 Vergil, for instance, pairs Styx with the Cocytus (*Aen.* 6.323).

16 This is the implication of *saevus et intranti populo* ('fierce as he was even to people entering,' *Theb.* 2.28).

17 This word has occasioned several conjectures. If we accept the emendation to *utque* by Eden (1998, 321), then Statius' passage, like Seneca's, has repetition of *ut* in its temporal sense.

> **sensit ut** *motus pedum,*
> *attollit hirtas angue vibrato comas*
> *missumque captat aure **subrecta** sonum,*
> *sentire **et** umbras solitus. ut propior stetit*
> *Iove natus antro...* (*HF* 788–792)

> **When** he **sensed** the movement of feet, his shaggy coat bristled with quivering snakes and he caught the sound with a **raised** ear, accustomed as he was to sense **even** shades. When Jupiter's son Hercules stood nearer to the cave...

As with Statius' Sphinx passage, here too intertextuality is not confined to a single source text. The description of Cerberus as *recubans* points to Vergil, where the guard dog is described with the same word when he meets Aeneas (*Aen.* 6.418) and, significantly, Hercules (*Aen.* 8.297). Moreover, Statius's subsequent description of the bones in Cerberus' lair (*iam sparsa solo turbaverat ossa*, *Theb.* 2.29) adopts a detail from Vergil's hymn to Hercules (*Aen.* 8.296–297, quoted above in the context of Statius' Sphinx), but is expressed in the language of Seneca's *Oedipus*, drawing from the passage we have already discussed: *albens ossibus sparsis solum* (*Oed.* 94).

Once again, then, we find Oedipus and the Sphinx juxtaposed with Hercules and Cerberus. As I have argued elsewhere, Oedipus and Hercules (particularly in their capacity as a monster slayers) constitute competing models of heroism in Statius' epic, but characters like Tydeus and Polynices who try to assume Herculean status are doomed to failure in the ultimately Oedipal universe of the *Thebaid*.[18] This previous discussion did not take into account the specifically Senecan nature of Hercules and Oedipus at this stage in the epic. Doing so underscores the futility of any attempts to emulate Herculean and reject Oedipal heroism. The Hercules that Seneca offers as a model is ultimately not the civilizing force found in Imperial propaganda or even the ambivalent figure immortalized by Vergil's *Aeneid*, but rather a fully tragic hero in the Oedipal mold, who gets no reward for his labours and instead rains destruction on his family, becoming (like Oedipus) a monster indistinguishable from those he has slain.[19]

---

18 Gervais 2015. See also Ripoll 1998a, 145–152 on "faux Hercules" in the epic. Henderson (1993) argues most persuasively for the Oedipal nature of the *Thebaid*.

19 Boyle 2011, 260 also makes this point, citing passages that describe Hercules as a *monstrum* worse than the Sphinx (*Oed.* 640–641, *Phoen.* 122; cf. *HF* 1279–1281). All three of the Flavian epicists wrestle with the ambiguities of Hercules: Hardie 1993a, 65–71 and Ripoll 1998a, 86–163. The Senecan portrayal of Hercules was particularly influential on Statius, as discussed by Rebeggiani 2018, 123–152, whose work I regret being unable to consult before writing this chapter.

3 *Phoenissae*

Statius incorporates into his *Thebaid* the mythology of Seneca's *Phoenissae*, which shows Jocasta still alive and attempting to intervene in the conflict between Polynices and Eteocles.[20] Statius divides this individual Senecan intervention into two scenes, with Jocasta confronting Polynices in Book 7 and Eteocles in Book 11.[21] He thereby ensures that the brothers do not in fact meet until the climax of the poem, when all hope for reconciliation has been lost and only fratricide remains. While these scenes constitute the clearest intertexts, Seneca's *Phoenissae* may be profitably compared with other parts of Statius' *Thebaid*.[22]

In *Thebaid* 2, I have found a few isolated intertexts. For instance, Statius narrates in flashback the murder of Laius, using the phrase *ensis impius* (*Theb*. 2.8–10):

> capulo nam largius illi
> transabiit animam cognatis ictibus **ensis**
> **impius** et primas Furiarum pertulit iras.

A kinsman's thrust had cut an **impious sword** clean through his life's breath, further than the hilt, striking the first blow of the Furies' rage.

This phrase is found as the clausula (*impius ensis*) of two lines in Ovid's *Metamorphoses*, describing Medea killing her children (7.396) and Roman *generi* waging war on their Sabine *soceri* (14.802). But the phrase appears in a more relevant context (and in enjambment, as in Statius) in *Phoenissae*, as Jocasta tries to stop her sons' fratricidal war: *clude vagina impium / ensem* ('stow your impious sword in its sheath,' 467–468). A similar phrase appears in Seneca's *Oedipus*, when the hero contemplates suicide after learning of his crimes: *aptat impiam capulo manum / ensemque ducit* ('he lays his impious hand on the hilt and draws the sword,' 935–936). Statius' phrase, read in a Senecan context, thus underscores *primas Furiarum pertulit iras*: Laius' murder is just the first in a series of impieties perpetrated by the house of Oedipus.

---

20 This version is found earlier in Stesichorus and Euripides: Smolenaars 1994, 213–214.

21 See Smolenaars 1994, 213–217 on Book 7 and Ganiban 2007, 159–165 on Book 11.

22 For instance, in the first half of the play, the exiled Oedipus offers a catalogue of infamous Theban ancestors (12–26), recalls his sinful life (243–269), and prays for his sons to commit a crime 'worthy of their father' (*patre... dignum*, 333); similar passages appear early in *Theb*. 1 (4–14, 60–72, 87).

Most of the resonances with Seneca's *Phoenissae* in *Thebaid* 2 are found in Tydeus' embassy to Eteocles. As is typical of Senecan intertexts, there are few striking verbal links; nevertheless, reading Tydeus and Eteocles' debate as a successor to the agon of Polynices and Eteocles in *Phoenissae* allows us to reinterpret or even undercut the arguments made by Statius' characters, particularly the disingenuous Eteocles. One cumulative effect of the intertext is to advance Tydeus as a substitute for Polynices in his conflict with Eteocles. This strengthens the identification of Tydeus with Polynices that is made throughout the poem both explicitly and implicitly.[23] It also once again defers a direct confrontation between the Theban brothers until the climax of the poem.

After Tydeus demands that Eteocles relinquish the Theban throne, Eteocles offers a long, rhetorically complex response. Among other tactics, he argues that Polynices should be happy with the fortune and noble family that he has acquired by marriage at Argos, which is superior to the poverty and squalor of Thebes (*Theb.* 2.430–442). This runs directly counter to an argument of Seneca's Polynices, who declares that he would be content with a small cottage, while his brother possessed a kingdom, as long as he could rule the cottage; as it is, he is subject to the whims and commands of the rich and lordly Argive royal family (*Phoen.* 592–598). Seneca's Polynices complains in particular that he has been given as 'a gift to his wife' (*coniugi donum*, *Phoen.* 595). Statius has his Eteocles echo this phrase, so that Polynices rules thanks to 'a gift from his wife' (*dono / coniugis*, *Theb.* 2.430–431) — a less embarrassing image that nevertheless hints at the sting hiding behind Eteocles' wish for his brother's happiness in Argos. Eteocles closes his speech by professing concern for his subjects, who would be in danger if he yielded the kingdom to the angered Polynices, then asserting that the Theban nobles love him and would thus not allow him to relinquish the throne (2.446–451). This too contradicts an argument in Seneca, whose tyrannical Eteocles declares that hatred and rule are natural companions, and that a ruler has more power over angered rather than loving subjects (654–659). Comparison with Seneca thus lays bare the Statian Eteocles' rhetoric: he offers his brother happiness that Polynices would not define as such, and espouses a ruler-subject relationship that is incompatible with his status as a tyrant.

---

23 See, e.g., Frings 1992, 47–54 and Korneeva 2011, 99–103. In Eteocles' reply to Tydeus' embassy, he calls him Polynices' 'mental image' (*illum / mente gerens*, 2.417–418; the translation is Shackleton Bailey's [2003]). The description of Tydeus' journey to Eteocles' kingdom before the embassy reverses the route taken by Polynices from Thebes in Book 1 (Gervais 2017, 203).

Tydeus' angry response to Eteocles threatens death and destruction for him and his people, as sarcastic 'rewards' for Eteocles' criminal behaviour; several lines later, the narrator again highlights Eteocles' crime and treachery:

> haec **praemia** morum
> ac **sceleris**, violente, **feres!** (*Theb.* 2.465–466)

These are the **rewards** you'll receive for your **sinful ways**, you savage!

> nec piger ingenio **scelerum fraudisque nefandae**
> rector eget. (*Theb.* 2.482–483)

Nor is the leader idle or lacking in wit for **sin and heinous deception**.

As usual, intertexts are not confined to Seneca. Most prominently, Tydeus' formulation echoes a taunt made by Vergil's Turnus (*haec praemia, qui me | ferro ausi temptare, ferunt*, 'these are the rewards received by those who dare to test me with steel,' *Aen.* 12.360–361), initiating an intertextual link between the two heroes that will be elaborated during Tydeus' monomachy.[24] But comparison with Seneca allows us to figure the *Thebaid* passages as intertextual replies to the repeated complaints of Polynices in *Phoenissae*:

> **fraudis** alienae dabo
> poenas; at ille **praemium scelerum feret?** (*Phoen.* 589–590)

Will I pay the penalty for another's **deception**, but **he'll receive a reward for his sins**?

> **sceleris et fraudis** suae
> poenas **nefandus** frater ut nullas **ferat?** (*Phoen.* 643–644)

So that my **heinous** brother **receives** no penalty for his **sin and deception**?

Statius' Eteocles will in fact immediately suffer for his crimes when his ambush of Tydeus utterly fails; the tyrant will next appear in Book 3 consumed with worry over this ambush, which Statius describes as a 'punishment for crime' (*scelerisque parati | supplicium*, *Theb.* 3.4–5).

Tydeus thus emerges, intertextually as Polynices' avenger. He also, at this stage in the epic, plays the part of a traditional, plainspoken epic hero (*Theb.* 2.391–396):

---

24 Gervais 2015; Gervais 2017, 230–231.

> *utque rudis fandi pronusque calori*
> *semper erat, iustis miscens tamen aspera coepit:*
> *"si tibi **plana fides** et **dicti** cura maneret*
> ***foederis**, ad fratrem completo **iustius** anno*
> *legatos hinc ire fuit teque ordine certo*
> *fortunam exuere et laetum descendere regno..."*

Since he was unpracticed in speaking and always prone to fury, he began with mixed words, harsh but just: "If you still maintained **plain good faith** and regard for your **spoken bond**, it was **more just** that legates travel from here to your brother at the end of your year and that you divest yourself of royal power in due order and descend happily from your throne..."

In this, he takes on the mantle of Polynices in the *Phoenissae* of Euripides (but not Seneca), who bookends his portion of the agon with Eteocles by declaring that he is speaking plainly in the service of truth and justice (469–472, 494–496). But we may also look to Seneca's *Phoenissae* to support this characterization of Tydeus (and here I will push verbal links with Seneca as far as I dare). The phrases *plana fides* and *dicti... foederis* in Tydeus' speech are unusual, found nowhere else in Latin poetry.[25] I have previously interpreted these oddities as symptoms of Tydeus' poor oratorical skills.[26] But *fides* and *foederis* appear (along with *ius* to match Statius' *iustius*) in more typical collocations[27] during a speech by Seneca's Oedipus, on the same topic as Tydeus' speech (*Phoen.* 280–284):

> *spernitur **pacti fides**:*
> *hic occupato cedere imperio negat;*
> ***ius** ille et **icti foederis** testes deos*
> *invocat et Argos exsulatque urbes movet*
> *Graias in arma.*

They despise the **good faith of the pact**: the one refuses to yield the power he has usurped, while the other calls on **justice** and calls the gods to witness **the treaty they struck**, and in his exile rouses Argos and the Greek cities to war.

---

25 This includes *foedus* + *dicere* in any form. Note *Theb.* 10.640, where *plana fides* appears as a manuscript variant alongside *plena fides*.

26 Gervais 2017, 208–209. His speech also features ambiguities, poor word choices, metrical infelicities, and repetitive arguments.

27 Seneca's *pacti fides* is a variation on the more common *pacta fides* (Ov. *Ep.* 6.41, 20.9, *F.* 3.485, Sen. *Phaed.* 953, Sil. 14.82; cf. also *pactique fides*, a manuscript variant at Ov. *Met.* 11.135); *ictum foedus* appears at Verg. *Aen.* 12.314, Phdr. 1.31.8, Luc. *BC* 10.371, Sil. 5.317.

I would suggest, then, that Tydeus' phrasing may be read as pointedly adapting Oedipus' so as to better fit Tydeus' character. Seneca's 'the good faith of the pact' becomes 'plain good faith', underscoring the high value Tydeus places on honesty and simplicity in interpersonal dealings. Seneca's 'the treaty they struck' becomes 'the treaty you spoke,' suggesting perhaps Tydeus' distrust of words, which Eteocles relies on at the expense of action[28] — the treaty Eteocles agreed to was, in the end, just words.

4 Thyestes

The shared theme of *odia fraterna* in Statius' *Thebaid* and Seneca's *Thyestes* is the subject of a short monograph by Frings (1992). And indeed, the Senecan brothers are an important model for Statius' Polynices and Eteocles, offering a tragic pair of rivals to complement and complicate Statius' various epic influences (from Achilles and Hector to Aeneas and Turnus to Caesar and Pompey). But in *Thebaid* 2 the meeting between the sons of Oedipus is still far off, and the familial tensions at Thebes are confined to the encounters of Eteocles with his grandfather Laius and with Tydeus, a surrogate Polynices.[29] Nevertheless, Seneca's *Thyestes* may be compared with *Thebaid* 2 in both specific details and larger structure: both begin with a ghost rising from the underworld (Tantalus and Laius), continue with the introduction of a tyrannical figure (Atreus and Eteocles), focus on the tyrant's plot to attack his brother, just arrived in his kingdom (Thyestes and Tydeus, Polynices' double), and conclude with that brother reduced to cannibalism (literally in the case of Thyestes, foreshadowed in the case of Tydeus). I will focus here on the links between Tantalus and Laius, Atreus and Eteocles, and Thyestes (along with Atreus) and Tydeus.

The opening of *Thebaid* 2 offers an extraordinarily rich set of intertexts: Laius' and Mercury's journey to Thebes may be compared to journeys at the openings of *Aeneid* 5 (Aeneas), *Argonautica* 2 (Jason), and *Punica* 2 (Fabius Maximus and Valerius Publicola), as well as the journeys of Priam in *Iliad* 24 and Caesar in *Bellum Civile* 5.237 ff.[30] Along with these epic intertexts, the ghosts in the prologues of Seneca's *Agamemnon* and, especially, *Thyestes* have long been recognized as models for Statius' scene: in each case, a ghost is summoned from the

---

28 Gervais 2017, 240.
29 See Frings 1992, 19–21 on Laius and Eteocles; her discussion of Tydeus (pp. 47–54) focuses on Books 1 and 9.
30 Gervais 2017, 59–60.

underworld to sow strife in the descendants' household. As usual, the intertext does not rely on specific verbal links, but rather important similarities and differences of detail: Frings, for example, has noted that the ghost of Tantalus in the *Thyestes* is summoned from the underworld by a Fury, goes unwillingly, and bears no ill will towards his grandsons, whereas the ghost of Laius is summoned by Mercury on Jupiter's orders, does not resist, and hates his grandsons.[31]

We may expand on these differences. Frings argues that the replacement of the Fury by Mercury shows that Olympian forces are "working hand-in-hand with the forces of the underworld."[32] In fact, the exact relationship between Olympian and infernal forces in the *Thebaid* is a point of contention (in both the poem and the scholarship), with debate partly centred on the relative power of Jupiter and the Furies.[33] This manifests itself when an anonymous shade in the underworld addresses Laius. Apparently unaware of the presence of Mercury, he wonders who has called Laius up to the world of the living (*Theb.* 2.20–22):

> ...*seu Iovis imperio, seu maior adegit Erinys*
> *ire diem contra, seu te furiata sacerdos*
> *Thessalis arcano iubet emigrare sepulcro.*

> ...whether by the command of Jupiter, or whether an Erinys more powerful drives you to face the day, or a raving priestess of Thessaly orders your departure from a secret tomb.

The first explanation is the correct one, but the shade's speculation points to some of the intertextual resonances in Laius' epiphany. *Iovis imperio* echoes language used by the ghost of Anchises in his epiphany to Aeneas (*imperio Iovis huc venio, Aen.* 5.725). The *sacerdos Thessalis* suggests Lucan's *Thessala vates* (*BC* 6.651), Erictho. The *maior Erinys* points not only to Vergil's Allecto, but also to the Furies that compel Seneca's ghosts, juxtaposed with the *imperium* of a Vergilian Jupiter to suggest the complex generic influences on Statius' scene. Furthermore, the description of the Fury as *maior* may be interpreted with reference to Seneca's *Thyestes*. Various explanations of the epithet have been advanced,[34] but the most straightforward reading is that the anonymous shade calls the Fury 'greater than Jupiter.' And indeed, Seneca's Tantalus offers a final resistance to his mission by praying to Jupiter as *magne divorum parens* (90). Immediately after this, the Fury compels Tantalus to follow her, leaving open the question at this point of whether

---

31 Frings 1992, 21.

32 Frings *ibid.*

33 Bibliography at Gervais 2017, xxxiii n. 100.

34 Namely, 'greater than Laius,' 'older than Jupiter,' or simply 'great': Gervais 2017, 68.

Jupiter is complicit in her actions or she is, simply, *maior* than the "great" Jupiter. Statius' invocation of a *maior Erinys*, placed beside *Iovis imperio* and read in the context of Seneca's *Thyestes*, thus suggests not only the cooperation of Olympian and infernal forces, but also a power struggle between the two.

At the climax of the epic, Jupiter cedes Thebes to the Furies, breaking with a tradition of Olympian spectatorship by turning away from the brothers' duel (*Theb.* 11.122–133).[35] But the Furies too give way in the end, as the brothers' fratricidal *furor* eclipses their own power (11.537–538). This final preeminence of Theban madness over destructive Olympian and infernal forces is anticipated during Laius' visit to Thebes, as the ghost sent by Jupiter hesitates to enter the palace (*Theb.* 2.65–70):

> *ventum erat ad Thebas; gemuit prope limina nati*
> *Laius et notos cunctatus inire penates.*
> *ut vero et celsis suamet iuga nixa columnis*
> *vidit et infectos etiamnum sanguine currus,*
> *paene retro turbatus abit: nec summa Tonantis*
> *iussa nec Arcadiae retinent spiramina virgae.*

> Here was Thebes. Laius groaned at the door of his son's house and was slow to enter the home he knew. But when he saw his very own yoke leaning on a lofty column and the chariot itself still stained with blood, he nearly turned to retreat in consternation; the high commands of the Thunderer did not hold him back, nor the breath of the Arcadian wand.

Except for this moment of fear and hesitation, Laius carries out his mission willingly, in contrast to the resistance offered by Seneca's Tantalus. But even this moment runs counter to the Senecan model. Whereas Laius groaned at the sight of his family home, the arrival of Tantalus causes *his* home to shudder (*Thy.* 103–104):

> *sentit introitus tuos*
> *domus et nefando tota contactu horruit.*

> The house feels you enter and shudders along its length at the evil encounter.

So great is the evil of the Theban house that it causes consternation even to the malign spirit sent to haunt it, and this surprising development is underscored by its contrast with Seneca's play. Furthermore, while Tantalus' resistance is overcome by the force of the Fury, Statius is explicit that it was not a divine force

---

35 Bernstein 2004, 64–69.

which overcame Laius' temporary hesitation. Statius' text has caused confusion,[36] but his implication seems to be that it is Laius' hatred for his descendants that drives him on. Unlike Seneca's Tantalus, but much like his grandsons at the end of the epic, Laius has no need for supernatural coercion, infernal or Olympian.

Laius emerges from the underworld at Taenarus. Statius' description of this hellmouth adapts some of its details from the description of the grove where Seneca's Atreus kills his nephews (*Theb.* 2.50–54; *Thy.* 668–677).[37] And Atreus emerges as a salient model once Laius meets Eteocles. Both Atreus and Eteocles exhibit the vices and passions stereotypical of 'the tyrant' in ancient thought.[38] For instance, Laius and Mercury find Eteocles full from a feast, sleeping on a luxurious bed of Assyrian fabrics (*Theb.* 2.90–93). Later, Tydeus encounters Eteocles high on a throne and surrounded by guards, savagely ruling his people; the description strongly alludes to Vergil's Dido, but in such a way as to contrast Eteocles' tyrannical nature with Dido's more positive portrayal (*Theb.* 2.384–388; *Aen.* 1.505–508).[39] Allusions to Lucan also suggest Eteocles' tyranny by associating him with Caesar.[40] Supplementing all of this are specific links between Laius' address to Eteocles (following the ghost's rise from the underworld) and Atreus' soliloquy in Act II (following the rise of Tantalus from the underworld). The two scenes occupy the same place in the structure of their respective texts, and share a similar purpose. Laius encourages Eteocles to attack his brother and drives him into a frenzy; Atreus, presumably influenced by the visitation of Tantalus to his home, encourages himself to do the same. Laius' words thus dramatize the implied effects of Tantalus on his grandson Atreus, supplying a scene that Seneca might have written.

The general themes and progressions of the two speeches are the same: an accusation of laziness for not taking action against Polynices or Thyestes, an assertion that they have not been humbled by exile, a claim that they too are plotting destruction for their brothers, and the threat that they will attack first if Eteocles or Atreus do not. Specific verbal links underscore these similarities. Two of the links are straightforward. First, Atreus resolves to 'dare' a savage and bloody

---

36 Dubner emends *nec... nec* in 69–70 to *sed... sed*; Shackleton Bailey emends to *nec... sed*. The emendations either fully or partially reverse the point made by the transmitted text.
37 Gervais 2017, 80.
38 As noted by Frings 1992, 21.
39 Gervais 2017, 207.
40 Gervais 2017, xliii–xliv.

crime of the sort that his brother would wish to commit against him (*aliquod au-dendum est nefas / atrox, cruentum, tale quod frater meus / suum esse mallet, Thy.* 193–195); more concisely, Laius encourages Eteocles to attack his brother by claiming that Polynices 'intends to dare the same thing' (*ausurumque eadem, Theb.* 2.117). Later, Atreus says that he must attack his brother before Thyestes has time to strengthen himself or 'prepare his forces' (*antequam se firmat aut vires parat, Thy.* 200); amplifying the sense of menace, Laius claims that Polynices is *already* strong and 'preparing his forces' against Eteocles (*iamque ille novis (scit Fama) superbit / conubiis viresque parat, Theb.* 2.108–109).

A verbal link between the start of each passage is more complex. Laius begins his speech by criticizing Eteocles for his inaction against his brother (*Theb.* 2.102–104):

> *non somni tibi tempus, **iners** qui nocte sub alta*
> *germani **secure iaces**, ingentia dudum*
> *acta vocant rerumque graves, **ignave**, paratus.*

> It's not your time for sleep, **sluggard**, **lying** in the deep night, **careless** of your brother! Long have mighty deeds been calling, **coward**, and grave preparations for things to come.

Laius' address to Eteocles as *iners* and *ignave* echoes Atreus' self-reproach in the first words of his soliloquy (*Thy.* 176–178):

> ***ignave, iners**, enervis et (quod maximum*
> *probrum tyranno rebus in summis reor)*
> *inulte*

> **Coward, sluggard**, weakling and (and, I think, the worst reproach for a tyrant in important matters) unavenged.

Eteocles is thus encouraged to follow the twisted morality of Atreus, for whom "only vengeance is proof of virtue."[41] Elsewhere in epic, *ignave* appears only once in Lucan (*BC* 5.487) as Caesar, another tyrannical model for Eteocles,[42] criticizes Antony for causing 'delays to his crimes' (*moras scelerum*, 5.470). But more interesting complexity emerges from a consideration of *Hercules Oetaeus*,[43] in which

---

41 Tarrant 1985, 116.
42 Gervais 2017, xliii–xliv.
43 Littlewood 2014, 515 summarizes the disputed authorship and date of this poem.

the dying Hercules criticizes Philoctetes for hesitating to light his pyre, using language identical to Atreus (*HO* 1719–1724):[44]

> quid dextra tremuit? num manus pavida impium
> scelus refugit? redde iam pharetras mihi,
> **ignave iners** enervis — en nostros manus
> quae tendat arcus! quid sedet pallor genis?
> animo faces invade quo Alciden vides
> voltu iacere.

Why does your right hand tremble? Don't tell me your frightened hand is fleeing from an impious crime. Give me back my quiver now, **coward**, **sluggard**, weakling — look at the hands that bend my bow! Why does pallor sit on your cheeks? Seize the torch with the same spirit that you see on the face of Hercules as he lies here.

This in turn may look back to Hercules' attempted suicide after killing his family in the earlier *Hercules furens* (*HF* 1279–1284):

> iamdudum mihi
> monstrum impium saevumque et immite ac ferum
> oberrat: agedum, dextra, conare aggredi
> ingens opus, labore bis seno amplius.
> **ignave**, cessas, fortis in pueros modo
> pavidasque matres?

For a long time an impious, savage, ungentle, and fierce monster has ranged before me: come, my right hand, try to undertake a mighty feat, bigger than your twelve labours. Do you delay, **coward**? Are you brave only against boys and frightened mothers?

As was the case earlier (section 2), Hercules once again emerges as a model, juxtaposed with a less noble character (Atreus here, Oedipus earlier). More precisely, Eteocles is encouraged by Laius to deadly conflict with his brother in the context not only of Seneca's tyrant Atreus, but also of his complex Hercules — noble in his stoic attitudes towards death, but tainted by family violence.

A final complexity emerges from Laius' claim that Eteocles is not concerned about his brother (*germani secure iaces*). These words may be linked to a motif that runs through *Thyestes* and traces the downfall of its protagonist. Initially, Thyestes resists the lure of power that Atreus offers him, preferring the simple life he had in exile (*o quantum bonum est / obstare nulli, capere **securas** dapes / humi iacentem!*, 'oh how good it is to quarrel with no one, to eat **carefree** meals, **lying**

---

44 This scene echoes language used earlier in the play, when Deianira tries to convince Hyllus to kill her and thereby show bravery worthy of his father Hercules (984–999).

on the ground,' *Thy.* 449–451).[45] Later, he indulges fully in the luxurious feast that Atreus has offered him, unaware of what is actually on the menu ([Atreus speaking] *nimis diu conviva* **securo iaces**, 'too long have you been **lying** at the feast **without care**,' 898). Finally, he wishes in vain for the earth to swallow him whole and inflict on him a punishment commensurate with his crimes (*immota tellus, pondus* **ignavum iaces?**, 'do you **lie** motionless, Earth, a **sluggish** mass?,' 1020 [cf. *ignave* at *Theb.* 2.104]). Most basically, this link between Eteocles and Thyestes increases the sense of menace that Laius wishes to convey: Polynices, perhaps, is plotting destruction for his unsuspecting brother like Atreus did for Thyestes. More broadly, the assimilation of Eteocles to both Atreus and Thyestes points to the inescapable similarities between the Senecan brothers, even as they struggle to differentiate themselves — a dynamic that becomes a controlling theme in Statius' epic of Oedipal family confusion.[46]

This confusion of identities, characteristic of the house of Oedipus, also affects Tydeus. As Augoustakis (2015) has discussed, the death of Tydeus at the end of *Thebaid* 8 assimilates him to both Thyestes and Atreus. Thyestes' cannibalism is the most obvious model for Tydeus' final moments, as he dies chewing on the severed head of his enemy Melanippus. Unlike Thyestes, however, Tydeus does not act out of ignorance, but rather confronts his meal with savage joy (*amens / laetitiaque iraque, Theb.* 8.751–752) and a desire for revenge. This, Augoustakis argues (387–388), recalls Seneca's Atreus as he prepares his revenge on his brother. Furthermore, Tydeus specifically mentioned Atreus when he begs Hippomedon to bring him the severed head, citing an "otherwise obscure reference to Hippomedon's origin from the house of Atreus" (387): *i, precor, Atrei si quid tibi sanguinis umquam, / Hippomedon* ('go, I beg you, if there was ever any blood of Atreus in you, Hippomedon,' 8.742–743). Augoustakis suggests that this "serves as an ironic reminder of the Thyestes story and Atreus' involvement in perpetrating an act of cannibalism" (387). More specifically, I would suggest, it characterizes Tydeus as a far more horrific Thyestes, ready and willing to commit his crime, and looking only for an Atreus to provide the meal.

Thyestes and Atreus are salient models for Tydeus at the end of *Thebaid* 2 as well. As Tydeus stands victorious and exhausted in the midst of his slaughtered

---

45 In addition to the link *secure iaces ~ securas... iacentem*, note also *capit ille dapes* of Eteocles at *Theb.* 2.93 (*dapes / dapem capere* is a rare phrase; besides *Thy.* 449, cf. Varro, *Men.* 443.1, Mart. 8.39.2).

46 As Schiesaro 2003, 139–151 argues, the Senecan brothers share important moral affinities; their differing actions are largely motivated by differing circumstances. On the prominence of doubles in the *Thebaid* (most notably, but not limited to, Polynices and Eteocles), see, e.g., Bonds 1985; Hardie 1993b; O'Gorman 2005; Korneeva 2011.

Theban attackers, Statius deploys the simile of a lion grown nauseous after gorging on a flock of sheep (*Theb.* 2.675–681). The gory details of this simile point ominously to Tydeus' emetic final act, and thus remind us of the cannibalistic, Senecan end to be suffered by Statius' aspiring Herculean hero.[47] But among the several epic models for this lion simile there is a link to Seneca's *Thyestes*, which uses a lion simile to describe Atreus as he slaughters Thyestes' sons (732–736).[48] Thus, even as Statius' simile looks ahead to Tydeus' Thyestean cannibalism, it also suggests the savage bloodlust that will assimilate him to Atreus. This link with Atreus is subtly underscored earlier in Statius' scene during the description of Chromis, the first important Theban to die in the battle (*Theb.* 2.613–628). Chromis' strange birth, Herculean attire, exhortation of his comrades, and cruel death collectively evoke scenes from Homer, Vergil, Ovid, Valerius Flaccus, and Silius Italicus.[49] Seneca's *Thyestes* is, however, a small presence amongst the various epic intertexts. Chromis is in the midst of speaking when Tydeus' spear flies into his mouth; his tongue is severed and swims out of his mouth on a gush of blood, still 'full of words'[50] (*illi voce repleta / intercepta natat prorupto in sanguine lingua, Theb.* 2.625–626). After this sudden injury, Chromis' body remains standing for a time before finally falling over in death (*stabat adhuc, donec transmissa morte per artus / labitur, Theb.* 2.482–628). The motifs of a severed tongue or head still speaking and a protracted death may be found elsewhere in Latin literature,[51] but they also appear during the deaths of the first two sons of Thyestes killed by Atreus: *querulum cucurrit murmure incerto caput* ('the head rolled away, complaining with an indistinct murmur,' *Thy.* 729); *educto stetit / ferro cadaver, cumque dubitasset diu / hac parte an illa caderet, in patruum cadit* ('the corpse stood still when the sword was drawn out, and after it had long hesitated over falling this way or that, it fell onto its uncle,' *Thy.* 723–725).

This final example is characteristic of the presence of Seneca in Statius: the point of contact with the *Thyestes* is signalled primarily by similarities of detail

---

[47] Note especially that the lion is *victus cibis* (*Theb.* 2.679), exhausted and nauseated by its large meal — but the words also suggest the cannibalistic meal that will condemn Tydeus. The final detail of the wool around the lion's mouth (2.681) may be compared with the brains that will later befoul Tydeus' mouth (8.760–761).

[48] Note especially *in caede multa victor* (*Thy.* 733), fragmented by Statius into *sanguine multo* (2.676), *mediis in caedibus* (678), *victusque cibis* (679). For other intertextual models, see Gervais 2017, 309–310.

[49] Gervais 2017, 284–290.

[50] I thus read *repleta* as a nominative modifying *lingua*; some take it as an ablative with *voce* ('with his voice choked' by blood and the spear).

[51] See, e.g., Verg. *G.* 4.525–526, Ov. *Met.* 5.95–96, Stat. *Theb.* 5.236–237.

Agis Marinis

Eteocles and Polynices in Statius' *Thebaid*: Revisiting Tragic Causality

Conspicuous within the *Thebaid* is the existence of a tragic crux, reminiscent of a situation emblematic of Greek tragedy, namely one in which the 'tragic' character appears to stand at the confluence of forces stemming from both inner compulsion and supernatural factors.[1] Within the framework of such an amalgam the limits of personal responsibility and, therefore, guilt are inevitably problematized. Further, it is exactly this amalgam which, without of course being required to submit to any rules of realism, seeks to elucidate the human predicament and embodies an essential part of the reflective quality of Greek tragedy. Confronted with this issue we equally need to address the question whether we are dealing with a view of human behaviour that seeks to underline its irrationality.

Moreover, there exist moments at which the two brothers, especially as we approach the duel, emerge as 'tragic' (or even 'tragically heroic') figures in the sense of being characters not entirely evil, yet who are beset by unrelenting adverse circumstances and supernatural influence leading them to *nefas*. This applies first and foremost to Polynices, to whom the epic initially acknowledges a moral edge, on the ground of which one might ask whether we could posit a tragic 'fault' — an Aristotelian *hamartia* — rather than inherent evil at the root of his actions and his plight. Finally, given that in Greek tragedy we are confronted with a notorious difficulty of disentangling character from praxis and superhuman causality, we need to address the question of to what extent Statius surrenders to this difficulty or even foregrounds it by exposing it in all its paradoxical nature. In our quest we will focus on Book 1 — the very beginning of the conflict — and Book 11, its disastrous conclusion.

May I express here my thanks to Carole Newlands and the anonymous readers for the "Trends in Classics" series for their valuable feedback on this paper.

1 On the question of the influence exerted by Greek literature on Flavian epic, see the volume edited by Augoustakis (2014); specifically on the influence of Greek tragedy on Statius' *Thebaid*, see Marinis 2015, with further references, which need not be reiterated here. In the same volume (Dominik, Newlands, and Gervais 2015), see also the contributions by Ahl and Criado. The influence of Greek tragedy is, of course, particularly felt in the Catalogue of Book 4 of the *Thebaid*; see Micozzi 2007 and Parkes 2012 (*passim*).

https://doi.org/10.1515/9783110709841-009

1 The Seeds of Conflict — Book 1

The tragic story of Eteocles and Polynices in the *Thebaid* is set in motion by the perverted prayer of Oedipus to the gods of the Underworld and Tisiphone.[2] Oedipus seeks the punishment of his sons, indignant at their behaviour towards him: *superbi | — pro dolor! —... insultant tenebris gemitusque odere paternos* ('haughtily — ah! The maddening sting! —... they mock my blindness and abhor their father's groans...,' 76–79).[3] The prayer ends with the description of the *nefas* that he avows to be wishing, namely for his sons 'to sunder with the sword the binding ties of kinship' (84–85); the concluding lines provide a glimpse of the frame of mind of the young princes: *da, Tartarei regina barathri, | quod cupiam vidisse nefas, nec tarda sequetur | mens iuvenum; modo digna veni, mea pignora | nosces* ('Grant me, queen of Tartarus' abyss, grant me to see[4] the evil that my soul desires, nor will the spirit of the youths be slow to follow; come but worthy of yourself, you shall know them to be true sons of mine,' 85–87).[5] From Oedipus' imprecation[6] — which effectively assumes the role of a tragic prologue[7] — we learn two things that cannot be ignored by the reader, even though they are uttered by the disgruntled father: first that *both* brothers behaved improperly towards him, demonstrating their *superbia*,[8] and secondly that the unspeakable *nefas* that he

---

2 Translations of Statian passages follow Mozley (1928), with modifications. For an analysis of this imprecation see Delarue 2000, 257–260; Aricò 2002, 169–174; more recent discussions in Hubert 2013, 111–113; Briguglio 2017, 12–25 and 182 ff.; Simms 2018, 236–245; esp. 242–243 on the Euripidean intertext of *Phoenissae*; also Franchet d'Espèrey 1999, 52–59; on its function as the real beginning of the epic, see ead. 2001b, 193–194.

3 "The grim truth is that Oedipus is grieved as much by his loss of power as his loss of sight" (Vessey 1971a, 377). On Oedipus' psychological attitude here, in comparison with his repentance in Book 11.617 ff., see Venini 1964, 204–205.

4 *Video* is paradoxical: as Briguglio notes, it signifies a step forward from the Senecan *audiam* (*Phoen.* 362). The *Thebaid* thus introduces itself as a 'tragic spectacle,' a post-Senecan epic. See Briguglio 2017, 179 referring also to Barchiesi 2001, 326.

5 Tisiphone assumes a key role in the unfolding of the epic, even usurping the role of the Muses. A key intertextual precedent is the Vergilian Allecto; see analysis by Hardie 1993, 62 ff.; also Ganiban 2007, 155–156; Briguglio 2017, 182 ff. The key role of Tisiphone goes in tandem with the crisis of divine providence attested in the epic; see now Bessone 2013, esp. 151–152.

6 On the reasons for Oedipus' curse of his sons in Greek literary tradition, see Marinis 2015, 360, esp. n. 99; Simms 2018, 241–242.

7 Also possessing a distinct programmatic character; see Ripoll 1998b, 324; Franchet d'Espèrey 2001b, 193–194; Bessone 2011, 98–100.

8 Though, as Vessey (1971a, 377) points out, Statius does not overly emphasize the issue of Oedipus' treatment by his sons.

wishes for his sons, though effected by the Fury, will be facilitated by themselves, who are to be proven as "true sons" of Oedipus.[9] What is clearly signalled here is the propensity towards *furor* innate in the family of Laius.[10] However, things are not so straightforward, as Oedipus (and certain modern readers of the *Thebaid*) seek to present them: *mens iuvenum* may not univocally be considered as being conditioned by heredity.

In fact, the narrator opts to elaborate on exactly this point. When the Fury arrives at Thebes, 'to cast upon the house its wonted gloom' (1.124):

> *protinus adtoniti fratrum sub pectore motus,*
> *gentilesque animos subiit furor aegraque laetis*
> *invidia atque parens odii metus, inde regendi*
> *saevus amor, ruptaque vices iurisque secundi*
> *ambitus impatiens, et summo dulcius unum*
> *stare loco, sociisque comes discordia regnis.*

> troubled dismay seized the brothers' hearts and the madness of their race inspired them, and envy that repines at others' happiness, and hate-engendering fear; and then fierce love of power, and breach of mutual covenant, and ambition that brooks no second place, the dearer joy of sole supremacy, and discord that attends on partnered rule.

With this passage (1.125–130) we enter into the much-debated question whether *furor* in the *Thebaid* — induced via the demonic impact of Tisiphone — marks a radical change in the individuals, thus rendering psychological analysis practically irrelevant, or if it merely brings to the fore emotional states and aspects of their mental constitution that are already there.[11] An attentive reading of the above passage will reveal that, apart from the 'madness of their race,' the rest of the emotional states and inner attitudes mentioned are humanly intelligible, even though hardly laudable, aspects of a mental constitution intoxicated with lust for power and unbridled ambition.[12] Significantly, the last one — 'discord that

---

9 Cf. Lactantius Placidus ad v. 87: *quos ad facinora scelerum tam pronos invenies, ut meos filios esse non dubites.*

10 See esp. Davis 1994, 473–474; Franchet d'Espèrey 2001b, 193. On the importance of inherited disposition in the *Thebaid*, see thorough analysis by Bernstein 2008, 64–104.

11 For the first view the seminal study is Schetter 1960, esp. 5–21; it has been first forcefully refuted by Venini (1964). For the first view (with various nuances), see also Dominik 1994, 1–75, Hershkowitz 1998, 247–301. A sense of 'parallel motivation' is affirmed chiefly by Ahl 1986, esp. 2851–52; Fantham 1997; Ripoll 1998b, esp. 329–330; Franchet d'Espèrey 1999, 45–69; now Briguglio 2017, 180–181. Further references in Marinis 2015, 358 esp. n. 85.

12 A difference from Greek tragedy is that the brothers in Statius are ignorant of their father's curse against them: the latter does not weight on their minds. On this point see Vessey 1971a, 378.

attends on partnered rule' (1.130)[13] — may actually be considered as a parameter naturally reinforcing the emotions named before.[14] In my view, we are encouraged by the narrator to consider Tisiphone as acting on a background of character traits that can be 'naturalistically' understood and explained.[15] The impact of the Fury certainly may at times bring about a radical and gratuitous change in its victim;[16] apart from this case, however, the existence of such an external force powerfully intervening and shaping human behaviour need not prevent but rather encourage an examination of the intelligibly human background by itself. This is similar to what we are effectively obliged to do in Aeschylean drama, where the spectre of the Erinys looms large — decidedly less so in Euripides, with his propensity for psychological characterization.

To return to the sequence of events in Book 1, with such an attitude the brothers take the precarious measure to rule in alternate years, as a solution to the deadlock (1.138–139). The narrator adds (1.144–151) that it was for no rich kingdom that they vied, but for the very sake of power and a 'starveling kingdom': *sed nuda potestas / armavit fratres, pugna est de paupere regno* (1.150–151).[17] Up to the point that Eteocles assumes power by lot and Polynices sees 'his reign deferred' (1.164–165), there is no sign whatsoever that there is any difference between the two brothers in terms of mentality. However, the narrator, in a rare rhetorical move, apostrophizes Eteocles, addressing him as 'fierce' (*saeve*, 165), who

---

13 We are dealing with a *topos* with strong presence in Roman literature; characteristically Seneca *Thyestes* 444: *non capit regnum duos*. See Briguglio 2017, 211.

14 See apt comments by Franchet d'Espèrey 1999, 62–64.

15 Hence, I would agree with Venini (1964, 202) that what the demonic intervention essentially does is to awaken ("risvegliare") the criminal inclination of the brothers, which has already been expressed through the maltreatment of their father. The Fury appears to bring certain emotions to a conscious light ("alla luce della consapevolezza"). However, as it will become clear further, I would not subscribe to an entirely 'psychological' interpretation of the behaviour of the brothers. More nuanced is Ahl's approach: "The impetus to action rests with the individual, and with inherent, even inherited characteristics of behavior and temperament. ... external forces cannot operate unless the individual is predisposed to behave as required." (1986, 2852).

16 As in the case of Amphiaraus; see Venini 1964, 211.

17 See Ahl 1986, 2827–2829; Franchet d'Espèrey 2001b, 199; now Briguglio 2017, 224–225. Certainly the Lucanian intertext (*exiguum dominos commisit asylum*, 'a scant enclosure engaged its masters in battle,' *Pharsalia* 1.97, on Romulus and Remus) is meant to be recalled. Franchet d'Espèrey (2003) also draws on René Girard in order to highlight the paradox of such a fierce conflict when essentially the stakes are low. It is worth noting, however, that this reference at the 'starveling kingdom' does not square with mentions of luxury in Thebes, further in the epic (e.g. 2.90–92, 11.397–399): see Coffee 2006, 441; id. 2009, 260–261. On the ambiguous expression *Thebis opibusque* at 1.318, see Briguglio 2017, 335.

proudly exults in his sole hold in power. The narrator's characterization of Eteocles is contradicted, though, by an anonymous Theban, 'one whose chief thought
it was to hurt by mean and venomous speech and never to bear the yoke of rulers
with submissive neck' (1.171–173). What the anonymous Theban — so unfavour-
ably introduced by Statius — says, appears scarcely illogical: he denounces the
instinctive affection bestowed by the multitude to Polynices, an affection that
does not consider the fact that the exile may not be sincere in his kindness of
speech (*adfatu bonus*, 1.190) but solely yearn for the love of the people in order to
acquire the kingdom more easily (1.173–196). The anonymous Theban thus effectively mitigates the condemnation of Eteocles. In this sense, the narrator's view
that he grudgingly accepts the yoke of rulers is not even properly true: he disrupts
both the tendency to condemn Eteocles and to be particularly favourable to Polynices. Further, the anonymous Theban's foregrounding of the negative legacy
of the Spartoi ominously places the *fraternae acies* right at the foundational moment of the new city (1.184–185).[18] Hence, by allowing the anonymous' voice to
be heard, Statius prevents the reader from forming any easy verdict, even if such
a verdict is encouraged by the narrator's own apostrophe to Eteocles. Thus, the
first book of the *Thebaid*, with its programmatic character, does not allow for any
substantially divergent appraisal of the brothers. Neither does the Council of the
Gods, which follows, encourage any distinction between the brothers whatsoever.[19] However, this essential 'identification' ought not to be regarded as an easy
guideline for the interpretation of the whole epic, but more aptly as a deeper truth
that shall be adapted to the situation each time, and to the demeanour of the
brothers.[20]

The narrator returns to Polynices as he traverses 'the waste places of Aonia'
(*deserta pererrat Aoniae*, 1.313–314):[21] 'Already he broods over the lost realm that

---

18 See Davis 1994, 435 and esp. 468–469 on the parallels between Theban past and present;
indeed "[w]e can only conclude that the pattern of Theban history that we have observed will
continue to replicate itself in the future" (469). Also Franchet d'Espèrey 2001b, 192–193.
19 The emphasis there is rather on the inherited tendency to crime and inherited guilt; see Davis
1994, 171–172. On the role of this Council within the function of causality in the *Thebaid*, see
Franchet d'Espèrey 2001b, esp. 194–197.
20 Generally on the similarity of the brothers, see analytically Frings 1992, 11–46; Korneeva
2011, 35–69; also Dominik 1994, 80; Taisne 1994, 72–73; Franchet d'Espèrey 1999, 35–36, 198;
Ganiban 2007, 191; Marinis 2015, 353–358. On 'doubles' in the *Thebaid* see also Gervais in this
volume.
21 On Polynices' wandering, see Taisne 2005, 667–669; Briguglio 2017, 33–48.

was his due, and cries that the long year stands motionless in its tardy constellations' (1.314–316).[22] A single thought has taken hold of his mind, namely how he could see Eteocles lose the throne and himself the king of Thebes: 'a lifetime would he bargain for that day' (1.319). A key divergence from Euripides' *Phoenissae* is the fact that Polynices leaves Thebes willingly before the expiration of his brother's yearly tenure; he is not driven out of the city by his brother.[23] Further, the very fact that Polynices is impatient to return to the throne and cannot bear the one year of waiting is itself telling of his 'princely pride' (*flatus ducis*, 1.321)[24] and his total absorption by his dream of securing regal power in Thebes: *spes anxia mentem / extrahit* ('fretful hope keeps his mind busy,' 1.322–323).[25] This expression acquires a deeper meaning in the light of the Euripidean play: ἐλπίδες δ' οὔπω καθεύδουσ', αἷς πέποιθα σὺν θεοῖς / τόνδ' ἀποκτείνας κρατήσειν τῆσδε Θηβαίας χθονός ('But my hope is lively, and with Heaven's help I am confident I shall kill my enemy and be ruler of this land of Thebes,' 634–635).[26] These are the last words of Polynices spoken in front of his mother and his brother, as Jocasta's vain attempt at a reconciliation of her sons is led to a close. Polynices' 'fretful hope,' then, a central motive sealing the duel and the fate of the brothers in *Phoenissae*, is introduced in the *Thebaid* right at the beginning of Polynices' wandering, which will lead him to Argos. But how is he led there? Here the narrator offers us a memorable 'either/or' enumeration of options — an *aporia*, which is left to us, programmatically, as an interpretative challenge and crux: *seu praevia ducit Erinys, / seu fors illa viae, sive hac immota vocabat / Atropos* ('whether it were the Fury piloting his steps, or the chance direction of the road, or the summoning of resistless Fate,' 1.326–328). Given the presence of authorial comments condemning the brothers — a privilege denied to the tragic poet[27] — it is important in itself that the narrator

---

22 The fact that in this context Polynices is called *Oedipodionides* (1.313) is telling of the power of heredity; see Davis 1994, 474–475; Ripoll 1998b, 326–327; Marinis 2015, 359 and n. 95; Briguglio 2017, 331.

23 Compare *Phoen.* 74–76; with Vessey 1971a, 380. Note that Polynices is equally presented as an exile in *Sept.* 637–638. It is worth noting, however, that in Seneca's *Phoenissae* it is not clear whether Polynices has indeed been banished from Thebes, despite the occurrence of expressions such as *profugus* (586) or *exul* (652); see Frank 1995, *ad loc.* Hence, Statius may have been influenced by a Senecan construal of Polynices' plight.

24 On Polynices' *superbia*, see esp.Vessey 1973, 92–93.

25 See comments by Franchet d'Espèrey 1999, 49–50.

26 Translations of passages from *Phoenissae* follow Vellacott (1972), with possible modifications.

27 As Bessone (2011, 100) aptly points out: "Quella che Stazio opera è insieme una 'tragedizzazione' dell'epica, e una 'epicizzazione' della tragedia: la voce del narratore epico interviene in fine a condannare l'azione rappresentata — con un gesto autoriale che al poeta tragico è negato."

expresses his *aporia* in this case.[28] Of equal significance is the fact that the expression of such an *aporia* effectively places him on the same 'level' as the reader.[29] This attempt at 'making sense' may justifiably be appraised as a sign that the enigma of 'character' admits of no easy resolution, whereas it is exactly this multiplicity of causal factors that unmistakably refers us to Greek tragedy.

2 Book 11: The Final Confrontation

Since the central quest of this article is to deal with the issue of causality determining the action of *both* brothers, I opt to focus on Books 1 and 11, omitting the presentation of the two brothers in the intervening books, in which one may clearly discern an authorial tendency towards painting a more favourable portrait of Polynices, while Eteocles emerges as *peior* and *nocens*.[30] By contrast, it is in Books 1 and 11 that the difference between the two brothers is less strongly pronounced.[31]

---

28 We may also note that the nocturnal tempest subsequently experienced by Polynices (1.345–353) mirrors the outburst of passions within himself; see Taisne 2005, 667–668, with reference to the Vergilian and Lucanian intertext; also Delarue 2008, 456–438.

29 Thus, I would not agree with Franchet d'Espèrey (2001a, esp. 27–28) who claims that the poet effectively espouses the last hypothesis in this as well as in other cases, e.g. 3.59–62 (Maeon's attempt at explaining why it is he who has been the sole survivor of the ambush on Tydeus); 10.831–836 (on Capaneus' motivation). As Snijder (1968, 70), for instance, notes on the passage 3.59–62, the three explanations adduced there "may cohere according to the Stoic view of the connectedness of all things, thus representing three aspects of the same occurrence."

30 This is the case in the Theban bacchant's allegorical comparison of the two brothers with rival bulls in 4.396–402; see Coffee 2006, 417–418; id. 2009, 243–246. On Eteocles in the *Thebaid*, see succinctly Ahl 1986, 2873–2876. Further, as Coffee (2006; id. 2009, 241–267) astutely points out, between the beginning and the end of the epic the two brothers demonstrate substantial ethical differences that can be appraised in terms of the "economics of violence." Namely, Eteocles is presented as the stereotypical merchant who does neither value human life nor refrain from effectively bargaining away the lives of others; he lusts after the pleasures of violence. On the contrary, Polynices is depicted as young Roman prodigal, whose drive to power leads to a waste of life and resources, but who at times expresses his regret and remorse at his behaviour.

31 As Franchet d'Espèrey has astutely shown (2011; also 1999, esp. 171–205) the *Thebaid* actually has two endings: one which opposes Eteocles to Polynices and is tragic in its essence and one which opposes Argos to Thebes and is properly epic. Ripoll (1998b, 335–338), similarly argues that the "interlaced threads" of tragedy and epic find their final *dénouement* in Book 12 since not only has the *devota domus* now been punished, but the cosmic order has been vindicated.

The fact that the brothers need the incitement of the Furies in order to engage in the duel is expressive enough not only of the grim character of such a struggle between siblings, but also of the fact that a clash between them is not self-evident. The fact that Tisiphone is in need of assistance from her sister, Megaera, in order to bring about the fateful duel is most eloquent. As she exclaims to her sister (102–108):

> ambo faciles nostrique; sed anceps
> volgus et adfatus matris blandamque precatu
> Antigonen timeo, paulum ne nostra retardent
> consilia, ipse etiam, qui nos lassare precando
> suetus et ultrices oculorum exposcere Diras,
> iam pater est: coetu fertur iam solus ab omni
> flere sibi.

Both are compliant and will do our will; but the mob is double-minded, and I fear his mother's words and Antigone's persuasive tongue, lest they somewhat hinder our design. Even he, who is wont to weary us with his entreaties and call on the Furies to avenge his eyes, already feels his fatherhood; already they say he weeps alone, far from the haunts of men.

Remarkably, the Fury recognizes in Jocasta, Antigone, and even Oedipus forces that are potentially capable of rendering difficult the realization of the brotherly clash.[32] This may with justification be counted as an 'independent' confirmation of the possibility of the awakening of human feelings in the brothers, as well as of the likelihood of *both* (103) changing course at the last minute and abstaining from the fatal clash — something which is noteworthy in two senses. Firstly, there is no distinction made between the two brothers as regards their propensity towards *nefas*, but also as regards the possibility of their being dissuaded from it. Secondly, on an intertextual level, the attempt at dissuasion, taken up from the previous tradition, namely the tragic tradition of Aeschylus, Euripides, and Seneca, is not merely considered as a narrative possibility, but more pointedly as a device threatening to alter the 'predestined' course of events.

In Aeschylus it is the chorus of Theban women who attempt to dissuade Eteocles from fighting his brother. The chorus, though initially described as παρθέ-νοι, subsequently address Eteocles as τέκνον,[33] assuming a more authoritative

---

32 In line 98 Tisiphone had already mentioned Fides and Pietas as potential obstacles, and Pietas will indeed appear later at the battlefield in order to avert the fatal duel.

33 See *Sept.* 686. Thus, the women may be also considered as 'mothers,' apart from their status as figuratively 'sisters' of Eteocles *qua* young παρθένοι. See Hutchinson 1985, 155; Ieranò 2002, 86–88; Gruber 2009, 192–193.

status.[34] In the *Thebaid*, when the Fury names *anceps volgus*, the mother and Antigone as possible agents who might influence the brothers, we may effectively identify three aspects of the chorus of *Seven*: 'sister,' 'mother,' and bearer of values pertaining to the community of Thebes, particularly the continuation of the οἶκος.[35]

It must be noted here that, although in Tisiphone's words no distinction is made between the brothers (as in Oedipus' initial prayer to her), yet Polynices — obviously as *melior frater* — is the target of distinctly more sustained efforts at dissuasion. In fact, it is only Jocasta who addresses Eteocles, and to no avail — the Euripidean subtext being clearly discernible there.[36] In the case of Polynices, it is first his dream of Argia, with tresses torn and torch in hand, at the walls of Thebes, which leads him to reconsider his stance. He becomes aware (*sentit... sentire*, 11.149–150) of his approaching doom and experiences fear. Yet, being immediately lashed by the Fury, *ardet inops animi, nec tam considere regno, / quam scelus et caedem et perfossi in sanguine fratris / exspirare cupit* ('he raged without restraint, and yearned not to be seated on his throne, but for crime and carnage and to expire in his slaughtered kinsman's blood,' 11.152–154).[37] The outcome of this grim synergy between Tisiphone and Polynices' own frame of mind[38] is an exacerbated instantiation of *ira* which renders Polynices a tragic *furiosus* in a Senecan and more generally 'tragic' sense.[39] Further, we are dealing here with a tacit yearning, which in the case of the Aeschylean Polynices is expressed as a voci-

---

[34] Indeed, choral speech may by definition be considered as a combination of a point of view which is both marginal in relation to the citizens — bearers of decision within the polis, but also authoritative at the same time. See analysis by Goldhill 1996; cf. also Foley 2003, 20–22; Mastronarde 2010, 88–152, 114–121.

[35] When we evaluate the confrontation between Eteocles and the Chorus after line 677 we need to take into account that the choral voice is prominent in its "hermeneutic" — to employ Claude Calame's terminology — not its "performative" aspect; see Calame 2013, esp. 41–42. To quote his words on the hermeneutic voice: "taking on an ethic move, this interpretive voice relies on the traditional wisdom and patrimony of heroic figures and examples, which were the twin foundations of the standard political and religious culture in fifth-century Athens." (*ibid.* 42).

[36] *Phoen.* 446 ff. However, as Vessey (1973, 274) rightly points out, in both Euripides and Seneca Jocasta's advice is rejected after discussion, whereas here there is "an apparent but illusory chance that her supplication may be successful but for the counteraction of the Fury."

[37] *Inops animi* implies "a loss of mental balance," as Bonds points out (1985, 228).

[38] On these two sources of *furor*, see Vessey 1971a, esp. 375. Polynices' propensity to violence has been prefigured in his fight with Tydeus before Adrastus' palace at 1.408–427; see analysis by Bonds 1985.

[39] See analysis by Ripoll (1998b, 330–335), focusing on the protypical case of Tydeus, *immodicum irae* (1.41); on Tydeus as a tragic character, see also Estèves 2005, 97–111.

ferous public vow: namely, either to engage his brother in a duel and die beside him or to banish him from the land (636–638). Remarkably, what is absent is the possibility of *both* surviving:[40] in both Aeschylus and Statius, Polynices does not seriously contemplate the possibility of killing his brother and surviving. What is particularly foregrounded is the futility of the struggle, a point raised often in connection with the *Thebaid*.[41]

Further, Polynices' encounter with Adrastus results in another moment of awareness, which is again thwarted by the Fury. In his long address to his father-in-law (11.155–192) the Theban prince vindicates his decision to go to battle as a sort of repayment of what Argos has offered to him, as well as a kind of atonement for the losses in human lives Argos has suffered due to him. Characteristic of his manner of thought is line 182: *quis tantus luce timor? sed digna rependam* ('Why such craven fear for my own life? But I will make due recompense'). The conclusion of his thought becomes very clear in line 185: *fratri concurro, quid ultra est?* ('I will fight my brother! What more remains to do?'). Of note is also the fact that he does not place the blame solely on himself, but also on the gods and the Fates.[42] We may draw here distinct parallels with the mentality of the Aeschylean Eteocles. More precisely, the notion that his abstention from fratricide equals cowardice recalls the way Eteocles counters the pleas of the women after line *Sept.* 677. When the women raise the issue of moral pollution ensuing from fratricide (682), Eteocles' reply is that he cannot act shamefully (αἰσχύνης ἄτερ… κακῶν δὲ κἀισχρῶν, 683; 685). In the ensuing epirrhematic exchange, the Chorus accurately points to Eteocles' passionate drive towards committing a crime: θυμοπληθὴς δορίμαργος ἄτα ('bursting passion and lust for battle,' 686–687) and ὠμοδακὴς ἵμερος ('wild craving,' 692). His reply centres firstly on the fact that the gods themselves want to see the family of Laius perishing (689–691, 702), and then, again, on the honour of the warrior (717). His last words on stage have a pronounced fatalistic tone: θεῶν διδόντων οὐκ ἂν ἐκφύγοις κακά ('When the gods send destruction there is no escape,' 719).[43]

---

40 On the absence of temporality and continuity, on the lack of any perspective of the future, as a consequence of the fixation on *nuda potestas* (and the concomitant allusion to Roman politics, especially the wars of 68–69), see Korneeva 2011, 104–106.

41 See Lefèvre 2008, 896 on this passage and *passim* on lack of sense ("Sinnlosigkeit") of human action, generally in the *Thebaid*.

42 *nec enim omnis culpa malorum / me penes, et superi mecum Parcaeque nocentes* ('for mine is not all the blame for these ills, but the gods and Fate share the guilt with me,' 188–189).

43 On the confluence of human responsibility and supernatural determination in Eteocles' stance, see esp. Brown 1977, 312–314; Sewell-Rutter 2007, 25–34, 158–161; Hermann 2013, 68–70.

The parallels are clear; both the Statian Polynices and the Aeschylean Eteocles are in a position very close to the final clash; they both realize *to a certain extent* the fact that they are about to commit a heinous crime:[44] such moments of moral awareness have an indelibly tragic hue, inevitably bringing to mind the Aristotelian notion of tragic *hamartia*, that presupposes a frame of mind of the tragic agent which is by no means straightforwardly evil. In this realization they are assisted by Adrastus (whose speech will ensue at 11.429 ff.) and the Chorus respectively, who share a common characteristic: they both represent the values of the hearth and the continuance of the family. Conspicuous in both cases is the fact that Oedipus' son does not realize the peculiar nature of fratricide, namely its singular weight as a crime, since he is unduly devoted to military valour: the Statian hero regards it as an expression of fear and cowardice to abstain from fighting his brother (*Theb.* 11.182), while the Aeschylean Eteocles considers the idea of not proceeding to the seventh gate as something unmanly.[45]

Further in the *Thebaid*, when Polynices finishes his speech to Adrastus, they both 'fall to weeping' (*ibant in lacrimas*, 11.193). As the poet comments, 'the aged king had begun to soothe his rage with gentle words' (*leni senior mulcere furentem / adloquio*, 196–197). We may recall here the Aeschylean Eteocles' spontaneous tear that falls as he learns from the Messenger that his brother is attacking the seventh gate.[46] In both cases tears are a sign of inner realization of the grim prospect of fratricide, as well as of the lack of a future for the family of Oedipus: both Polynices in Statius and the Aeschylean Eteocles do not really discern any future prospect other than death (*Theb.* 11.190–192; *Sept.* 690–691). Tears are thwarted in the *Thebaid* by

---

44 To quote from the *Poetics* (13.1453a12–17): "The well-made plot, then, ought to be single rather than double... with a change... from prosperity to adversity, caused not by depravity but by a great error of character either like that stated, or better rather than worse." The phrase "like that stated" refers to "someone not preeminent in virtue and justice, and one who falls into adversity not through evil and depravity, but through some kind of error" (13.1453a7–10; translation by S. Halliwell 1995). On the notion of tragic *hamartia*, see, among a vast bibliography, Lucas 1968, 143–145; Halliwell 1986, 202–237; Schmitt 2008, 443–473.

45 Χο. νίκην γε μέντοι καὶ κακὴν τιμᾷ θεός. / Ἐτ. οὐκ ἄνδρ' ὁπλίτην τοῦτο χρὴ στέργειν ἔπος. ('Cho. Even unvaliant victory wins the gods approval. Et. That is not a motto for a man in arms to accept,' 716–717. We may discern here "his failure properly to register the enormity of fratricide," as Lawrence (2013, 65) points out.

46 *Sept.* 653–657: ὦ θεομανές τε καὶ θεῶν μέγα στύγος, / ὦ πανδάκρυτον ἁμὸν Οἰδίπου γένος· / ὤμοι πατρὸς δὴ νῦν ἀραὶ τελεσφόροι. / ἀλλ' οὔτε κλαίειν οὔτ' ὀδύρεσθαι πρέπει, / μὴ καὶ τεκνωθῇ δυσφορώτερος γόος. ('O house that gods drive mad, that gods so deeply hate, O house of endless tears, our house of Oedipus! It is his curse that now bears fruit in us his sons. Yet there is no time for either tears or groans, for fear this agony bear interest more crushing still').

the Fury herself, in the shape of Phereclus,[47] whilst in Aeschylus it is effectively the curses (ἀραί) of Oedipus which Eteocles senses will now transpire (655).[48]

Returning to the *Thebaid*, as Polynices heads to the gates, Eteocles offers sacrifice to Jupiter (11.205 ff.), one that is not, however, accepted by the supreme god. Eteocles' prayer (210–225) is followed by very potent adverse omens, such as the flame flying in his face and the bull, who was about to be sacrificed, dashing wildly and overturning the altar. Despite the grim omens, Eteocles orders the sacrificial rite to be renewed: 'with feigned countenance' he tries to 'screen his anxious fears' (*Theb.* 11.233). His subsequent comparison to Heracles is telling of his psychology and certainly entails a positive aspect: as when the latter felt the fire enwrapping his bones on mount Oeta, he continued the offering he had begun 'still resolute and enduring the agony' (*durus adhuc patiensque mali, Theb.* 11.237).[49] This extended comparison endows Eteocles with a stance of "tragically heroic resolve";[50] to which we shall return shortly.

Immediately after the sacrifice scene, Aepytus arrives in a rush, breaking to Eteocles the news of his brother assailing the gates and challenging him. Significantly, as he makes this announcement, *flent maesti retro comites, et uterque loquenti / adgemit* ('Behind him his sorrowing comrades weep, each echoing the speaker with their groans,' 11.246–247). The flowing of tears, now in the Theban camp, are a sign of realization of the gravity of fratricide. Still, not on the part of the monarch: he undergoes an inner torment (11.237) but does not let tears drop from his eyes. However, he realizes the enormity of fratricide and expresses in words his wish that he might be spared from the ordeal of fighting Polynices: he exclaims to Jupiter that now it was the time to exact punishment, *quid meruit Capaneus?* ('What did Capaneus deserve?,' 11.249). The key feeling is hate — Eteocles even indulges in it.[51]

---

47 Who urges Polynices to rush to the gates; as he flies off, he indeed senses 'the looming shadow of the goddess' (*Theb.* 11.204).

48 Also, in his subsequent epirrhematic exchange with the women, Eteocles, replying to their exhortations not to let himself be overcome by the frenzy of battle, asserts in a fatalistic key that 'to this ritual my own father's wicked curse appoints me, haunting me with dry pitiless eyes' (*Sept.* 695–696).

49 Tragic grandeur, but in a decidedly different sense, is emitted via the intertextual affinity between the suicide of Maeon in Book 3 (77–104) and Seneca's *Heracles Oetaeus*; see Ripoll 1998b, 334–335; also Vessey 1973; 114–115; Dominik 1994, 154–156.

50 Marinis 2015, 355. We may recall here, for instance, Sophocles' *Trachiniae*. Indeed, *pace* Bonds (1985, 235) I would not characterize the Statian Eteocles as "a stage villain."

51 *turbatus inhorruit altis / rex odiis, mediaque tamen gavisus in ira est* ('A thrill of profound hatred shook the king, yet he rejoices in mid rage,' 249–250). This stance is further elaborated

Meanwhile, the comrades of the king (*regni comites*) call him to desist from the brotherly fight, to stay on his throne and let the army confront Polynices (*Theb.* 11.257–262). The recurrence of the word *comites* is a fairly sure indicator that we are dealing with the same people who in lines 246–247 are described weeping and groaning as they hear Aepytus' announcement that Polynices is threatening at the gates. As in the case of the chorus' intervention in *Seven against Thebes* (677–719), it is again no eponymous person but an anonymous group of people who try to change the mind of Oedipus' son; moreover a group expressing in a conspicuous way their emotion.

By transferring female emotion to the *comites*, Statius deploys in a very eloquent manner the Aeschylean subtext: the feelings they express with tears and groans, by no means typical of the attendants of a king preparing for battle, assume an extraordinary character, reflecting the moral outrage of fratricide. These are tears that in *Seven* belong not merely to the women, but also potentially to Eteocles himself. In fact, the supressed tears of Eteocles (at *Sept.* 656–657) are representative of a more general attitude of male tragic heroes who consider it shameful to cry.[52] Most characteristic is Heracles in Sophocles' *Trachiniae* (1070–1075), as well as in Euripides' *Heracles* (1354–1356).[53] The Sophoclean hero, in his agony, considers himself particularly pitiful because he is crying and sobbing like a girl, something that had never occurred to him before, since "without a groan" he always followed his course.[54] The demeanour of the emblematic Heracles of Greek tragedy helps us read anew the Statian comparison of the sacrificing Eteocles to Heracles in agony, conducting the rites on mount Oeta. Heracles is described there, as we have seen, as 'resolute and enduring his agony,' (11.237) but not for long: *mox grande coactus / ingemuit, victorque furit per viscera Nessus* ('soon beneath the stress he groaned aloud, while triumphant Nessus raged throughout his vitals,' 11.237–238). The hero's endurance is thus projected as being difficult to sustain; by analogy, Eteocles' 'feigned countenance' (11.233) is something unnatural and certainly fragile. Hence, the emotive outbreak of his *comites*, contextually marked as feminine, would be equally apt for Eteocles, who would still be Herculean even if he allowed himself to cry. Like his Aeschylean

---

through the simile of the bull (251–256) who is impatient to engage in a fight, full of wrath, as well as knowledge of the challenge ahead of him (*adgnovitque minas*, 253).

52 Cf. Jason's unheroic tears in Valerius Flaccus' *Argonautica* (3.369–371), discussed by Papaioannou in her chapter in this volume.

53 See Suter 2009, 67–68.

54 ἀστένακτος αἰὲν εἱπόμην κακοῖς (1074).

counterpart, however, he does not,[55] but the suggestions of his *comites* actually end up shaking his resolve to proceed with fighting his brother.

It is in this very moment that Creon sees him 'in doubt and shrinking from action' (*dubium et pugnas cunctantem*, 11.268). He cannot bear the loss of his son, Menoeceus, who sacrificed himself at the injunction of Teiresias for Thebes to be saved.[56] He considers Eteocles 'guilty of Heaven's Furies and the war' (*Eumenidum bellique reum*, 11.271). The rationale of Creon's challenge to Eteocles (11.269–275) is that the king ought to risk his life and pay for the war instigated by himself.[57] Eteocles, in his reply (11.298–308) accuses him of being driven by the ambition to succeed him as king.[58] He vows revenge, but only after his fight with Polynices: *sed arma, / arma prius famuli! coeant in proelia fratres* ('but first — arms, arms, my servants! Let the brothers meet in battle,' 11.305–306).[59] Eteocles' final call to bring him arms thus happens after a very personal challenge by Creon and not as merely the practical consequence of his decision to confront his brother. Moreover, what the latter's intervention succeeds in rousing within Eteocles is a certain kind of shame, yet in a sense even more perverted than the one driving the protagonist of *Seven against Thebes*. In the Aeschylean play Eteocles is driven by the notion of duty characterizing the ἀνὴρ ὁπλίτης (717), whilst in Statius it is again shame and affirmation of courage, but this time bereft of any patriotic quality. What is common, however, is a sense of impending doom, of the impossibility of changing one's fate — most characteristically in line 717, featuring the last words of Eteocles on stage:[60] θεῶν

---

55 With the difference that in Statius it is hatred and anger, rather than manly virtue which is at the forefront.

56 The sacrifice of Menoeceus is inherited from Euripides (*Phoen.* 834–1018; with comments by Mastronarde 1994, 391–393); on its Statian reworking see Vessey 1971b; id. 1973 117–122; Ganiban 2007, 138–144; Papadopoulou 2008, 115–116; Marinis 2015, 357–358. On Creon in Euripides' *Phoenissae* see Medda 2013, 266–270.

57 His characterization of Teiresias as 'wicked' (*profanus Teiresias*, 288–289) is indicative of a mode of thought which does not really stem from the respect of moral and religious values. It stems from his personal grief and indignation due to the loss of his son; it is clear that the issue of fratricide as a *nefas* threatening to happen in Thebes does not enter into his consideration.

58 Recalling thus his father in Sophocles' *Oedipus Tyrannus* (532–542). One may actually argue that Eteocles' stance acts as a mirror for the characterization of other persons as well: when he accuses Creon (11.300) of harbouring 'ambition' (*spes*) and 'concealed desire' (*occulta cupido*), he projects on him his own character traits, yet he is still fairly accurate and thus *exposes* the real motives behind Creon's tirade.

59 Cf. Eteocles' address to his attendants in *Seven against Thebes* (675–676): φέρ' ὡς τάχος / κνημῖδας, αἰχμῆς καὶ πετρῶν προβλήματα ('Run, bring my greaves, to protect me against spear and stone'); see Marinis 2015, 355.

60 Cf. 702–704. On the whole scene and the final confrontation between Eteocles and Polynices in *Seven*, see Zeitlin 1982, 153–160.

διδόντων οὐκ ἂν ἐκφύγοις κακά ('When the gods send destruction there is no escape').[61] In Statius we are told about the 'anxious fears' (*magnos timores*, 11.233) that Eteocles tries to conceal during the ill-omened sacrifice; these fears betray a grim sense of the future. Thus, if the king's attitude is determined by 'deep hatred' (*altis odiis*, 11.249–250),[62] his resolve can well be softened, as we have seen, when he hears the pleas of his attendants.

If Creon is urging Eteocles to engage in the fight, it is Jocasta who will make the last attempt to prevent him from acting thus. The mother, who had emerged *velut Eumenidum antiquissima* and 'in all the mighty majesty of her sorrow' in Book 7 (477–478),[63] now appears again in a frenzied manner: *ibat / scissa comam voltusque et pectore nuda cruento, / non sexus decorisve memor* ('she went with face and tresses torn, and naked blood-stained breast, reckless of gender and dignity,' 11.316–318). The poet proceeds by further comparing her to the mother of Pentheus climbing to the mountain 'to bring the promised head to fierce Lyaeus' (11.318–320), an image which brings unmistakably to mind Euripides' *Bacchae*.[64] The maenadic behaviour and appearance of Jocasta more broadly recalls the mythical history of Thebes,[65] which Eteocles himself had deployed within his prayer to Jupiter.[66] Meanwhile, it also evokes Jocasta's Senecan incarnation,[67] as well as her earlier attempt at preventing fratricide in the *Thebaid* — to which we shall return — that had ended with the episode of the maddening of the holy tigers of Bacchus.[68] On the other hand, the connection with *Seven against Thebes* is of particular note. In that play the very conflict is emblematically portrayed in a key of Bacchic frenzy, via the Dionysiac element conspicuous in the central adversary, among the seven, Hippomedon: ἔνθεος δ Ἄρει / βακχᾷ πρὸς ἀλκήν, θυιὰς

---

61 Translations of passages from *Seven against Thebes* follow Vellacott 1961 (with occasional modifications).

62 Compare also his hatred towards Creon conveyed through the simile of the serpent at lines 308–314.

63 On these expressions see Smolenaars 1994, 223–224; regarding Jocasta's intervention in Book 7, see also further in this paper.

64 In fact, it is not merely her appearance that is "frenzied" in the sense of lack of *decorum*, but also the strength (*robur*) that she acquires as she runs to her son, such that nobody can keep pace with her (11.321–323).

65 Cf. *Theb.* 1.327–328: the maenadic rites have left their imprint in the very landscape of Boeotia. For an overview of the multiple intertextual affinities of this comparison, see Voigt 2015; also Ganiban 2007, 164–165; Augoustakis 2010, 33, 65–66; Bessone 2011, 178–179. Note that Bacchus is already mentioned at 1.11; see Carrara 1986, 156–158; Briguglio 2017, 119–120.

66 "Let our own Bacchus and Alcides strive to repay you" (11.224–225).

67 See Sen. *Phoen.* 363–367, 427, 434–441; *Oed.* 1004–1007.

68 See 7.564–607.

ὥς, φόβον βλέπων ('Ares has entered into him; a Bacchant, drunk with lust of war — his eyes strike terror,' *Sept.* 497–498).[69] At the same time, the frenzied character of the brotherly fight in particular is eloquently expressed by the Chorus in their attempt at dissuading Eteocles from proceeding to the seventh gate: μή τί σε θυμο-/πληθὴς δορίμαργος ἄτα φερέτω ('Do not let bursting passion and lust for battle carry you away,' *Sept.* 686–687); in their next reply, Eteocles' martial urge is described as ὠμοδακὴς ἵμερος ('wild craving,' 692). This manic character of the brotherly struggle is expressed, after their death, in unambiguously Dionysiac terms within the Chorus' lament.[70] While the main thrust of the Statian comparison is the lack of *decorum* — *non sexus decorisve memor* (11.318) —, the reference to Agave and Pentheus clearly highlights the parallel between the two families, those of Pentheus and Oedipus, and the divine punishment exacted on both.[71] Frenzy is in both cases the key means through which this punishment is realized. In *Seven* Eteocles is driven by the θυμοπληθὴς δορίμαργος ἄτα, whilst the Statian Jocasta's frenzied appearance in the *Thebaid* can be read as a reflection[72] of what is taking place: the parallel of the Chorus' lament in the Aeschylean tragedy is closer.[73]

Eteocles is fastening his helm as his mother appears, 'mighty to behold' (*ingens*) 'and he and all his company grew pale with fear, and his squire took back the spear he was proffering' (*et ipse metu, famulumque expalluit omnis / coetus, et oblatam retro dedit armiger hastam*, 11.327–328). Jocasta's speech (329–353) is a forceful, poignant plea aimed at persuading her son to retreat.[74] Now it is apparently too late, however, for Eteocles to change course, despite the initial fear (*metu*, 327) he experiences. He proceeds towards the gates with no further regard for his mother's words. Actually, he repels her, as we learn — in a manner reminding us of dramatic literature — through her own speech: *quid oppositam capulo*

---

69 Central within the structure of the Shield Scene; see analysis of this metaphor in Marinis 2012.

70 ἔτευξα τύμβωι μέλος / θυιὰς αἱματοσταγεῖς / νεκροὺς κλύουσα δυσμόρως / θανόντας ('I begin a chant for the tomb, in frenzied grief, on hearing they are killed, bodies dripping with blood, an evil death their fate,' 835–838). See Marinis 2012, 33–35.

71 Note the epithet *saevus* for Dionysos: *saevo Lyaeo* (320).

72 A 'reflection' in the sense that her outwardly pious attempt at a mediation is somehow undercut by this apparently inherent tendency towards 'madness'; see Hershkowitz 1998, 280–282; Ganiban 2007, 159–160; Augoustakis 2010, 65–66.

73 As Voigt (2015, §§ 22–26) points out — noting the Homeric and Vergilian reminiscences — a key facet of Jocasta's *persona* here is that of the grieving mother, since her intervention "is also motivated by her grief" (§ 26); see also Newlands 2012, 110–117; Voigt 2016, 67–68.

74 See comments by Bernstein 2013, 142–143; Simms 2014, 178–179.

parmaque repellis? ('why do you repel me from your path with shield and sword?,' 11.343).[75] Eteocles' lack of any response whatsoever to the fact that 'all beseech him, here all make lament' (*te cuncta rogant, hic plangimus omnes*, 11.350) is eloquent indeed. Both here and earlier, Eteocles' resolve recalls his Aeschylean counterpart whose determination to proceed to the seventh gate is accompanied by a reluctance to extend his discussion with the women.[76] The divergence from Jocasta's attempt at changing Polynices' mind, back in Book 7, is worth noting: he had turned to kiss, in front of the army, his mother, and his sisters, Ismene and Antigone, and for a moment 'the kingdom is forgot' (7.534–537);[77] in fact, in this 'sentimentality' we may discern an unmistakably Euripidean echo.[78] However, the subsequent intervention of Tydeus, mindful of righteous anger (538), not unlike Creon in Book 11, as well the episode with the demise of the tigers of Bacchus, had condemned Jocasta's intervention to failure.[79]

To return to Book 11, while Jocasta makes her vain attempt to keep Eteocles away from battle, Antigone 'in another region' (*parte ex alia*, 354) hastens through all the tumult and climbs to the summit of the wall (354–357).[80] Here the transparent intertextual background of the teichoscopy in Euripides' *Phoenissae*[81] helps drive home the deeply emotional and solicitous manner of Antigone's plea.[82] Instead of the emphasis, by the old Tutor, on the need for a girl not to be seen publicly, here Antigone's indifference to *decorum*[83] is telling of her love of her brother and of her deep concern for the house of Oedipus, for her family:

---

75 The futility of Jocasta's words is reflected in the fact that she urges Eteocles to distinguish between her and his father, Oedipus: *genetrix te, saeve, precatur, non pater* ('it is your mother, not your father entreats you, cruel one,' 346–347). However, it is the house of Oedipus that is under the spell of madness, not merely one member of it.

76 'Say what you have to say, and finish; no long speech. ... My will is set; not all your words can blunt it now' (λέγοιτ' ἂν ὧν ἄνη τις· οὐδὲ χρὴ μακράν. ... τεθηγμένον τοί μ' οὐκ ἀπαμβλυνεῖς λόγῳ, 713; 715).

77 See comments by Smolenaars 1994, 243–244.

78 Cf. Polynices' exchange with his mother in *Phoen.* 357–442; note particularly his tears and pain in 370–373.

79 Generally on Jocasta's intervention in Book 7 (and its Euripidean intertext), see Vessey 1973, 270–274 (involving a comparison with her role in Book 11); Smolenaars 1994, 213–253; Augoustakis 2010, 62–68; Simms 2014, 175–178; Dietrich 2015, 307–313; Newlands 2016, 166–167.

80 On Antigone's appearance in Book 11, see Augoustakis 2010, 67–68; Manioti 2016, 129–131.

81 Ll. 88–201; see discussion by Mastronarde 1994, 167–173; Medda 2013, 241–246.

82 For analytical discussion of the scene, see Augoustakis 2013, 165–170; also Lovatt 2006, 65–66; ead. 2009, 244–246.

83 Note particularly the affirmation *nec casta retardat / virginitas* ('nor does maidenly chastity delay her,' 355–356). Further, now the old servant does not lead her to the walls, but can scarcely keep pace (357–358). Compare esp. with *Phoen.* 88–105, 93–201.

suorum / Antigone devota malis ('Antigone, faithful to her kinsmen's sufferings,' 11.370–371), as she herself declares. In this sense, her 'indecorous' rush to the walls, can be likened to the rush, in Aeschylus, of the παρθένοι of Thebes to the acropolis, in order to beseech the gods[84] and later to prevent Eteocles from confronting his brother.[85] In both cases, female presence in public space, amidst preparations for war or the duel, disconcerting as it may be for male protagonists, is the only authoritative vindication of the claims of γένος, of the family. Interestingly, Jocasta's attempt at dissuading Eteocles, though vain, checks him for a while; Antigone refers to Jocasta's entreaties (375–376) and finishes her speech with the affirmation that Eteocles 'does not come to your challenge' (381–382). In this sense, Jocasta's venture does at least accomplish something, namely to reinforce Antigone's argument. Indeed, Tisiphone was right in predicting that the sister would potentially be able to change Polynices' mind: after hearing her, 'his rage began somewhat to grow faint' (382–383), notwithstanding the resistance of the Fury. The description of his reaction is telling: not only does he slow down, but 'groans burst from him' and 'his casque confesses tears, his ire is blunted, and he feels shame both to depart and to have come in guilt' (382–387). This is one of the eminently 'tragic' moments in which, as already noted, the protagonists experience an awakening to the grim reality of the situation and their moral predicament. However, this reaction will be very short-lived: the Fury herself thrusts Jocasta aside, shatters the gate and hurls Eteocles to the battlefield. The subsequent verbal exchange between the brothers (389–395) is telling indeed of the hate that prevails. The narrator, having quoted the words of both, considers it necessary to explain Polynices' feelings: 'in his heart he chafes at the other's numerous train, and his royal helm and the purple trappings of his charger and his buckler's glancing gold' — though his own armour and apparel is by no means second-rate (397–399).[86] This is a key motive, foregrounded by the narrator exactly because it reflects Polynices' inner mental workings — beside any supernatural influence. In any case, the Furies are now in control (*Furiis hortantibus*, 403).

Neither the reaction of the people ('the wretched common folk,' 416), who lament, nor of Adrastus (424–435) can lead to any change of the situation. Adrastus understands well what the narrator has already foregrounded: Polynices' lust for power is at the root of his behaviour; he thus offers him the very

---

84 On the parodos of *Seven against Thebes*, see analysis in Stehle 2005 and Giordano-Zecharya 2006.
85 See discussion above.
86 On the idea of wealth emanating from this description and the concomitant issue of the 'poverty' of Thebes, see above n. 17.

kingdom of Argos in order to satiate this desire: *sceptri si tanta cupido est...* (433).[87] We may recall here the 'frenzied' mind as a driving force — a hallmark of the 'tragic plot': more precisely, the ὠμοδακὴς ἵμερος ascribed to Eteocles by the Chorus in *Seven against Thebes* (692), as well as the ἔρως of fratricide proclaimed by both brothers in Euripides' *Phoenissae* (622). The descent of Pietas on the battlefield (11.457 ff.) is of no avail, either, since the goddess is being upbraided by Tisiphone and retreats to heaven.[88] Now, if it is exactly *sceptri cupido* that will lead to Polynices' demise when he attempts to wrest the regal insignia from his fallen brother 557 ff., his prayer during the duel (504–508) draws our attention to another key facet of his psychological constitution: *piabo manus et eodem pectora ferro / rescindam, dum me moriens his sceptra tenentem / linquat et hunc secum portet minor umbra dolorem* ('I will atone my deed and rend my breast with the same sword, so that my rival die and leave me with the sceptre in my grasp, and, my vassal in the shades, take that sorrow with him to the tomb,' 506–508).[89] As has been the case earlier (152–154), Polynices does not appear to contemplate his survival; it is a merely symbolic, effectively nonsensical 'victory' over his brother that he envisions.[90] The expression *piabo manus* recalls Book 9, where Polynices, distraught by Tydeus' loss and considering himself responsible for it, exclaims *qua nam hoc ego morte piabo?* 'With what death shall I atone for this?' (60).[91] Further, *piabo manus* acquires depth through the reminiscence of the Aeschylean admonition of the chorus to Eteocles, namely that there is no fading to the pollution of fratricide (οὐκ ἔστι γῆρας τοῦδε τοῦ μιάσματος, 682).[92] Hence, as the Aeschylean Eteocles

---

87 See comments by Ganiban (2007, 168–169), foregrounding the intertextual hint to Vergil's Latinus in *Aeneid* 12.18–53.

88 Characteristically, she draws her mantle over her eyes and flees in order to express her complaints to Jupiter (11.495–496). This reluctance to watch the *nefas* being committed echoes Jupiter's command *auferte oculos!* (11.126). In a manner reminding us of Greek tragedy, in which heinous acts are never depicted on stage, the Statian narrative "interrogates the exemplary potential of spectacle"; so Bernstein (2004, 117), who offers a thorough analysis of the modes of viewing in Book 11.

89 The whole prayer actually recalls Oedipus' imprecation in Book 1, to which Polynices himself refers in lines 504–506. See Ganiban 2007, 186, esp. n. 36; Korneeva 2011, 97–98, rightly pointing to the epithet *caecus* used of Polynices in line 517; now Bessone 2018, 97–99, who emphasizes the 'overturning' of the language of prayer here.

90 "Die Hybris ist pervertiert, sie stößt, ohne Ziel, allenthalben ins Leere" (Lefèvre 2008, 897).

91 See comments by Coffee 2006, 443–444; id. 2009, 262–264. We are also reminded of the notion of *piaculum*, the propitiatory sacrifice (as, for instance, in Verg. *Aen.* 6.153, 569).

92 See Marinis 2015, 355; cf. Hutchinson 1985, 154. It may also be read against the background of the momentous pollution created by the cannibalistic act of Tydeus in Book 8 of the *Thebaid*:

does not realize the enormity of fratricide and proceeds regardless, with his mind fixed on the ideal of ἀνδρεία (martial valour), similarly the Statian Polynices fails to realize the fact that the fratricide will render him effectively equal to his brother and both damned. The constant interplay between supernatural causation and human character finds its final culmination in the ultimate fight of the two brothers — *sine more, sine arte* (11.524)[93] — when 'no more need is there of Furies': 'they only marvel and praise as they watch, and grieve that human rage exceeds their own' (537–538).[94] The final apostrophe of the narrator to the brothers,[95] the *damnatio* and the wish for forgetfulness seal the notion of their shared guilt, forming the climax of the tragic story.[96]

3 Final Thoughts

One may actually argue that the very fact that Polynices appears to hold, at the beginning at least, the moral high ground in the *Thebaid*, can be read as an intertextual allusion pointing to Euripides' *Phoenissae*, more specifically to the tragically ironic 'interchangeability' of the brothers which soon becomes evident in the Euripidean play — yet which equally seals the conclusion of *Seven against Thebes*. Further, the fact that the *furor* informing the demeanour of the central characters is split between the impact of the personified Tisiphone and the emotions of the human actors, need not be merely appraised as a factor rendering more difficult the conception of causality in human behaviour. It may in fact be

---

there the goddess Pallas, who flees the battlefield, does not enter heaven before her eyes are "purged" by the *mystica lampas* and the river Ilissos (*purgavit*, 765–766); see comments in Augoustakis 2016, 354–356.

93 See comments by Bonds 1985, 232.

94 It is worth noting that the description of the duel (11.497–573) can be regarded as owing more to the aesthetic sublime of Vergil than to the tragic horror encountered in Senecan tragedy; see analysis by Estèves (2005) 112–118. Hence — due to the immensity of *nefas* — "le récit travaille davantage à donner *l'idée* d'une grandeur de l'horreur qu'à en livrer *l'image*" (*ibid.* 118). The author (*ibid.* 101 ff.) underlines the contrast with the presentation of Tydeus' savage action in Book 8 (esp. 751–766). On the narration of the duel see also Ganiban 2007, 190–195; McNelis 2007, 145–148.

95 Ll. 574–579; see Franchet d'Espèrey 2011, 286–288.

96 The wish for forgetfulness is expressed via the enigmatic utterance *et soli memorent haec proelia reges* ('and let only kings alone recount that combat,' 579); on this anti-epic utterance and its import as the conclusive moment of the "crescendo in negativo" forming the *tragic* exposition of the myth of *Seven against Thebes*, see analysis in Bessone 2011, 75–101.

considered as a rhetorical trope capable of shedding light on the eminently human background of action, which even the terrible figure of Tisiphone needs to manipulate in order to bring about the unspeakable *nefas*. Finally, notwithstanding all the differences between the two genres and the two eras, Statius has succeeded in provoking a scholarly debate on character and responsibility just as vigorous as the one engendered by Aeschylus and Euripides — by the Aeschylean Eteocles most characteristically.

Carole Newlands
Afterword

We have come a long way since Flavian epic in schools and universities was generally dismissed as belonging to a lesser metal. The current volume, which pairs antiquity's two grandest genres, epic and tragedy, is witness to the innovative and stimulating work now being done by Flavian scholars. The Flavian poets were the inheritors of a well-established canon of Greek and Latin texts; they had prodigious poetic memories as well. They lived in a society where texts circulated more easily and travelled further afield than ever before, and they could count on a growing literate audience for their work. Yet their task was formidable, to rebuild the Roman epic tradition after Lucan's dazzling deconstruction of the genre. This volume has shown how central tragedy was to that endeavour.

The challenges of understanding these epic poems is complicated, however, not only by their rich and complex intertextuality, but also by the fragmentary nature of our evidence for ancient tragedy. Since Roman Republican tragedy survives only in fragments, Seneca remains our main source for Roman tragedy. The situation is better for Greek tragedy, but nonetheless many ancient Greek plays are likewise fragmentary and known to us only by name. (If we had more than the few fragments of Euripides' *Hypsipyle*, how, I wonder, might that change our perception of the central *Hypsipyle* episode in the *Thebaid*?). Yet this volume shows that it is not simply a matter of chance survival that makes Senecan tragedy (along with Lucan's *Bellum Civile*) so important for the Flavian epic poets. Rather, the lessons in the nature of monarchical power conveyed by Seneca in his dramas and in his prose works have a major impact on Flavian epic plots.[1]

One of the major achievements of this volume lies in its focus on Flavian epic as a distinct literary and socio-historical phenomenon. The contributors' sophisticated analyses of Valerius Flaccus' *Argonautica*, Silius Italicus' *Punica*, and Statius' *Thebaid* are contextualized within a shared understanding of "the tragic" as an important element in the reconstruction of the epic tradition under the Flavians. Beginning with Aristotle, whose thinking about tragedy includes remarks on epic, the two literary genres have been closely connected. Seeking to sharpen the meaning of "the tragic," this volume explores the relationship between epic and tragedy through diverse modalities of reception. The contributors draw upon an impressively wide variety of intertexts through which to engage with formal,

---

1 Briguglio 2017, 11.

https://doi.org/10.1515/9783110709841-010

hermeneutic, ethical, and socio-political issues. Aeschylus, Sophocles, and Euripides receive their due here, along with the Roman tragic poets. The essays of Cowan and Marinis, for instance, explore complex ethical issues in Statius' *Thebaid* through the poem's multiple allusions to Greek tragic texts. Augoustakis skillfully navigates the fragmentary evidence for Roman Republican drama, while Bernstein, Gervais, and Manuwald make Senecan tragedy the focus for their respective discussions of the problematic hero in the *Punica*, the *Thebaid*, and the *Argonautica*. The engagement of the three Flavian epics with Roman as well as Greek tragic sources thus emerges clearly from this volume as a defining feature of the revitalized genre. Furthermore, the central obsession of all three epics with kingship (or with its equivalent, powerful, charismatic military leadership), for instance, is an important element of Roman Republican tragedy that becomes fully developed in Senecan tragedy and in Flavian epic. Yet the volume also makes clear that the models of the three epic poets were lateral as well as vertical; they cross-referenced one another's work as well as intelligently appropriating the past.

Another major contribution made by this volume lies in the variety of critical perspectives it presents. Several of the articles reflect upon the tensions between the two genres of epic and tragedy, involving, for instance, the power of tragic thought to disrupt the epic narrative (Manuwald; Papaioannou). Others show how tragic themes or motifs can function formally and metatextually to draw attention to the shift within epic to the tragic mode at dramatically heightened moments (Gervais, Parkes). Tragic episodes and figures can also be subverted, however, as when in the *Thebaid* Argia takes over the Sophoclean Antigone's role as guardian of Polynices' corpse (Parkes). Cowan's essay brings the three Flavian epics closely together in his study of *anagnorisis* as a formal marker of Greek tragedy, one that is deployed by all three Flavians in what he names the 'hypertragic' context of civil war. Thus, despite the differences among the three Flavian epic poems, this volume suggests that the common identity of Flavian epic rests not upon a traditional interest in heroism alone but rather upon a shared interest in two simultaneously tragic and historically contemporary themes, namely civil war and kingship, including the dangers of absolute power.

As Hardie observed, the themes of generational continuity and political power are acute problems for the survival of the principate through the first century CE, and they are often closely intertwined in imperial epic, particularly in civil war narratives.[2] These themes are linked, as Papaioannou and Marinis point out in their introduction, by the notion of inherited guilt. In particular, the idea

---

2 Hardie 1993a, 93.

of the *filius degener* (the son who cannot match his father), a figure introduced by Vergil for Neoptolemus, Achilles' son (*Aen.* 2.549), runs through the literature of the first century CE, appearing prominently in Lucan's *Bellum Civile* and Senecan tragedy.[3] Its most moving and ironic instantiation, perhaps, occurs in Silius' *Punica*, where, Bernstein argues, Hannibal as the son of the failed leader Hamilcar doubles the sense of tragic decline in the Carthaginian dynasty. The plots of Flavian tragic epic thus are centred not only on power and fall but also on degradation, a powerful concept that is dramatically interwoven with the history of two imperial dynasties that declined from their initial promise, the Julio-Claudian and the Flavian. Vergil wrote the *Aeneid* shortly after the end of the late Republican civil wars; his epic expressed hope that Augustus was inaugurating a new stable regime that would endure. The Flavians wrote under the shadow of another civil war, recently fought in the streets of Rome itself, rather than abroad, and culminating in the *nefas* of the burning down of the Capitoline Temple itself. They also, as several essays here acknowledge, wrote in the potent shadow of the tragic-Lucanian narrative of civil war and decline.[4] And, as Ash reminds us, we should not forget that these three epic poets, who had lived through the fresh trauma of the civil war of 69 CE, wrote for a contemporary audience whose responses would also have been shaped by the horrifying local experience of internecine conflict.[5]

As Parkes and other contributors make clear, there are of course formal differences between tragedy and epic: for instance, in the former, the lack of an omniscient, third-person narrative voice, and in the latter, the opportunity for amplitude in time and space. There is necessarily a fundamental difference in style and diction between tragedy and epic. And yet there is also overlap between the two genres in this period, particularly as regards similarities of topic and theme. The Flavian epics display a poetics of horror inherited from Seneca and Lucan, and they share profound ethical and political sensibilities. Thus, to adopt Curley's term, Flavian epic displays a "generic synergy," creating in sum something more powerful than the individual poems.[6]

Cowan here has argued that marking an episode as 'tragic' is both a formal marker of generic affiliation and a trope for understanding that 'the tragic' im-

---

3 See *degener* in *PHI* for Lucan and Seneca, showing the marked increase in the use of the word.
4 Briguglio 2017, 4–7. See also Henderson 1998, 220: "the post-Lucanian tragedy of the Caesars of 69 CE."
5 Ash 2015, 218. An insight developed now by Rebeggiani 2018.
6 Curley 2013, 13.

plies a particular worldview. What emerges strongly from the papers in this volume is the fundamental, tragic outlook of Flavian epic, embedded not only in intertexts but in lived experience. Contrary to the optimistic outlook expressed by Jupiter at the start of the *Aeneid*, the outlook of the three Flavian epics (allowing for the fact that we do not have Valerius' ending, and Silius' work may be lacking one book) seems fundamentally tragic in their sense or fear of history as simultaneously repetitive and entropic, a process whose inbuilt degeneration is resisted only by the boldness and dynamism of the epic poets' pens.[7]

How might the Flavian epic poets have encountered tragic drama? The circumstances for the reception of tragedy in Flavian society are not fully understood. Suetonius reports that the emperor Nero performed tragic scenes before a vast public, making tragedy spectacle (Suet. *Nero* 20–24), but a debate continues over whether Seneca's tragedies were ever staged in a theatre rather than being recited. We may wonder whether classical Greek tragedies enjoyed some sort of revival under the philhellene emperors Titus and Domitian. Certainly, the live performance of tragedy lived on through the spectacle of pantomime. Statius, as Suetonius and Juvenal tell us, wrote a pantomime libretto called *Agave* (named after the mother of Pentheus). This was performed by the pantomime actor Paris, who was killed in 83 CE — a sign, according to Suetonius, of the decline of Domitian's reign into cruelty (*Dom.* 10.1).[8] Writing pantomime libretti was derided by Seneca the Elder and others as a degraded form of literary composition. Yet if Suetonius' story is true, Statius' *Agave* was written for a top-of-the line performer; the story also suggests the poet's deep interest in the flexibility of tragedy in imperial Rome as regards both genre and gender. There is also plenty of evidence for the popularity of recitation — in private homes or in hired venues — as a way of publicizing and trying out one's work before an audience.[9] In Tacitus' *Dialogus*, Maternus' tragedies are performed at recitals, including a *Thyestes* (*Dial.* 3–4), a play of dynastic degeneracy that obviously appealed to the Romans; in addition to Seneca's play of that name, we know of a *Thyestes* by the Augustan poet Varius that was much admired (but is no longer extant).[10] Thus the Flavian epic poets

---

7 In the Roman cultural imagination political strife, in particular, civil strife, was seen as cyclical; see Ginsberg and Krasne 2018 and their quotation (p. 1) of Tac. *Hist.* 1.50.2–4, esp. the telling phrase on the fear of the triumph of degeneracy, *deteriorem fore qui vicisset*.

8 Sen. *Suas.* 2.19; Juv. 7.86–87. For an excellent introduction to pantomime in the imperial age see Jory 2008.

9 There is a substantial bibliography on recitation. For a succinct overview see Newlands 2011, 19–20.

10 Cf. Quint. *Inst.* 10.1.98; Tarrant 1985.

probably had access to tragic drama not only through texts but through panto-mime and recitation, both highly charged performative modes. Goldberg has en-couraged us to think of recitation as appealing to an audience who would appreci-ate the power of words over spectacle.[11] The psychological power of declamatory rhetoric was in part key to the survival of Senecan tragedy and to its appeal in the Renaissance, as well as in the Flavian period. And yet the spectacular need not be separated from the verbal. As Gianpiero Rosati has argued, a crucial feature of Flavian aesthetics was "its peculiar tendency to spectacularize reality while at the same time stimulating a visual perception of it" such that either the viewer or the reader was emotionally engaged in a vivid appreciation of a work of art or text.[12]

This volume, ambitious in its goals, is a welcome addition to recent important monographs on the relationship between individual Roman epics and tragedy, notably by Panoussi (Vergil), Bessone (Statius), and Curley (Ovid).[13] Of course not all bases can be covered in these eight essays. Gender is not a major concern of this volume, nor is the powerful female voice of Greek and Roman tragedy which crosses over into Flavian epic, particularly the *Thebaid*. Where then might we go from here? Attention has been directed to Lucan's use not only of Greek and Ro-man tragedies but also of Hellenistic tragic histories.[14] Woodman has cited evi-dence that Tacitus read all three Flavian epic poets.[15] And Ash, reminding us that Silius Italicus was a participant in the civil war of 69 CE, has argued that in the *Histories* Tacitus suggests the increasing moral degeneracy of the Flavian army through allusion to the Carthaginian army in the *Punica*.[16] Moreover, Ginsberg and Krasne have recently issued an important collection of essays exploring the Flavian literary response to the fresh trauma of the civil war of 69 CE.[17] Perhaps then it is time to further the momentum represented by that volume and this pre-sent one by exploring not only how the epic poets drew on literary texts but also how historiographical writing, after the Flavian era, was shaped by Flavian epic.

---

11 Goldberg 1996.

12 Rosati 2017, 134.

13 For further works see also Papaioannou and Marinis in this volume, p. 3 n. 10. Giusti (2018) makes a convincing argument throughout her monograph that is relevant to this present volume, namely, the importance of tragedy as a common thread woven into the *Aeneid* that invites Ro-man self-evaluation in relation to war.

14 Marti 1964; Ripoll 2016.

15 Woodman 2009, 36–37.

16 Ash 1999, 63–69.

17 See also note 5 above.

Bibliography

Adamietz, J. (1970), 'Jason und Hercules in den Epen des Apollonios Rhodios und Valerius Flaccus', *A&A* 16, 29–38.

Adamietz, J. (1976), *Zur Komposition der Argonautica des Valerius Flaccus*, Munich.

Adams, B.B. (2000), *Coming-to-Know: Recognition and the Complex Plot in Shakespeare*, New York.

Ahl, F. (1986), 'Statius' *Thebaid*: A Reconsideration', *ANRW* 2.32.5, 2803–2912.

Ahl, F. (1991), *Sophocles' Oedipus: Evidence and Self-Conviction*, Ithaca, NY.

Ahl, F. (2015), 'Transgressing Boundaries of the Unthinkable: Sophocles, Ovid, Vergil, Seneca, and Homer Refracted in Statius' *Thebaid*', in: W.J. Dominik/K. Gervais/C.E. Newlands (eds), *Brill's Companion to Statius*, Leiden/Boston, 240–265.

Allan, W. (2013), 'The Ethics of Retaliatory Violence in Athenian Tragedy', *Mnemosyne* 66, 593–615.

Ambühl, A. (2005), '*Thebanos imitata rogos* (*BC* 1,552). Lucans *Bellum civile* und die Tragödien aus dem thebanischen Sagenkreis', in: C. Walde (ed.), *Lucan im 21. Jahrhundert*, Munich, 261–294.

Ambühl, A. (2019), 'Intergeneric Influences and Interactions', in: C. Reitz/S. Finkmann (eds), *Structures of Epic Poetry*, vol. 1: '*Foundations*', Berlin/Boston, 167–192.

Anderson, M.J. (2008), 'Myth', in: J. Gregory (ed.), *A Companion to Greek Tragedy*, Malden, MA, 121–135.

Anderson, W.S. (1997), *Ovid, Metamorphoses Books 1–5*, Norman, OK.

Anderson, W.S. (2002), 'Resistance to Recognition and "Privileged Recognition" in Terence', *CJ* 98, 1–8.

Antoniadis, Th. (2017), 'Epic as Elegy: Generic Interplay in the Scenes of Lament and Separation in Valerius Flaccus' *Argonautica* 2 & 3', *Mnemosyne* 70, 631–653.

Arcellaschi, A. (1990), *Médée dans le théâtre latin d'Ennius à Sénèque*, Rome.

Aricò, G. (1981), 'Contributo alla riconstruzione degli *Skyrioi* euripidei', in: I. Gallo (ed.) *Studi salernitani in memoria di R. Cantarella*, Salerno, 215–230.

Aricò, G. (1983), 'L'*Ars Poetica* di Orazio e la tragedia romana arcaica', *QCTC* 1, 67–93.

Aricò, G. (1998), '*.. spirat tragicum* (Horace, *epist.* 2, 1, 166). Réflexions sur le tragique romain archaïque', *Pallas* 49, 73–90.

Aricò, G. (2002), '*Crudelis vincit pater*. Alcune note su Stazio e il mito tebano', in: A. Aloni/E. Berardi/G. Besso/S. Cecchin (eds), *I Sette a Tebe. Dal mito alla letteratura. Atti del Seminario Internazionale, Torino 21–22 Febbraio 2001*, Bologna, 169–184.

Ariemma, E.M. (2008), '*Odia fraterna, fraternae acies*: i gemelli gladiatori in Silio Italico (*Pun.* 16.527–48)', *Lexis* 26, 325–369.

Ariemma, E.M. (2010), '*Fons cuncti Varro mali*: The Demagogue Varro in *Punica* 8–10', in: A. Augoustakis (ed.), *Brill's Companion to Silius Italicus*, Leiden, 241–276.

Arnott, W.G. (1996), *Alexis: The Fragments. A Commentary*, Cambridge.

Ash, Rh. (1999), *Ordering Anarchy: Armies and Leaders in Tacitus' Histories*, London.

Ash, Rh. (2015), 'War Came in Disarray', in: W.J. Dominik/C.E. Newlands/K. Gervais (eds), *Brill's Companion to Statius*, Leiden, 207–220.

Augoustakis, A. (2003), '*Lugendam Formae sine Virginitate Reliquit*: Reading Pyrene and the Transformation of Landscape in Silius' *Punica* 3', *AJPh* 124, 235–257.

Augoustakis, A. (2005), 'Two Greek Names in Silius Italicus' *Punica*', *RhM* 148, 222–224.

https://doi.org/10.1515/9783110709841-011

Augoustakis, A. (2010), *Motherhood and the Other. Fashioning Female Power in Flavian Epic*, Oxford.

Augoustakis, A. (2013), '*Teichoskopia* and *Katabasis*: The Poetics of Spectatorship in Flavian Epic', in: G. Manuwald/A. Voigt (eds), *Flavian Epic Interactions*, Berlin/Boston, 157–175.

Augoustakis, A. (ed.) (2014), *Flavian Poetry and its Greek Past*, Leiden.

Augoustakis, A. (2015), 'Statius and Senecan Drama', in: W.J. Dominik/C.E. Newlands/K. Gervais (eds), *Brill's Companion to Statius*, Leiden, 377–392.

Augoustakis, A. (2016a), *Statius, Thebaid 8. Edited with an Introduction, Translation, and Commentary*, Oxford.

Augoustakis, A. (2016b), 'Achilles and the Poetics of Manhood: Re(de)fining Europe and Asia in Statius' *Achilleid*', *CW* 109, 195–219.

Balula, J.P.R. (2015), 'Contributos para a leitura das *Troianas* de Séneca', *Ágora. Estudos Clássicos em Debate* 7, 299–322.

Barchiesi, A. (1995), 'Figure dell'intertestualità nell'epica romana', *Lexis* 13, 49–67 (English translation: 'Tropes of intertextuality in Roman epic', in: id., *Speaking Volumes, Narrative and Intertext in Ovid and Other Latin Poets*, London 2001, 129–140).

Barchiesi, A. (1997), *The Poet and the Prince. Ovid and Augustan Discourse*, Berkeley.

Barchiesi, A. (2001), 'Genealogie letterarie nell'epica imperiale. Fondamentalismo e ironia', in: E.A. Schmidt (ed.), *L'histoire immanente dans la poésie latine*, Vandœuvres-Genève (Entretiens sur l'antiquité classique 47), 315–347.

Barchiesi, A. (2005), 'Masculinity in the 90s: The Education of Achilles in Statius and Quintilian', in: M. Paschalis (ed.), *Roman and Greek Imperial Epic*, Herakleion, 47–75.

Barchiesi, A. (2006), 'Music for Monsters: Ovid's *Metamorphoses*, Bucolic Evolution, and Bucolic Criticism', in: M. Fantuzzi/T. Papanghelis (eds), *Brill's Companion to Greek and Latin Pastoral*, Leiden, 403–425.

Baertschi, A. (2015), 'Epic Elements in Senecan Tragedy', in: G.W.M. Harrison (ed.), *Brill's Companion to Roman Tragedy*, Leiden, 169–195.

Barker, E.T.E. (2009), *Entering the Agon: Dissent and Authority in Homer, Historiography, and Tragedy*, Oxford.

Beacham, R.C. (1991), *The Roman Theater and Its Audience*, Cambridge, MA.

Belfiore, E.S. (2005), *Murder among Friends: Violation of Philia in Greek Tragedy*, Oxford.

Bernstein, N.W. (2003), 'Ancestors, Status, and Self-Presentation in Statius' *Thebaid*', *TAPhA* 133, 353–379.

Bernstein, N.W. (2004), '*Auferte Oculos*: Modes of Spectatorship in Statius, *Thebaid* 11', *Phoenix* 58, 62–85.

Bernstein, N.W. (2008), *In the Image of the Ancestors: Narratives of Kinship in Flavian Epic*, Toronto.

Bernstein, N.W. (2013a), 'Ritual Murder and Suicide in Statius' *Thebaid*', in: A. Augoustakis (ed.), *Ritual and Religion in Flavian Epic*, Oxford, 233–248.

Bernstein, N.W. (2013b), '*Distat opus nostrum, sed fontibus exit ab isdem*: Declamation and Flavian Epic', in: G. Manuwald/A. Voigt (eds), *Flavian Epic Interactions*, Berlin/Boston, 139–156.

Bernstein, N.W. (2017), *Silius Italicus, Punica 2. Edited with an Introduction, Translation, and Commentary*, Oxford.

Bessone, F. (2011), *La Tebaide di Stazio: Epica e potere*, Pisa/Roma.

Bessone, F. (2013), 'Religion and Power in the *Thebaid*', in: A. Augoustakis (ed.), *Ritual and Religion in Flavian Epic*, Oxford, 145–161.

Bessone, F. (2018), 'Signs of Discord: Statius's Style and the Traditions on Civil War', in: L.D. Ginsberg/D.A. Krasne (eds), *After 69 CE — Writing Civil War in Flavian Rome*, Berlin/ Boston, 89–108.

Bexley, E. (2016), 'Recognition and the Character of Seneca's *Medea*', *CCJ* 62, 31–51.

Billerbeck, M. (1986), 'Stoizismus in der römischen Epik neronischer und flavischer Zeit', *ANRW* II.32.5, 3116–3151.

Billerbeck, M. (1999), *Seneca, Hercules furens. Einleitung, Text, Übersetzung und Kommentar*, Leiden/Boston/Köln.

Billerbeck, M. (2014), '*Hercules furens*', in: G. Damschen/A. Heil, with the assistance of Mario Waida (eds), *Brill's Companion to Seneca. Philosopher and Dramatist*, Leiden/Boston, 425–433.

Biondi, G.G. (1984), *Il nefas argonautico: mythos e logos nella Medea di Seneca*, Bologna.

Bispham, E.H./T.J. Cornell/J.W Rice/C.J. Smith (eds) (2013), *The Fragments of the Roman Historians: Introduction*, vol. 1, Oxford.

Blum, J. (2019), '"What Country, Friends, is This?" Geography and Exemplarity in Valerius Flaccus' *Argonautica*', in: T. Biggs/J. Blum (eds), *The Epic Journey in Greek and Roman Literature*, Cambridge, 59–88.

Bonds, W.S. (1985), 'Two Combats in the *Thebaid*', *TAPhA* 115, 225–235.

Bowie, A. (1990), 'The Death of Priam: Allegory and History in the *Aeneid*', *CQ* 40, 470–481.

Boyle, A.J. (1997), *Tragic Seneca: An Essay in the Theatrical Tradition*, London.

Boyle, A.J. (2006), *Roman Tragedy: An Introduction*, London/New York.

Boyle, A.J. (ed. and tr.) (2011), *Seneca, Oedipus. Edited with Introduction, Translation and Commentary*, Oxford.

Braund, S.M./Gill, C. (eds) (1997), *The Passions in Roman Thought and Literature*, Cambridge.

Briguglio, S. (2017), *Fraternas Acies: Saggio di commento a Stazio, Tebaide, 1, 1–389*, Alessandria.

Brink, C.O. (1971), *Horace on Poetry*, vol. 2: *The 'Ars Poetica'*, Cambridge.

Brown, A.L. (1977), 'Eteocles and the Chorus in the *Seven Against Thebes*', *Phoenix* 31, 300–318.

Brown, J. (1994), *Into The Woods: Narrative Studies in the Thebaid of Statius with Special Reference to Books IV-VI*, Diss. University of Cambridge.

Bruère, R.T. (1959), '*Color Ovidianus* in Silius' *Punica* 8–17', *CPh* 54, 228–245.

Buckley, E. (2013), 'Visualising Venus: Epiphany and *Anagnorisis* in Valerius Flaccus' *Argonautica*', in: C. Vout/H. Lovatt (eds), *Epic Visions: Visuality in Greek and Latin Epic and Its Reception*, Cambridge, 78–98.

Buckley, E. (2014), 'Valerius Flaccus and Seneca's Tragedies', in: M. Heerink/G. Manuwald (eds), *Brill's Companion to Valerius Flaccus*, Leiden, 307–325.

Burck, E. (1976), 'Die Befreiung der Andromeda bei Ovid und der Hesione bei Valerius Flaccus (*Met.* 4.663–764; *Argon.* 2.451–578)', *WS* 89, 221–238.

Burck, E. (1981), 'Epische Bestattungsszenen: Ein literarischer Vergleich', in: id. (ed.), *Vom Menschenbild in der römischen Literatur*, vol. II, Heidelberg, 429–487.

Calame, C. (2013), 'Choral Polyphony and the Ritual Functions of Tragic Songs', in: R. Gagné/ M. Govers Hopman (eds), *Choral Mediations in Greek Tragedy*, Cambridge, 35–57.

Carrara, P. (1986), 'Stazio e i primordia di Tebe: Poetica e polemica nel prologo della *Tebaide*', *Prometheus* 12, 146–158.

Castelletti, C. (2014), 'Aratus and the Aratean Tradition in Valerius' *Argonautica*', in: A. Augoustakis (ed.), *Flavian Poetry and Its Greek Past*, Leiden, 49–72.

Cave, T. (1988), *Recognitions: A Study in Poetics*, Oxford.

Chaudhuri, P. (2014), *The War with God: Theomachy in Roman Imperial Poetry*, Oxford.

Coffee, N. (2006), 'Eteocles, Polynices, and the Economics of Violence in Statius' *Thebaid*', *AJPh* 127, 415–452.

Coffee, N. (2009), *The Commerce of War: Exchange and Social Order in Latin Epic*, Chicago/London.

Collard, J./E. Cropp (2008), *Euripides*, vol. VII: *Fragments, Aegeus-Meleager*, Cambridge, MA (Loeb Classical Library).

Conte, G.B. (1986), *The Rhetoric of Imitation: Genre and Poetic Memory in Vergil and Other Latin Poets*, transl. Ch. Segal, Ithaca, NY.

Conte, G.B. (1992), 'Empirical and Theoretical Approaches to Literary Genre', in: K. Galinsky (ed.), *The Interpretation of Roman Poetry: Empiricism or Hermeneutics?*, Frankfurt am Main, 104–123.

Conte, G.B. (1994), *Latin Literature: A History*, transl. G.W. Most, Baltimore/London.

Conte, G.B. (2007), *The Poetry of Pathos: Studies in Vergilian Epic*. Ed. S.J. Harrison, Oxford.

Cordes, L.S. (2009), 'Der Weg zur Anagnorisis. Eine personenbezogene Analyse der Kompositionsstrukturen in Senecas *Oedipus*', *Hermes* 137, 425–446.

Cowan, R. (2010), 'A Stranger in a Strange Land: Medea in Roman Republican Tragedy', in: H. Bartel/A. Simon (eds), *Unbinding Medea: Interdisciplinary Approaches to a Classical Myth from Antiquity to the 21st Century*, London, 39–52.

Cowan, R. (2013), 'Haven't I Seen You Before Somewhere? Optical Allusions in Republican Tragedy', in: G.W.M. Harrison/V. Liapis (eds), *Performance in Greek and Roman Theatre*, Leiden, 311–342.

Cowan, R. (2014), 'My Family and Other Enemies: Valerian Villains and Argonautic Antagonists', in: M. Heerink/G. Manuwald (eds), *Brill's Companion to Valerius Flaccus*, Leiden/Boston, 229–248.

Cowan, R. (2017), 'Bloated Buskins: Seneca and the Satiric Idea of Tragedy', in: C.V. Trinacty/C.M. Sampson (eds), *The Poetics of Senecan Tragedy = Ramus* 46, 75–117.

Criado, C. (1999), 'Tragicidad y epicidad de la Tisífone estaciana', *CFC (Estudios Latinos)* 16, 141–161.

Criado, C. (2015), 'The Constitutional Status of Euripidean and Statian Theseus: Some Aspects of the Criticism of Absolute Power in the *Thebaid*', in: W.J. Dominik/K. Gervais/C.E. Newlands (eds), *Brill's Companion to Statius*, Leiden/Boston, 291–306.

Curley, D. (2013), *Tragedy in Ovid: Theater, Metatheater, and the Transformation of a Genre*, Cambridge.

Dangel, J. (1995), *Accius, Oeuvres (Fragments)*, Paris.

Davis, P.J. (1994), 'The Fabric of History in Statius' *Thebaid*', in: C. Deroux (ed.), *Studies in Latin Literature and Roman History*, vol. 7, Brussels, 464–483.

Davis, P.J. (2010), 'Jason at Colchis: Technology and Human Progress in Valerius Flaccus', *Ramus* 39, 1–13.

Davis, P.J. (2015), 'Argo's Flavian Politics: the Workings of Power in Valerius Flaccus', in: H. Baltussen/P.J. Davis (eds), *The Art of Veiled Speech: Self-Censorship from Aristophanes to Hobbes*, Philadelphia, 157–175.

Dee, N. (2013), 'Wasted Water: The Failure of Purification in the *Thebaid*', in: A. Augoustakis (ed.), *Ritual and Religion in Flavian Epic*, Oxford, 181–198.

Delarue, F. (2000), *Stace, poète épique: Originalité et cohérence*, Leuven/Paris.

Delarue, F. (2003), 'Le romanesque dans l'*Achilléide* de Stace', *Ars Scribendi* 1 [online at: http://ars-scribendi.ens-lyon.fr/spip.php?article10].

Delarue, F. (2008), 'Prélude aux ténèbres: Le temps et la nuit dans le chant I de la *Thébaïde*', in: L. Castagna/C. Riboldi (eds), *Amicitiae templa serena: Studi in onore di Giuseppe Aricò*, vol. 1, Milan, 445–470.

Delz, J. (1995), 'Zur Neubewertung der lateinischen Epik flavischer Zeit', in: G. Reggi (ed.), *Aspetti della poesia epica latina. Atti del corso d'aggiornamento per docenti di latino e greco del Canton Ticino, Lugano 21–22–23 ottobre 1993*, Lugano, 143–172.

De Witt, N. (1907), 'The Dido Episode as a Tragedy', *CJ* 2, 283–288.

Dietrich, J.S. (2015), 'Dead Woman Walking: Jocasta in the *Thebaid*', in: W.J. Dominik/K. Gervais/C.E. Newlands (eds), *Brill's Companion to Statius*, Leiden/Boston, 307–321.

Dinter, M. (2008), 'Epic from Epigram: The Poetics of Valerius Flaccus' *Argonautica*', *AJPh* 130, 533–566.

Dominik, W.J. (1994), *The Mythic Voice of Statius: Power and Politics in the* Thebaid, Leiden.

Dominik, W.J. (2003), 'Hannibal at the Gates: Programmatising Rome and *Romanitas* in Silius Italicus' *Punica* 1 and 2', in: A.J. Boyle/W.J. Dominik (eds), *Flavian Rome: Culture, Image, Text*, Leiden, 469–497.

Dominik, W.J. (2010), 'The Reception of Silius Italicus in Modern Scholarship', in: A. Augoustakis (ed.), *Brill's Companion to Silius Italicus*, Leiden, 425–447.

Dominik, W.J./C. Newlands/K. Gervais (eds) (2015), *Brill's Companion to Statius*, Leiden/Boston.

Dräger, P. (1995), 'Jasons Mutter-Wandlung von einer griechischen Heroine zu einer römischen Matrone', *Hermes* 123, 470–489.

Duckworth, G.E. (1956), 'Fate and Free Will in Vergil's "Aeneid"', *CJ* 51, 357–364.

Duff, J.D. (ed. and tr.) (1934), *Silius Italicus: Punica*. 2 volumes, Cambridge, MA (Loeb Classical Library).

Easterling, P.E. (1988), 'Tragedy and Ritual', *Mètis* 3, 87–109.

Eden, P.T. (1998), 'Problems of Text and Interpretation in Statius, *Thebaid* I-VI', *CQ* 48, 320–324.

Edwards, M.J. (1999), 'The Role of Hercules in Valerius Flaccus', *Latomus* 58, 150–163.

Ehlers, W.W. (ed.) (1980), *Gai Valeri Flacci Setini Balbi Argonauticon libros octo*, Stuttgart.

Eigler, U. (1988), *Monologische Redeformen bei Valerius Flaccus*, Frankfurt am Main.

Elliott, J. (2008), 'Ennian Epic and Ennian Tragedy in the Language of the *Aeneid*: Aeneas' Generic Wandering and the Construction of the Latin Literary Past', *HSCPh* 104, 241–272.

Estèves, A. (2005), '"Color" épique et 'color' tragique dans la *Thébaïde* de Stace: Recits de 'nefas' et stratégies narratives (viii, 751–765 et xi, 524–579)', *Latomus* 64, 96–120.

Falcetto, R. (1998), 'L' *Andromeda* di Euripide: proposta di ricostruzione', in: *Quaderni del Dipartimento di filologia, linguistica e tradizione classica* 9 (1997), Bologna, 55–71.

Falcone, M.J. (2016), *Medea sulla scena tragica repubblicana: Commento a Ennio, Medea exul; Pacuvio, Medus; Accio, Medea sive Argonautae*, Tübingen.

Fantham, E. (1979), 'Statius' Achilles and his Trojan Model', *CQ* 29, 457–462.

Fantham, E. (2006), 'The Perils of Prophecy: Statius' Amphiaraus and His Literary Antecedents', in: R.R. Nauta/H.-J. van Dam/J.J.L. Smolenaars (eds), *Flavian Poetry*, Leiden, 147–162.

Fantham, E. (2011), 'Statius' *Thebaid* and the Genesis of Hatred', in: ead., *Roman Readings. Roman Response to Greek Literature from Plautus to Statius and Quintilian*, Berlin/New York, 577–606 [= 'Envy and Fear the Begetter of Hate: Statius' *Thebaid* and the Genesis of Hatred', in: S. Braund/C. Gill (eds), *The Passions in Roman Thought and Literature*, Cambridge 1997, 185–212.]

Fantuzzi, M. (2012), *Achilles in Love: Intertextual Studies*, Oxford.

Farmer, M.C. (2016), *Tragedy on the Comic Stage*, Oxford.

Feeney, D.C. (1991), *The Gods in Epic: Poets and Critics of the Classical Tradition*, Oxford.

Feeney, D. (2004), '*Tenui ... latens discrimine*: Spotting the Differences in Statius' *Achilleid*', *MD* 52, 85–105.

Fenik, B.C. (1960), *The Influence of Euripides on Vergil's Aeneid*, Diss. Princeton University.

Ferenczi, A. (2014), 'Philosophical Ideas in Valerius Flaccus' *Argonautica*', in: M. Heerink/ G. Manuwald (eds), *Brill's Companion to Valerius Flaccus*, Leiden/Boston, 136–153.

Fernandelli, M. (2002–3), 'Vergilio e l'esperienza tragica. Pensieri fuori moda sul libro IV dell'*Eneide*', *Incontri triestini di filologia classica* 2, 1–54.

Filippi, M. (2015), 'The Reception of Latin Archaic Tragedy in Ovid's Elegy', in: G.W.M. Harrison (ed.), *Brill's Companion to Roman Tragedy*, Leiden, 196–215.

Finkmann, S. (2014), 'Collective Speech and Silence', in: A. Augoustakis (ed.), *Flavian Poetry and its Greek Past*, Leiden, 73–94.

Fitch, J.G. (1976), 'Aspects of Valerius Flaccus' Use of Similes', *AJPh* 106, 113–124.

Fitch, J.G. (1987), *Seneca's Hercules Furens. A Critical Text with Introduction and Commentary*, Ithaca/London.

Fitch, J.G. (ed. and tr.) (2002), *Seneca, Tragedies*, vol. I: *Hercules, Trojan Women, Phoenician Women, Medea, Phaedra*, Cambridge, MA (Loeb Classical Library).

Fitch, J.G. (ed. and tr.) (2004), *Seneca, Tragedies*, vol. II: *Oedipus, Agamemnon, Thyestes. [Seneca], Hercules on Oeta, Octavia*, Cambridge, MA (Loeb Classical Library).

Foley, H. (2003), 'Choral Identity in Greek Tragedy', *CPh* 98, 1–30.

Fowler, A. (1982), *Kinds of Literature: an Introduction to the Theory of Genres and Modes*, Oxford.

Fowler, D.P. (2000), *Roman Constructions: Readings in Postmodern Latin*, Oxford.

Franchet d'Espèrey, S. (1988), 'Une étrange descente aux enfers: le suicide d'Éson et Alcimédé (Valerius Flaccus, *Arg.* I 730–851)', in: D. Porte/J.-P. Neraudau (eds), *Hommages à Henri Le Bonniec: Res Carae*, Brussels, 193–197.

Franchet d'Espèrey, S. (1999), *Conflit, violence et non-violence dans la* Thébaïde *de Stace*, Paris.

Franchet d'Espèrey, S. (2001a), 'Le problème des motivations multiples (sive...sive...) dans la *Thébaïde* de Stace', in: A. Billault (ed.), Ὀπώρα. *La belle saison de l'hellénisme. Études de littérature antique offertes au Recteur Jacques Bompaire*, Paris, 23–31.

Franchet d'Espèrey, S. (2001b), 'La causalité dans le chant I de la *Thébaïde* de Stace: où commence la *Thébaïde*?', *RÉL* 79, 188–200.

Franchet d'Espèrey, S. (2003), '*Nuda potestas armavit fratres*. Le paradoxe du pouvoir et du conflit dans la *Thébaïde* de Stace', in: ead./V. Fromentin/S. Gotteland/J.-M. Roddaz (eds), *Fondements et crises du pouvoir*, Bordeaux, 109–117.

Franchet d'Espèrey, S. (2011), 'Finir l'histoire: la voix du poète aux chants 11 et 12 de la *Thébaïde* de Stace', in: E. Raymond (ed.), *Vox poetae. Manifestations auctoriales dans l'épopée gréco-latine, Actes du colloque organisé les 13 et 14 novembre 2008 par l'Université Lyon 3*, Paris, 285–298.

Frank, M. (1995), *Seneca's Phoenissae: Introduction and Commentary*, Leiden/New York.
Frings, I. (1992), *Odia fraterna als manieristiches Motiv: Betrachuntungen zu Senecas* Thyest *und Statius'* Thebais, Stuttgart/Mainz.
Fuà, O. (1986), 'Il rifacimento eroico di Esone in Valerio Flacco. L'addio a Giasone (I.320–347)', *GIF* 38, 267–273.
Fucecchi, M. (1999), 'La vigilia di Canne nei *Punica* e un contributo alla storia dei rapporti fra Silio Italico e Lucano', in: P. Esposito/L. Nicastri (eds), *Interpretare Lucano: miscellanea di studi*, Naples, 305–342.
Gainsford, P. (2003), 'Formal Analysis of Recognition Scenes in the *Odyssey*', *JHS* 123, 41–59.
Gale, M.R. (1997), 'The Shield of Turnus (*Aeneid* 7.783–792)', *G&R* 44, 176–196.
Galinsky, K. (1968), '*Aeneid* 5 and the *Aeneid*', *AJPh* 89, 157–185.
Galinsky, K. (1972a), *The Herakles Theme. The Adaptations of the Hero in Literature from Homer to the Twentieth Century*, Oxford.
Galinsky, K. (1972b), 'Hercules Ovidianus (*Metamorphoses* IX.1–272)', *WS* 85, 93–116.
Galinsky, K. (2003),'Greek and Roman Drama in the *Aeneid*', in: D. Braund/C. Gill (eds), *Myth, History and Culture in Republican Rome*, Exeter, 275–294.
Galli, D. (2002) [2005], 'Influssi del *Thyestes* di Seneca nel libro I degli *Argonautica* di Valerio Flacco', *Aevum(ant)* 2, 231–242.
Galli, D. (2014), 'Dionysius Scytobrachion's *Argonautica* and Valerius', in: A. Augoustakis (ed.), *Flavian Epic and its Greek Past*, Leiden/Boston, 137–151.
Ganiban, R.T. (2007), *Statius and Vergil: The Thebaid and the Reinterpretation of the Aeneid*, Cambridge/New York.
Ganiban, R.T. (2010), 'Vergil's Dido and the Heroism of Hannibal in Silius' *Punica*', in: A. Augoustakis (ed.), *Brill's Companion to Silius Italicus*, Leiden, 73–98.
Gantz, T. (1993), *Early Greek Myth: A Guide to Literary and Artistic Sources*, Baltimore.
Garson, R.W. (1964), 'Some Critical Observations on Valerius Flaccus' *Argonautica* I', *CQ* 14, 267–279.
Garstang, J.B. (1950), 'The Tragedy of Turnus', *Phoenix* 4, 47–58.
Garthwaite, J. (1989), 'Statius' Retirement from Rome: *Silvae* 3.5', *Antichthon* 23, 81–91.
Gärtner, U. (1994), *Gehalt und Funktion der Gleichnisse bei Valerius Flaccus*, Stuttgart.
Gervais, K. (2013), *Statius, Thebaid 2: Edited with a Commentary*, Diss. University of Otago.
Gervais, K. (2015), 'Tydeus the Hero? Intertextual Confusion in Statius, *Thebaid* 2', *Phoenix* 69, 56–78.
Gervais, K. (2017), *Statius, Thebaid 2: Edited with an Introduction, Translation, and Commentary*, Oxford.
Gildenhard, I./Revermann, M. (2010), 'Introduction', in: I. Gildenhard/M. Revermann (eds), *Beyond the Fifth Century: Interactions with Greek Tragedy from the Fourth Century BCE to the Middle Ages*, Berlin/New York, 1–35.
Gildenhard, I./Zissos, A. (1999), '"Somatic Economies": Tragic Bodies and Poetic Design in Ovid's *Metamorphoses*', in: P. Hardie/A. Barchiesi/S. Hinds (eds), *Ovidian Transformations: Essays on Ovid's Metamorphoses and its Reception*, Cambridge, 162–181.
Ginsberg, L./Krasne, D. (eds) (2018), 'Introduction', in: L. Ginsberg/D. Krasne (eds), *After 69 CE: Writing Civil War in Flavian Rome*, Berlin/Boston, 1–21.
Giordano-Zecharya, M. (2006), 'Ritual Appropriateness in *Seven Against Thebes*. Civic Religion in a Time of War', *Mnemosyne* 59, 53–74.
Giusti, E. (2018), *Carthage in Vergil's Aeneid: Staging the Enemy under Augustus*, Cambridge.

Gladhill, B. (2009), 'The Poetics of Alliance in Vergil's *Aeneid'*, *Dictynna* 6 [online at: http://dictynna.revues.org/260].

Goldberg, S. (1996), 'The Fall and Rise of Roman Tragedy', *TAPhA* 126, 265–286.

Goldhill, S. (1991), *The Poet's Voice: Essays on Poetics and Greek Literature*, Cambridge.

Goldhill, S. (1996), 'Collectivity and Otherness — The Authority of the Tragic Chorus: Response to Gould', in: M.S. Silk (ed.), *Tragedy and the Tragic. Greek Theatre and Beyond*, Oxford, 244–256.

Grewe, S. (1998), 'Der Einfluß von Senecas *Medea* auf die *Argonautica* des Valerius Flaccus', in: U. Eigler/E. Lefèvre, in collaboration with G. Manuwald (eds), *Ratis omnia vincet: Neue Untersuchungen zu den Argonautica des Valerius Flaccus*, Munich, 173–190.

Griffin, J. (1992), 'Of Genres and Poems: Response to G.B. Conte', in: K. Galinsky (ed.), *The Interpretation of Roman Poetry: Empiricism or Hermeneutics?*, Frankfurt am Main, 124–133.

Griffith, M. (2009), 'Apollo, Teiresias, and the Politics of Tragic Prophecy', in: L. Athanassaki/R.P. Martin/J.F. Miller (eds), *Apolline Politics and Poetics: International Symposium*, Athens, 473–500.

Gruber, M.A. (2009), *Der Chor in den Tragödien des Aischylos. Affekt und Reaktion*, Tübingen.

Halliwell, S. (1986), *Aristotle's Poetics*, London.

Halliwell, S. (1987), *The Poetics of Aristotle. Translation and Commentary*, London.

Halliwell, S. (ed. and tr.) (1995), *Aristotle, Poetics,* in Aristotle, vol. XXIII, including *Longinus, On the Sublime; Demetrius, On Style*, Cambridge, MA (Loeb Classical Library).

Hardie, P.R. (1990), 'Ovid's Theban History: The First 'Anti-*Aeneid*'?', *CQ* 40, 224–235.

Hardie, P.R. (1991), 'The *Aeneid* and the *Oresteia*', *PVS* 20, 29–45.

Hardie, P.R. (1992), 'Augustan Poets and the Mutability of Rome', in: A. Powell (ed.), *Roman Poetry and Propaganda in the Age of Augustus*, London, 59–82.

Hardie, P.R. (1993a), *The Epic Successors of Vergil: A Study in the Dynamics of a Tradition*, Cambridge.

Hardie, P.R. (1993b), 'Tales of Unity and Division in Imperial Latin Epic', in: J.H. Molyneux (ed.), *Literary Responses to Civil Discord*, Nottingham, 55–71.

Hardie, P.R. (1997), 'Vergil and Tragedy', in: C. Martindale (ed.), *The Cambridge Companion to Vergil*, Cambridge, 318–326.

Hardie, P.R. (2004), 'Approximative Similes in Ovid: Incest and Doubling', *Dictynna* 1 [online at: http://journals.openedition.org/dictynna/166].

Hardie, P.R. (2012), *Rumour and Renown: Representations of Fama in Western Literature*, Cambridge.

Harper Smith, A. (1987), *A Commentary on Valerius Flaccus' Argonautica II*, Diss. Oxford University.

Harrison, E.L. (1972–3), 'Why Did Venus Wear Boots? Some Reflections on *Aeneid* 1.314f.', *PVS* 12, 10–25 [republished in P.R. Hardie (ed.), *Critical Assessments of Classical Authors: Vergil*, vol. 4, London, 59–75].

Harrison, E.L. (1989), 'The Tragedy of Dido', *EMC* 33 (n.s. 8), 1–21.

Harrison, S.J. (2007), *Generic Enrichment in Vergil and Horace*, Oxford.

Heath, M. (1996), *Aristotle, Poetics: Translated with an Introduction and Notes*, London.

Heerink, M.A.J. (2007), 'Going a Step Further: Valerius Flaccus' Metapoetical Reading of Propertius' Hylas', *CQ* 57, 606–620.

Heerink, M.A.J. (2016). 'Vergil, Lucan and the Meaning of Civil War in Valerius Flaccus' *Argonautica*', *Mnemosyne* 69, 511–525.

Heerink, M./Manuwald, G. (eds) (2014), *Brill's Companion to Valerius Flaccus*, Leiden/Boston.

Heldmann, K. (1974), *Untersuchungen zu den Tragödien Senecas*, Wiesbaden.

Helm, R. (1892), *De P. Papinii Statii Thebaide*, Berlin.

Henderson, J. (1993), 'Form Remade/Statius' *Thebaid*', in: A.J. Boyle (ed.), *Roman Epic*, London, 162–191.

Henderson, J. (1998), *Fighting for Rome: Poets and Caesars, History and Civil War*, Cambridge.

Hermann, F.-G. (2013), 'Eteocles' Decision in Aeschylus' *Seven Against Thebes*', in: D. Cairns (ed.), *Tragedy and Archaic Greek Thought*, Swansea, 39–80.

Hershkowitz, D. (1997), '*Parce metu, Cytherea*: 'Failed' Intertext Repetition in Statius' *Thebaid*, or, Don't Stop Me If You've Heard This One Before', *MD* 39, 35–52.

Hershkowitz, D. (1998a), *The Madness of Epic: Reading Insanity from Homer to Statius*, Oxford.

Hershkowitz, D. (1998b), *Valerius Flaccus: Argonautica. Abbreviated Voyages in Silver Latin Epic*, Oxford.

Herington, C.J. (1970), *The Author of the Prometheus Bound*, Austin, TX.

Heslin, P.J. (2005), *The Transvestite Achilles: Gender and Genre in Statius' Achilleid*, Cambridge.

Heslin, P.J. (2008), 'Statius and the Greek Tragedians on Athens, Thebes and Rome', in: J.J.L. Smolenaars/H.-J. van Dam/R.R. Nauta (eds), *The Poetry of Statius*, Leiden/Boston, 111–128.

Hinds, S. (1998), *Allusion and Intertext: Dynamics of Appropriation in Roman Poetry*, Cambridge.

Hinds, S. (2000), 'Essential Epic: Genre and Gender from Macer to Statius', in: M. Depew/ D. Obbink (eds), *Matrices of Genre: Authors, Canons, and Society*, Cambridge MA/London, 221–244.

Hinds, S. (2020), 'Pre- and Post-Digital Poetics of 'Transliteralism': Some Greco-Roman Epic Incipits', in: N. Coffee/C. Forstall/L. Galli Milić/D. Nelis (eds), *Intertextuality in Flavian Epic Poetry: Contemporary Approaches*, Berlin, 421–446.

Holford-Strevens, L. (1999), 'Sophocles at Rome', in: J. Griffin (ed.), *Sophocles Revisited: Essays Presented to Sir Hugh Lloyd-Jones*, Oxford, 219–259.

Horsfall, N. (2000), *Vergil, Aeneid 7: A Commentary*, Leiden.

Horsfall, N. (2016), *The Epic Distilled: Studies in the Composition of the Aeneid*, Oxford.

Hubert, A. (2013), '*Malae preces* and their Articulation in the *Thebaid*', in: A. Augoustakis (ed.), *Ritual and Religion in Flavian Epic*, Oxford, 109–126.

Hull, K.W.D. (1979), 'The Hero-Concept in Valerius Flaccus' *Argonautica*', in: C. Deroux, (ed.), *Studies in Latin Literature and Roman History*, vol. 1, Brussels, 379–409.

Hulls, J.-M. (2014), 'Greek Author, Greek Past: Statius, Athens, and the Tragic Self', in: A. Augoustakis (ed.), *Flavian Poetry and its Greek Past*, Leiden, 193–213.

Hunter, R.L. (1985), *The New Comedy of Greece and Rome*, Cambridge.

Hunter, R.L. (ed. and comm.) (1989), *Apollonius of Rhodes: Argonautica Book III*, Cambridge.

Hunter, R.L. (ed. and comm.) (2015), *Apollonius of Rhodes: Argonautica Book IV*, Cambridge.

Hurka, F. (2003), *Textkritische Studien zu Valerius Flaccus*, Stuttgart.

Hutchinson, G.O. (1985), *Aeschylus: Septem contra Thebas. Edited with Introduction and Commentary*, Oxford.

Hutchinson, G.O. (2013), *Greek to Latin: Frameworks and Contexts for Intertextuality*, Oxford.

Ieranò, G. (2002), 'La città delle donne. Il sesto canto dell'*Iliade* e il *Sette contro Tebe* di Eschilo', in: A. Aloni/E. Berardi/G. Besso/S. Cecchin (eds), *I Sette a Tebe. Dal mito alla letteratura. Atti del Seminario Internazionale, Torino 21–22 febbraio 2001*, Bologna, 73–92.

Innes, D.C. (1979), 'Gigantomachy and Natural Philosophy', *CQ* 29, 165–171.

Jocelyn, H.D. (1967), *The Tragedies of Ennius*, Cambridge.

Jocelyn, H.D. (1988), 'Valerius Flaccus and Ennius', *LCM* 13, 10–11.

Jory, J. (2008), 'The Pantomime Dancer and his Libretto', in: E. Hall/R. Wyles (eds), *New Directions in Ancient Pantomime*, Oxford, 157–168.

Juhnke, H. (1972), *Homerisches in römischer Epik flavischer Zeit. Untersuchungen zu Szenennachbildungen und Strukturentsprechungen in Statius' Thebais und Achilleis und in Silius' Punica*, Munich.

Kearns, E. (2013),'Pindar and Euripides on Sex with Apollo', *CQ* 63, 57–67.

Keith, A.M. (2000), *Engendering Rome: Women in Latin Epic*, Cambridge.

Keith, A.M. (2002), 'Sources and Genres in Ovid's *Metamorphoses*', in: B. Weiden Boyd (ed.), *Brill's Companion to Ovid*, Leiden/Boston, 235–259.

Keith, A.M. (2010), 'Dionysiac Theme and Dramatic Allusion in Ovid's *Metamorphoses* 4', in: I. Gildenhard/M. Revermann (eds), *Beyond the Fifth Century: Interactions with Greek Tragedy from the Fourth Century BCE to the Middle Ages*, Berlin/New York, 181–211.

Keith, A.M. (2013), '*Sexus muliebris* in Flavian Epic', *EuGeStA* 3, 282–302.

Kennedy, P.F./Lawrence, M. (eds) (2008), *Recognition: The Poetics of Narrative. Interdisciplinary Studies on Anagnorisis*, New York.

Kennedy, P.F. (2016), *Recognition in the Arabic Narrative Tradition: Discovery, Deliverance and Delusion*, Edinburgh.

Kircher, N. (2018), *Tragik bei Homer und Vergil. Hermeneutische Untersuchungen zum Tragischen im Epos*, Heidelberg.

Klaassen, E.K. (2010),'Imitation and the Hero', in: A. Augoustakis (ed.), *Brill's Companion to Silius Italicus*, Leiden, 99–126.

Kleywegt, A.J. (2005), *Valerius Flaccus, Argonautica, Book 1: A Commentary*, Leiden.

Klimek-Winter, R. (1993), *Andromeda Tragödien: Sophokles-Euripides-Livius Andronicus-Ennius-Accius. Text, Einleitung und Kommentar*, Berlin.

Kline, A.S. (tr.) (2002), *Vergil, The Aeneid. A Translation into English Prose* (Poetry in Translation) [online at: https://www.poetryintranslation.com/PITBR/Latin/Vergilhome.php].

Klotz, A. (ed.) (1953), *Scenicorum Romanorum Fragmenta (=SRF)*, vol. 1: *Tragicorum Fragmenta*, Munich.

Knauer, G.N. (1964), *Die Aeneis und Homer. Studien zur poetischen Technik Vergils mit Listen der Homerzitate in der Aeneis*, Göttingen.

Korneeva, T. (2011), *Alter et ipse: identità e duplicità nel sistema dei personaggi della* Tebaide *di Stazio*, Pisa.

Krasne, D.A. (2011), *Mythic Recursions: Doubling and Variation in the Mythological Works of Ovid and Valerius Flaccus*, Diss. University of California at Berkeley [online at: https://digitalassets.lib.berkeley.edu/etd/ucb/text/Krasne_berkeley_0028E_11344.pdf].

La Penna, A. (1980), 'Mezenzio: una tragedia della tirannia e del titanismo antico', *Maia* 32, 3–30.

La Penna, A. (2002), 'La collana di Armonia e il bàlteo di Pallante: Una nota su Vergilio e Accio', *Maia* 54, 259–262.

Lawrence, S. (2013), *Moral Awareness in Greek Tragedy*, Oxford.

Lee, M.O. (1982), *Fathers and Sons in Vergil's Aeneid: Tum Genitor Natum*, Albany.

Lefèvre, E. (2008), 'Sinn und Sinnlosigkeit in Statius' *Thebais*', in: L. Castagna/Ch. Riboldi (eds), *Amicitiae templa serena. Studi in onore di Giuseppe Aricò*, vol. 2, Milan, 885–905.

Leigh, M. (1997), *Lucan: Spectacle and Engagement*, Oxford.

Leo, F. (1912), *Plautinische Forschungen zur Kritik und Geschichte der Komödie*. 2nd edn, Berlin.

Levin, D.N. (1971), *Apollonius' Argonautica Re-examined: The Neglected First and Second Books*, Leiden.

Liberman, G. (1996), 'Le *Prométhée délivré* attribué à Eschyle, un passage de Valérius Flaccus et un vase d'Apulie', *REA* 98, 273–280.

Liberman, G. (ed. and tr.) (2003), *Valerius Flaccus, Argonautiques: Chants I-IV*, Paris.

Littlewood, C.A.J. (2004), *Self-Representation and Illusion in Senecan Tragedy*, Oxford.

Littlewood, C.A.J. (2014), '*Hercules Oetaeus*', in: G. Damschen/A. Heil, with the assistance of M. Waida (eds), *Brill's Companion to Seneca. Philosopher and Dramatist*, Leiden/Boston, 515–521.

Littlewood, R.J. (2011), *A Commentary on Silius Italicus' Punica 7: Edited with Introduction and Commentary*, Oxford.

Littlewood, R.J. (2017), *A Commentary on Silius Italicus' Punica 10: Edited with Introduction, Translation, and Commentary*, Oxford.

Lovatt, H. (2005), *Statius and Epic Games: Sports, Politics and Poetics in the Thebaid*, Cambridge.

Lovatt, H. (2006), 'The Female Gaze in Flavian Epic: Looking out from the Walls in Valerius Flaccus and Statius', in: R.R. Nauta/H.-J. van Dam/J.J.L. Smolenaars (eds), *Flavian Poetry*, Leiden, 59–78.

Lovatt, H. (2010), 'Interplay: Silius and Statius in the Games of *Punica* 16', in: A. Augoustakis (ed.), *Brill's Companion to Silius Italicus*, Leiden, 155–176.

Lovatt, H. (2013a), *The Epic Gaze: Vision, Gender and Narrative in Ancient Epic*, Cambridge.

Lovatt, H. (2013b), 'Competing Visions: Prophecy, Spectacle and Theatricality in Flavian Epic', in: A. Augoustakis (ed.), *Ritual and Religion in Flavian Epic*, Oxford, 53–70.

Lovatt, H. (2015), 'Following after Valerius: Argonautic Imagery in the *Thebaid*', in: W.J. Dominik/C. Newlands/K. Gervais (eds), *Brill's Companion to Statius*, Leiden, 408–424.

Lucas, D.W. (1968), *Aristotle Poetics*, Oxford.

Lüthje, E. (1971), *Gehalt und Aufriß der Argonautica des Valerius Flaccus*, Diss. University of Kiel.

Lyne, R.O.A.M. (1987), *Further Voices in Vergil's Aeneid*, Oxford.

Mac Góráin, F. (2009), *Tragedy and the Dionysiac in Vergil's Aeneid*, Diss. Oxford University.

Mac Góráin, F. (2013), 'Vergil's Bacchus and the Roman Republic', in: J. Farrell/D. Nelis (eds), *Augustan Poetry and the Roman Republic*, Oxford, 124–145.

Mac Góráin, F. (2018), 'Vergil's Sophoclean Thebans', *Vergilius* 64, 131–156.

Mader, G. (1997),'*Duplex nefas, ferus spectator*: Spectacle and Spectator in Act 5 of Seneca's *Troades*', in: C. Deroux (ed.), *Studies in Latin Literature and Roman History VIII*, Bruxelles, 319–351.

Maguinness, W.S. (1963), 'L'inspiration tragique de l'*Énéide*', *AC* 32, 477–490.

Manioti, N. (2016), 'Becoming Sisters: Antigone and Argia in Statius' *Thebaid*', in: N. Manioti (ed.), *Family in Flavian Epic*, Leiden/Boston, 122–142.

Manuwald, G. (1999), *Die Cyzicus-Episode und ihre Funktion in den Argonautica des Valerius Flaccus*, Göttingen.

Manuwald, G. (2000), 'Der Tod der Eltern Iasons. Zu Valerius Flaccus, *Arg.* 1, 693–850', *Philologus* 144, 325–338.

Manuwald, G. (2004), 'Hesione und der 'Weltenplan' in Valerius Flaccus' *Argonautica*', in: F. Spaltenstein (ed.), *Untersuchungen zu den Argonautica des Valerius: Ratis omnia vincet III*, Munich, 145–163.

Manuwald, G. (2011), *Roman Republican Theatre*, Cambridge.

Manuwald, G. (ed. and comm.) (2015), *Valerius Flaccus: Argonautica Book III*, Cambridge.

Marinis, A. (2012), 'Dionysiac Metaphor in Aeschylus' *Seven Against Thebes*', *MD* 69, 9–43.

Marinis, A. (2015), 'Statius' *Thebaid* and Greek Tragedy: the Legacy of Thebes', in: C. Newlands/W. Dominik/K. Gervais (eds), *Brill's Companion to Statius*, Leiden, 343–361.

Marks, R. (2005), *From Republic to Empire: Scipio Africanus in the Punica of Silius Italicus*, Frankfurt am Main.

Marks, R. (2010a),'Silius and Lucan', in: A. Augoustakis (ed.), *Brill's Companion to Silius Italicus*, Leiden, 127–153.

Marks, R. (2010b),'The Song and the Sword: Silius's *Punica* and the Crisis of Early Imperial Epic', in: D. Konstan/K.A. Raaflaub (eds), *Epic and History*, Malden, MA, 185–211.

Marks, R. (2020),'Searching for Ovid at Cannae: A Contribution to the Reception of Ovid in Silius Italicus' *Punica*', in: N. Coffee/C. Forstall/L. Galli Milić/D. Nelis (eds), *Intertextuality in Flavian Epic Poetry: Contemporary Approaches*, Berlin, 87–106.

Marshall, C.W. (2000), 'Location! Location! Location! Choral Absence and Dramatic Space in Seneca's *Troades*', in: G.W.M. Harrison (ed.), *Seneca in Performance*, London, 27–51.

Marshall, C.W. (2014), *The Structure and Performance of Euripides' Helen*, Cambridge.

Marti, B. (1964), 'Tragic History and Lucan's *Pharsalia*', in: C. Henderson Jr. (ed.), *Classical, Mediaeval and Renaissance Studies in Honor of Berthold Louis Ullman*, vol. 1, Rome, 165–204.

Mastronarde, D.J. (1994), *Euripides: Phoenissae. Edited with Introduction and Commentary*, Cambridge.

Mastronarde, D.J. (2010), *The Art of Euripides: Dramatic Technique and Social Context*, Cambridge.

McAuley, M. (2016), *Reproducing Rome: Motherhood in Vergil, Ovid, Seneca, and Statius*, Oxford.

McClure, L. (2015), 'Tokens of Identity: Gender and Recognition in Greek Tragedy', *ICS* 40, 219–236.

McGuire, D.T. (1997), *Acts of Silence: Civil War, Tyranny, and Suicide in the Flavian Epics*, Hildesheim/New York.

McHardy, F. (2005), 'From Treacherous Wives to Murderous Mothers: Filicide in Tragic Fragments', in: F. McHardy/J. Robson/D. Harvey (eds), *Lost Dramas of Classical Athens: Greek Tragic Fragments*, Exeter, 129–150.

McKeown, J.C. (1998), *Ovid: Amores. Text, Prolegomena and Commentary. Volume III: A Commentary on Book Two*, Leeds.

McNelis, C. (2007), *Statius' Thebaid and the Poetics of Civil War*, Cambridge.

McNelis, C. (2015), 'Statius' *Achilleid* and the *Cypria*', in: M. Fantuzzi/C. Tsagalis (eds), *The Greek Epic Cycle and its Ancient Reception: A Companion*, Cambridge, 578–595.

Medda, E. (2013), *La saggezza dell'illusione. Studi sul teatro Greco*, Pisa.

Mehmel, F. (1934), *Valerius Flaccus*, Diss. University of Hamburg.

Micozzi, L. (2007), *Il catalogo degli eroi. Saggio di commento a Stazio Tebaide 4, 1–344*, Pisa.

Miles, S. (2009), *Strattis, Comedy and Tragedy*, Diss. University of Nottingham [online at: http://etheses.nottingham.ac.uk/887/].

Mleynek, S.S. (1999), *Knowledge and Mortality. Anagnorisis in Genesis and Narrative Fiction*, New York.

Moles, J.L. (1982–3), 'Vergil, Pompey and the *Histories* of Asinius Pollio', *CW* 76, 287–288.

Montiglio, S. (2012), *Love and Providence: Recognition in the Ancient Novel*, Oxford.

Morgan, Ll. (1999), *Patterns of Redemption in Vergil's Georgics*, Cambridge.

Morgan, Ll. (2000), 'The Autopsy of C. Asinius Pollio', *JRS* 90, 51–69.

Mozley, J.H. (ed. and tr.) (1928), *Statius*, vol. I: *Silvae, Thebaid I–IV*; vol. II: *Thebaid V–XII, Achilleid*, Cambridge, MA (Loeb Classical Library).

Mozley, J.H. (ed. and tr.) (1934), *Valerius Flaccus: Argonautica*, Cambridge, MA (Loeb Classical Library).

Mueller, M. (2010), 'Athens in a Basket: Naming, Objects, and Identity in Euripides' *Ion*', *Arethusa* 43, 365–402.

Munteanu, D. (2002), 'Types of Anagnorisis: Aristotle and Menander. A Self-Defining Comedy', *WS* 115, 111–126.

Murgatroyd, P. (2009), *A Commentary on Book 4 of Valerius Flaccus' Argonautica*, Leiden.

Murnaghan, S. (1987), *Disguise and Recognition in the Odyssey*, Princeton.

Myers, K.S. (ed. and comm.) (2009), *Ovid, Metamorphoses: Book 14*, Cambridge.

Narducci, E. (1973), 'Il tronco di Pompeo', *Maia* 25, 317–325.

Nelis, D. (2001), *Vergil's Aeneid and the Argonautica of Apollonius Rhodius*, Leeds.

Newlands, C. (ed.) (2011), *Statius, Silvae: Book II*, Cambridge.

Newlands, C.E. (2012), *Statius, Poet Between Rome and Naples*, London.

Newlands, C.E. (2016), 'Fatal Unions: Marriage at Thebes', in: N. Manioti (ed.), *Family in Flavian Epic*, Leiden/Boston, 143–173.

Nugent, S.G. (1996), 'Statius' Hypsipyle: Following in the Footsteps of the *Aeneid*', *Scholia* 5, 46–71.

O'Gorman, E. (2005), 'Beyond Recognition: Twin Narratives in Statius' *Thebaid*', in: M. Paschalis (ed.), *Roman and Greek Imperial Epic*, Herakleion, 29–45.

O'Hara, J.J. (1990), *Death and the Optimistic Prophecy in Vergil's Aeneid*, Princeton.

Ogden, D. (2008), *Perseus*, London/New York.

Otis, B. (1970), *Ovid as an Epic Poet*. 2nd edn, Cambridge.

Padel, R. (1992), *In and Out of the Mind: Greek Images of the Tragic Self*, Princeton.

Pagán, V.E. (2000), 'The Mourning After: Statius *Thebaid* 12', *AJPh* 121, 423–452.

Panoussi, V. (2002), 'Vergil's Ajax: Allusion, Tragedy, and Heroic Identity in the *Aeneid*', *ClAnt* 21, 95–134.

Panoussi, V. (2009), *Greek Tragedy in Vergil's Aeneid: Ritual, Empire and Intertext*, Cambridge.

Papadopoulou, Th. (2008), *Euripides, Phoenician Women*, London.

Parkes, R. (2008), 'The Return of the Seven: Allusion to the *Thebaid* in Statius' *Achilleid*', *AJPh* 129.3, 381–402.

Parkes, R. (2012), *Statius, Thebaid 4: Edited with an Introduction, Translation, and Commentary*, Oxford.

Parkes, R. (2013), 'The Long Road to Thebes: The Geography of Journeys in Statius' *Thebaid*', in: M. Skempis/I. Ziogas (eds), *Geography, Topography, Landscape: Configurations of Space in Greek and Roman Epic*, Berlin/Boston, 405–426.

Parkes, R. (2014), 'The Epics of Statius and Valerius Flaccus' *Argonautica*', in: M. Heering/G. Manuwald (eds), *Brill's Companion to Valerius Flaccus*, Leiden/Boston, 326–339.

Parkes, R. forthcoming. 'Statius and the Epic tradition', in: L. Fratantuono/C. Stark (eds), *A Companion to Latin Epic: 14–96 CE*, Malden, MA.

Paschalis, S. (2015), *Tragic Palimpsests: The Reception of Euripides in Ovid's Metamorphoses*, Diss. Harvard University.

Pavlock, B. (1985), 'Epic and Tragedy in Vergil's Nisus and Euryalus Episode', *TAPhA* 115, 207–224.

Perutelli, A. (1982), 'Pluralità di modelli e discontinuità narrativa: l'episodio della morte di Esone in Valerio Flacco (1,747 sgg.)', *MD* 26, 123–140.

Phelan, J. (1989), *Reading People, Reading Plots: Character, Progression, and the Interpretation of Narrative*, Chicago/London.

Piot, M. (1965), 'Hercule chez les poètes du Ier siècle après Jésus-Christ', *REL* 43, 342–358.

Polleichtner, W. (2013), '*Scaenis decora apta futuris*: Das Theater und die *Aeneis*', in: M. Baumbach/W. Polleichtner (eds), *Innovation aus Tradition: Literaturwissenschaftliche Perspektiven der Vergilforschung*, Trier, 139–165.

Pollmann, K. (2004), *Statius, Thebaid 12: Introduction, Text, and Commentary*, Paderborn.

Poortvliet, H.M. (1991), *C. Valerius Flaccus, Argonautica Book II: A Commentary*, Amsterdam.

Putnam, M.C.J. (1995), *Vergil's Aeneid: Interpretation and Influence*, Chapel Hill/London.

Quint, D. (1993), *Epic and Empire: Politics and Generic Form from Vergil to Milton*, Princeton.

Raeburn, D. (tr.) (2004), *Ovid, Metamorphoses*. With an introduction by D. Feeney, London (Penguin Classics).

Rebeggiani, S. (2016), 'Orestes, Aeneas, and Augustus: Madness and Tragedy in Vergil's *Aeneid*', in: P.R. Hardie (ed.), *Augustan Poetry and the Irrational*, Oxford, 56–73.

Rebeggiani, S. (2018), *The Fragility of Power: Statius, Domitian and the Politics of the Thebaid*, Oxford.

Reed, J.D. (2007), *Vergil's Gaze: Nation and Poetry in the Aeneid*, Princeton.

Richardson, N.J. (1983), 'Recognition Scenes in the *Odyssey* and Ancient Criticism', *PLLS* 4, Liverpool, 219–235.

Riley, K. (2008), *The Reception and Performance of Euripides' Herakles: Reasoning Madness*, Oxford.

Rimell, V. (2015), *The Closure of Space in Roman Poetics: Empire's Inward Turn*, Cambridge.

Ripoll, F. (1998a), *La morale héroique dans les épopées latines d'époque flavienne: tradition et innovation*, Leuven/Paris.

Ripoll, F. (1998b), 'La *Thébaïde* de Stace entre épopée et tragédie', in: M.-H. Garelli-François (ed.), *Rome et le tragique. Colloque international 26, 27, 28 mars 1998*, Pallas 49, 323–340.

Ripoll, F. (2003a), 'Un héros barbare dans l'épopée latine: Masinissa dans les *Punica* de Silius Italicus', *AC* 72, 95–111.

Ripoll, F. (2003b), 'Jason héros épique et tragique au chant VII des *Argonautiques* de Valérius Flaccus', *Vita Latina* 169, 70–82.

Ripoll, F. (2004), 'L'inspiration tragique au chant VII des *Argonautiques* de Valérius Flaccus', *REL* 82, 187–208.

Ripoll, F. (2007), '*Regum placidissimus*: le roi Lycomède dans l'*Achilléide* de Stace', *Vita Latina* 177, 50–62.

Ripoll, F. (2008), 'La «tragédie» d'Éson au chant I des *Argonautiques* de Valérius Flaccus', *LEC* 76, 383–396.

Ripoll, F. (2016), 'Peut-on considérer la *Pharsale* comme une "épopée tragique?"', in: V. Berlincourt/L. Galli Milić/D. Nelis (eds), *Lucan and Claudian: Context and Intertext*, Heidelberg, 61–76.

Robiano, P. (2008), 'La scène de reconnaissance de Chariton, *Chéréas et Callirhoé*', *Hermes* 136, 426–437.

Robinson, M. (2011), *A Commentary on Ovid's Fasti, Book 2*, Oxford.

Ronconi, A. (1979), 'Orazio e I poeti latini arcaici', *Studia di poesia latina in onore di A. Traglia*, vol. 2, Rome, 501–524.

Rosati, G. (2005), 'Elegy after the Elegists: From Opposition to Assent', in: F. Cairns (ed.), *PLLS* 12, Cambridge, 133–150.

Rosati, G. (2017), '*Et latet et lucet*: Ovidian Intertextuality and the Aesthetics of Luxury in Martial's Poetry', *Arethusa* 50, 117–142.

Rosenbloom, D. (2006), *Aeschylus, Persians*, London.

Rossi, A. (2004), *Contexts of War: Manipulation of Genre in Vergilian Battle Narrative*, Ann Arbor.

Russo, T.G. (ed.) (2013), *Recognition and Modes of Knowledge: Anagnorisis from Antiquity to Contemporary Theory*, Edmonton.

Rutherford, R.B. (2007), 'Why should I mention Io? Aspects of Choral Narration in Greek Tragedy', *CCJ* 2007, 1–39.

Sacerdoti, A. (2008), 'Seneca's *Phaedra* and the Last Book of Statius' *Thebaid*: *Properate, Verendi Cecropidae*', *Phoenix* 62, 281–289.

Sauer, Ch. (2011), *Valerius Flaccus' dramatische Erzähltechnik*, Göttingen.

Scaffai, M. (1986), 'Il tiranno e le sue vittime nel 1 l. degli *Argonautica* di Valerio Flacco', in: *Munus amicitiae: scritti in memoria di Alessandro Ronconi*, Florence, 233–261.

Scafoglio, G. (2007), 'Vergil and the *Astyanax* of Accius', *CQ* 57, 781–787.

Schetter, W. (1960), *Untersuchungen zur epischen Kunst des Statius*, Wiesbaden.

Schierl, P. (2006), *Die Tragödien des Pacuvius*, Berlin.

Schiesaro, A. (1997), 'Passion, Reason and Knowledge in Seneca's Tragedies', in: S.M. Braund/ C. Gill (eds), *The Passions in Roman Thought and Literature*, Cambridge, 89–111.

Schiesaro, A. (2003), *The Passions in Play: Thyestes and the Dynamics of Senecan Drama*, Cambridge.

Schmitt, A. (tr. and comm.) (2008), *Aristoteles, Poetik*, Berlin.

Schütz, I. (1950), *Hercules als 'mythisches exemplum' in der römischen Dichtung. Seine Gestaltung und seine Bedeutung*, Diss. University of Hamburg.

Scott, W.C. (2009), *The Artistry of the Homeric Simile*, Hanover, NH.

Seaford, R. (1994), *Reciprocity and Ritual: Homer and Tragedy in the Developing City-State*, Oxford.

Segal, C. (1999–2000), 'Lament and Recognition: A Reconsideration of the Ending of the *Bacchae*', *ICS* 24–5, 273–291.

Seo, J.M. (2013), *Exemplary Traits: Reading Characterization in Roman Poetry*, New York.

Sewell-Rutter, N.J. (2007), *Guilt by Descent: Moral Inheritance and Decision Making in Greek Tragedy*, Oxford.

Shackleton Bailey, D.R. (ed. and comm.) (1977), *Cicero, Epistulae ad Familiares*, 2 vols, Cambridge.

Shackleton Bailey, D.R. (ed. and tr.) (2003), *Statius*, vol. I: *Silvae*; vol. II: *Thebaid*, Books 1–7; vol. III: *Thebaid*, Books 8–12, *Achilleid*, Cambridge, MA (Loeb Classical Library).

Simms, R.C. (2014), 'Chronology and Canonicity in Jocasta's Intercessions in Statius' *Thebaid*', *ICS* 39, 171–189.

Simms, R.C. (2018), '*iam pater est*: Oedipus in Statius's *Thebaid*', *ICS* 43, 234–257.

Sissa, G. (2006), 'A Theatrical Poetics: Recognition and the Structural Emotions of Tragedy', *Arion* 14, 35–92.

Smith, R.A. (2011), *Vergil*, Malden, MA.

Smolenaars, J.J.L. (1994), *Statius, Thebaid VII: A Commentary*, Leiden.

Smolenaars, J.J.L. (2004), 'La sfinge in Stat. *Theb.* 2,496–523: un'analisi intertestuale', in: P. Esposito/E.M. Ariemma (eds), *Lucano e la tradizione dell'epica latina. Atti del convegno internazionale di studi Fisciano - Salerno, 19–20 ottobre 2001*, Università degli studi di Salerno, Naples, 69–84.

Smolenaars, J.J.L. (2008), 'Statius *Thebaid* 1.72: Is Jocasta Dead or Alive? The Tradition of Jocasta's Suicide in Greek and Roman Drama and in Statius' *Thebaid*', in: J.J.L. Smolenaars/H.-J. van Dam/R.R. Nauta (eds), *The Poetry of Statius*, Leiden/Boston, 215–237.

Snell, B. (1971), *Tragicorum Graecorum Fragmenta*, vol. 1, Göttingen.

Soerink, J. (2014a), *Beginning of Doom. Statius Thebaid 5.499–753: Introduction, Text, Commentary*, Diss. University of Groningen.

Soerink, J. (2014b), 'Tragic/Epic: Statius' *Thebaid* and Euripides' *Hypsipyle*', in: A. Augoustakis (ed.), *Flavian Poetry and its Greek Past*, Leiden/Boston, 171–191.

Sommerstein, A.H. (ed. and tr.) (2008), *Aeschylus, Persians, Seven against Thebes, Suppliants, Prometheus Bound*, Cambridge, MA (Loeb Classical Library).

Sourvinou-Inwood, C. (1994), 'Something to Do with Athens: Tragedy and Ritual', in: R. Osborne/S. Hornblower (eds), *Ritual, Finance, Politics: Athenian Democratic Accounts Presented to David Lewis*, Oxford, 269–290.

Sourvinou-Inwood, C. (2005), 'Greek Tragedy and Ritual', in: R. Bushnell (ed.), *A Companion to Tragedy*, Malden, MA/Oxford, 7–24.

Spaltenstein, Fr. (2002), *Commentaire des Argonautica de Valérius Flaccus (livres 1 et 2)*, Brussels.

Spaltenstein, Fr. (2004), *Commentaire des Argonautica de Valérius Flaccus (livres 3, 4 et 5)*, Brussels.

Stabryła, S. (1970), *Latin Tragedy in Vergil's Poetry*, Wroclaw.

Stehle, E. (2005), 'Prayer and Curse in Aeschylus' *Seven Against Thebes*', CPh 100, 101–122.

Stinton, T.C.W. (1975), '*Hamartia* in Aristotle and Greek Tragedy', CQ 25, 221–254.

Stockes, C. (2018), 'Band of Brothers: Fraternal Instability and Civil Strife in Silius Italicus' *Punica*', in: L. Ginsberg/D. Krasne (eds), *After 69 CE – Writing Civil War in Flavian Literature*, Berlin, 253–270.

Stover, T. (2006), *Fables of the Reconstruction: A Reading of Valerius Flaccus' Argonautica*, Diss. The University of Texas at Austin.

Stover, T. (2009), 'Apollonius, Valerius Flaccus and Statius: Argonautic Elements in *Thebaid* 3.499–647', AJPh 130, 79–83.

Stover, T. (2012), *Epic and Empire in Vespasianic Rome: A New Reading of Valerius Flaccus' Argonautica*, Oxford.

Suter, A. (2009), 'Tragic Tears and Gender', in: T. Fögen (ed.), *Tears in the Graeco-Roman World*, Berlin/New York, 59–83.

Sweeney, R.D. (ed.) (1997), *Lactantius Placidus, In Statii Thebaida Commentum Vol. I*, Stuttgart.

Taisne, A.-M. (1994), *L'esthétique de Stace: la peinture des correspondances*, Paris.

Taisne, A.-M. (2005), 'L'art de Stace au chant I de la *Thébaïde*', Latomus 64, 661–677.

Tarrant, R.J. (1985), *Seneca's Thyestes: Edited with Introduction and Commentary*, Atlanta.

Tarrant, R.J. (1995), 'Greek and Roman in Seneca's Tragedies', HSCPh 97, 215–230.

Tarrant, R.J. (ed. and comm.) (2012), *Vergil, Aeneid: Book XII*, Cambridge.

Thomas, R.F. (1986), 'Vergil's *Georgics* and the Art of Reference', *HSCPh* 90, 171–198.

Thomas, R.F. (1999), *Reading Vergil and His Texts: Studies in Intertextuality*, Ann Arbor.

Tipping, B. (2007), '*Haec tum Roma fuit*: Past, Present, and Closure in Silius Italicus' *Punica*', in: S.J. Heyworth/P.G. Fowler/S.J. Harrison (eds), *Classical Constructions: Papers in Memory of Don Fowler, Classicist and Epicurean*, Oxford, 221–241.

Torrance, I. (2011), 'In the Footprints of Aeschylus: Recognition, Allusion, and Metapoetics in Euripides', *AJPh* 132, 177–204.

Trinacty, C. (2014), *Senecan Tragedy and the Reception of Augustan Poetry*, Oxford.

Trinacty, C. (2017), 'Retrospective Reading in Senecan Tragedy', in: C.V. Trinacty/C.M. Sampson (eds), *The Poetics of Senecan Tragedy = Ramus* 46, 175–196.

Tschiedel, H.J. (1998), 'Prometheus und die Argonauten', in: U. Eigler/E. Lefèvre, in collaboration with G. Manuwald (eds), *Ratis omnia vincet. Neue Untersuchungen zu den Argonautica des Valerius Flaccus*, Munich, 293–305.

Ugolini, Gh. (1995), *Untersuchungen zur Figur des Sehers Tiresias*, Tübingen.

Várhelyi, Z. (2007), 'The Specters of Roman Imperialism: The Live Burials of Gauls and Greeks at Rome', *ClAnt* 26.2, 277–304.

Vellacott, P. (tr.) (1961), *Aeschylus, Prometheus Bound and Other Plays*, London.

Vellacott, P. (tr.) (1972), *Euripides, Orestes and Other Plays*, London.

Venini, P. (1964), 'Furor e psicologia nella *Tebaide* di Stazio', *Athenaeum* 42, 201–213.

Vessey, D.W.T.C. (1971a), '*Exitiale genus*: Some Notes on Statius, *Thebaid* I', *Latomus* 30, 375–382.

Vessey, D.W.T.C. (1971b), 'Menoeceus in the *Thebaid* of Statius', *CPh* 66, 236–243.

Vessey, D.W.T.C. (1973), *Statius and the Thebaid*, Cambridge.

Vessey, D.W.T.C. (1982),'The Dupe of Destiny: Hannibal in Silius, *Punica* III', *CJ* 77, 320–335.

Vian, F. (1974), *Apollonios de Rhodes Argonautiques Chants I-II*, Paris.

Voigt, A. (2015), 'The Intertextual Matrix of Statius' *Thebaid* 11.315–23', *Dictynna* 12 [online at: http://dictynna.revues.org/1149].

Voigt, A. (2016), 'The Power of the Grieving Mind: Female Lament in Statius's *Thebaid*', *ICS* 41, 59–84.

von Albrecht, M. (1964), *Silius Italicus: Freiheit und Gebundenheit römischer Epik*, Amsterdam.

Walde, C. (1992), *Herculeus labor. Studien zum pseudosenecanischen Hercules Oetaeus*, Frankfurt am Main/Bern/New York/Paris.

Walter, A. (2014), *Erzählen und Gesang im flavischen Epos*, Berlin/Boston.

Weber, C. (2002), 'The Dionysus in Aeneas', *CPh* 97, 322–343.

Wigodsky, M. (1972), *Vergil and Early Latin Poetry*, Wiesbaden.

Wijsman, H.J.W. (1996), *Valerius Flaccus, Argonautica, Book V: A Commentary*, Leiden.

Wilson, M. (2004), 'Ovidian Silius', *Arethusa* 37, 225–249.

Wilson, M. (2013),'The Flavian *Punica?*', in: G. Manuwald/A. Voigt (eds), *Flavian Epic Interactions*, Berlin, 13–28.

Wiseman, T.P. (1998), *Roman Drama and Roman History*, Exeter.

Witt, C. (2005), 'Tragic Error and Agent Responsibility', *Philosophic Exchange* 35, 2–19.

Wlosok, A. (1976), 'Vergils Didotragödie. Ein Beitrag zum Problem des Tragischen in der *Aeneis*', in: H. Görgemanns/E. Schmidt (eds), *Studien zum antiken Epos*, Meisenheim am Glan, 228–250.

Wohl, V. (2015), *Euripides and the Politics of Form*, Princeton.

Woodman, A.J. (2009), 'Tacitus and the Contemporary Scene', in: A.J. Woodman (ed.), *The Cambridge Companion to Tacitus*, Cambridge, 31–43.

Wright, M. (2005), *Euripides' Escape-Tragedies: A Study of Helen, Andromeda, and Iphigenia among the Taurians*, Oxford.

Zeitlin, F.I. (1982), *Under the Sign of the Shield: Semiotics and Aeschylus' Seven Against Thebes*, Rome [reprinted with a new Postscript: Lanham 2009].

Zeitlin, F.I. (2012), 'A Study in Form: Recognition Scenes in the Three Electra Plays', *Lexis* 30, 361–78.

Zissos, A. (1997), *Voyage and Progress: Studies in the Argonautica of Valerius Flaccus*, Diss. Princeton University.

Zissos, A. (2004), 'Terminal Middle: The *Argonautica* of Valerius Flaccus', in: S. Kyriakidis/ F.D. Martino (eds), *Middles in Latin Poetry*, Bari, 311–344.

Zissos, A. (2008), *Valerius Flaccus, Argonautica: Book 1. A Commentary*, Oxford.

Zissos, A. (2009), 'Shades of Vergil: Seneca's *Troades*', *MD* 61, 191–210.

Zissos, A. (2014), 'Stoic Thought and Homeric Reminiscence in Valerius Flaccus' *Argonautica*', in: M. Garani/D. Konstan (eds), *The Philosophizing Muse: The Influence of Greek Philosophy on Roman Poetry*, Newcastle upon Tyne, 267–297.

Zorzetti, N. (1990), 'Tragici latini', in: *Enciclopedia Vergiliana* , vol. 5, Rome, 245–247.

Zwierlein, O. (1984), *Senecas Hercules im Lichte kaiserzeitlicher und spätantiker Deutung. Mit einem Anhang über 'tragische Schuld' sowie Seneca-Imitationen bei Claudian und Boethius*, Wiesbaden 1984.

Zwierlein, O. (ed.) (1986), *L. Annaei Senecae Tragoediae, incertorum auctorum Hercules [Oetaeus] Octavia*, Oxford (repr. with corr. 1993).

List of Contributors

Antony Augoustakis is Professor of Classics at the University of Illinois at Urbana–Champaign. He is the author of *Statius, Thebaid 8* (Oxford 2016), *Motherhood and the Other: Fashioning Female Power in Flavian Epic* (Oxford 2010) and *Plautus' Mercator* (Bryn Mawr 2009). He has edited and co-edited numerous volumes, most recently *Fides in Flavian Literature* (Toronto 2019) and *Campania in the Flavian Poetic Imagination* (Oxford 2019). He is in the final stages of a commentary on Silius Italicus' *Punica* 3, co-edited with Joy Littlewood. He serves as editor of *The Classical Journal*.

Neil W. Bernstein is Professor in the Department of Classics & World Religions at Ohio University, where he has taught since 2004. He is the author of *Seneca: Hercules Furens* (Bloomsbury 2017); *Silius Italicus, Punica 2* (Oxford 2017); *Ethics, Identity, and Community in Later Roman Declamation* (Oxford 2013); and *In the Image of the Ancestors: Narratives of Kinship in Flavian Epic* (Toronto 2008). He has been a Distinguished Scholar in Residence at the University of Western Ontario; an NEH Fellow at the National Humanities Center, North Carolina; and a Fulbright lecturer at National Taiwan University, Taipei.

Robert Cowan is Senior Lecturer in Classics at the University of Sydney, having previously held posts in Exeter, Bristol, and Oxford. His research interests range over much of Greek and Latin poetry, and he has published on Sophocles, Aristophanes, Plautus, Lucretius, Catullus, Cicero, Cinna, Ticida, Virgil, Horace, Ovid, Columella, Martial, Suetonius, and Juvenal, as well as ancient graffiti and the operatic reception of Greek tragedy. His main specialisms are Imperial epic and Republican tragedy.

Kyle Gervais (PhD Otago) is an Associate Professor of Classical Studies at the University of Western Ontario. He is author of *Statius, Thebaid 2: Edited with an Introduction, Translation, and Commentary* (Oxford) and co-editor of *Brill's Companion to Statius*. He has published articles and chapters on classical, late antique, and medieval Latin poetry, as well as classical reception in popular culture.

Gesine Manuwald is Professor of Latin at University College London (UCL). Her research interests include Roman epic, Roman drama, Roman oratory, and the reception of classical literature, especially in Neo-Latin texts. She has published widely on all these areas, including a commentary on Valerius Flaccus' *Argonautica* 3 (Cambridge 2015).

Agis Marinis is Assistant Professor of Greek Philology and Drama at the University of Patras (Greece). The focus of his current research is the intersection of Pindaric poetry and religion, on which a monograph is forthcoming from Routledge. He has also published on Aeschylus' *Seven against Thebes*, as well as on the presence of Theban myth in Greek and Roman poetry.

Carole Newlands is Professor of Classics at the University of Colorado at Boulder. Her principal areas of research are Augustan and post-Augustan poetry; late Antique and Medieval poetry; and Classical reception. She is the author of *Playing with Time: Ovid and the Fasti* (Ithaca 1995), and she has co-edited (with J.F. Miller) *The Wiley-Blackwell Handbook to Ovid* (2014). Her recent work on Statius includes two monographs, *Statius' Silvae and the Poetics of Empire* (Cambridge 2002), and *Statius: Poet between Rome and Naples* (London 2012); a commentary on Statius' *Silvae* 2 for the Cambridge Greek and Latin series (2011); and she has co-edited with W.J. Dominik and K. Gervais the *Brill's Companion to Statius* (2015).

Sophia Papaioannou is Professor of Latin at the National and Kapodistrian University of Athens. Her research interests embrace Ancient Epic, Latin poetry and Roman Comedy, and she has published many books and articles on these topics. She is currently working on a book that explores the reception of the Latin tradition in Nonnus' *Dionysiaca*.

Ruth Parkes is Senior Lecturer in Classics at the University of Wales Trinity Saint David, Wales. She works on the epic tradition through the ages, particularly with regards to the works of Statius and Claudian. She has written numerous articles on classical and post-classical texts and is the author of a commentary on Book 4 of Statius' *Thebaid* (2012).

Index Rerum et Nominum

https://doi.org/10.1515/9783110709841-013

Index Auctorum Antiquorum et Locorum

https://doi.org/10.1515/9783110709841-014